THE

Well-Gardened

MIND

The Restorative Power
of Nature

SUE STUART-SMITH

SCRIBNER

New York   London   Toronto   Sydney   New Delhi

Scribner
An Imprint of Simon & Schuster, Inc.
1230 Avenue of the Americas
New York, NY 10020

For Tom

All truly wise thoughts have been thought already thousands of times; but to make them truly ours, we must think them over again honestly, till they take root in our personal experience.

Johann Wolfgang von Goethe

Contents

1. Beginnings   1

2. Green Nature: Human Nature   23

3. Seeds and Self-Belief   45

4. Safe Green Space   67

5. Bringing Nature to the City   87

6. Roots   109

7. Flower Power   135

8. Radical Solutions   157

9. War and Gardening   183

10. The Last Season of Life   209

11. Garden Time   237

12. View from the Hospital   257

13. Green Fuse   277

Acknowledgments   289

Selected General Sources on Nature, Gardens, and Health   295

Notes   297

Illustration Credits   323

Index   325

CHAPTER 1

Beginnings

Sue and Tom with baby Rose, planting the first
hedges in the courtyard at the Barn, 1988.

Come forth into the light of things,
Let Nature be your teacher.
William Wordsworth (1770–1850)

Long before I wanted to be a psychiatrist, long before I had any
inkling that gardening might play an important role in my life, I
remember hearing the story of how my grandfather was restored
after the First World War.

He was born Alfred Edward May, but was always known as Ted. Little more than a boy when he joined the Royal Navy, he trained as a Marconi wireless operator and entered the submarine service. In the spring of 1915, during the Gallipoli campaign, the submarine he was serving on ran aground in the Dardanelles. Most of the crew survived, only to be taken prisoner. Ted kept a tiny diary in which he documented the early months of his captivity in Turkey, but his subsequent time in a series of brutal labor camps is not recorded. The last of these was a cement factory on the shores of the Sea of Marmara from which he eventually escaped by sea in 1918.

Ted was rescued and treated on board a British hospital ship, where he recovered just enough strength to attempt the long journey home overland. Eager to be reunited with his fiancée, Fanny, whom he had left behind as a fit young man, he turned up on her doorstep in a battered old raincoat with a Turkish fez on his head. He was barely recognizable, weighing, as he did, little more than eighty pounds and having lost all his hair. The four-thousand-mile journey had, he told Fanny, been "horrendous." On top of everything else he had endured during the preceding years, that journey took a severe toll on his health. When he underwent the naval medical examination, his malnutrition was found to be so advanced that he was given little more than a few months to live.

But Fanny nursed him faithfully by feeding him tiny amounts of soup and other sustenance on an hourly basis, so that gradually he was able to digest food again. Ted began the slow process of regaining his health, and he and Fanny were married soon after. In that first year, he would sit for hours stroking his bald head with two soft brushes, willing his hair to grow back. When it finally did, it was prolific, but it was white.

Love and patient determination enabled Ted to defy the gloomy prognosis he had been given, but his POW camp experiences stayed with him and his terrors were worst at night. He was especially afraid of spiders and crabs because they had crawled all over the prisoners as they tried to sleep. For years to come, he couldn't stand being alone in the dark.

The next phase of Ted's recovery began in 1920, when he signed up for a yearlong course in horticulture, one of many initiatives set up in the postwar years with the aim of rehabilitating ex-servicemen who had been damaged by the conflict. After this, he traveled to Canada in search of a new life and in the hope that working the land might further improve his physical and mental strength. At that time the Canadian government was running programs to encourage ex-servicemen to migrate, and thousands of men who had returned from the war made that long Atlantic crossing.

Ted labored on the wheat harvest in Winnipeg and then found more settled employment as a gardener on a cattle ranch in Alberta. Fanny joined him for some of the two years he spent there, but for whatever reason their dream of starting a new life in Canada did not come to fruition. Nevertheless, Ted returned to England a stronger, fitter man.

A few years later he and Fanny bought a smallholding with an orchard in Hampshire. In his spare time, he kept pigs, bees, and hens as well as growing flowers, fruit, and vegetables. For five years during the Second World War he worked at The Admiralty wireless station in London, and my mother remembers his pigskin suitcase which traveled up with him on the train, packed full of home-slaughtered meat and home-grown vegetables. He and the suitcase used to return carrying supplies of sugar, butter, and tea. She relates with some pride how the family never ate margarine during the war and that Ted even grew his own tobacco.

I remember his good humor and the warmth of his spirit, a warmth that emanated from a man who seemed to my childish eyes to be robust and at ease with himself. He wasn't intimidating and he didn't wear his traumas on his sleeve. He spent hours tending his garden and his greenhouse and was almost always attached to a pipe, with his tobacco pouch never far away. Ted's long and healthy life—he lived into his late seventies, and his reconciliation to some of the appalling abuses he experienced—is attributed in our family mythology to the restorative effects of gardening and working the land.

Ted died suddenly in his late seventies, when I was twelve, from an aneurysm that ruptured while he was out walking with his much loved Shetland sheepdog. The local paper ran an obituary entitled "Once youngest submariner dies." It reveals that he was reported dead twice during the war and that when he escaped with a group of captive soldiers from the cement factory, they lived for twenty-three days on water alone. The closing words document his love of gardening: "He devoted much of his leisure time to the cultivation of his extensive garden, and achieved fame locally as the grower of several rare orchids."

Somewhere inside her, my mother must have drawn on this when my father's death, in his late forties, left her a relatively young widow. In the second spring afterward, she found a new home and took on the task of restoring the neglected cottage garden. Even then, in my youthful, self-preoccupied state, I noticed that alongside the digging and the weeding, a parallel process of reconciling herself to her loss was taking place.

At that stage of my life, gardening was not something I thought I would ever devote much time to. I was interested in the world of literature and was intent on embracing the life of the mind. As far as I was concerned, gardening was a form of outdoor housework, and I would no more have plucked a weed than baked a scone or washed the curtains.

My father had been in and out of the hospital during my university years, and he died just as I started my final year. The news came by phone one morning at around 5 a.m., and as soon as dawn broke I walked out through the quiet Cambridge streets into the park and down to the river. It was a bright, sunny October day, and the world was green and still. The trees and the grass and the water were somehow consoling, and in those peaceful surroundings, I found it possible to acknowledge to myself the awful reality, that beautiful as the day was, my father was no longer alive to see it.

Perhaps this green and watery place reminded me of happier times and of the landscape that had first made an impression on me as a child? My father kept a boat on the river Thames, and when my brother and I were small, we spent many weekends and holidays on the water, once making an expedition up to the river's source, or as near to it as we could get. I remember the stillness of the early morning mists and the feeling of freedom playing in the summer meadows and fishing with my brother, what was then our favorite pastime.

During my last few terms at Cambridge, poetry took on a new emotional significance. My world had irrevocably changed, and I clung to verses that spoke of the consolations of nature and the cycle of life. Dylan Thomas and T. S. Eliot were sustaining, but above all I turned to Wordsworth, the poet who himself had learned:

> To look on nature, not as in the hour
> Of thoughtless youth; but hearing oftentimes
> The still, sad music of humanity.

Grief is isolating and is no less so when it is a shared experience. A loss that devastates a family generates a need to lean on one another, but at the same time everyone is bereft, everyone is in a state of collapse. There is an impulse to protect one another from too much raw emotion, and it can be easier to let feelings surface away from people. Trees, water, stones, and sky may be impervious to human emotion, but they don't reject us either. Nature is unperturbed by our feelings, and because there is no contagion, we can experience a kind of consolation that helps assuage the loneliness of loss.

In the first few years that followed my father's death, I was drawn toward nature, not in gardens, but by the sea. His ashes had been committed to the waters of The Solent near his family home on the south coast. It is a busy channel full of boats and ships, but it was on the long, solitary beaches of north Norfolk, with barely a boat in sight, that I found greatest solace. The wide horizons were the widest I had ever seen. It felt like the edge of the known world and seemed as close to my father as I could be.

Having studied Freud for one of my exam papers, I had developed an interest in the workings of the mind. I gave up the idea of staying on to do a PhD in literature and decided that as soon as I completed my English degree, I would change direction, study the sciences, and train to be a doctor. Then, in the third year of my medical training, I married Tom Stuart-Smith, for whom gardening was a way of life. I decided that if he loved it, then I would too, but if I were being honest, I'd say that I was still a garden skeptic. Gardening seemed at that point to me to be another chore that had to be done, although it was nicer (as long as the sun was shining) to be outdoors rather than indoors.

A few years after, along with our tiny baby, Rose, we moved to the Barn, close to Tom's family home at Serge Hill in Hertfordshire. Over the next few years Rose was joined by Ben and Harry, and at the same time we hurled ourselves into making a garden from scratch. The Barn, as we had named our new home, was surrounded by an open field, and its position on a north-facing hill exposed to the winds meant that above all, we needed shelter. We carved out some plots from the stony field around us, planting trees and hedges and making enclosures of wattle fencing as well as laboring over the ground to improve it. None of this could have happened without an enormous amount of help and encouragement from Tom's parents and a number of willing friends. When we held stone-picking parties, Rose, along with her grandparents, aunts, and uncles, joined in the task of filling up endless buckets with rocks and pebbles that needed to be carted away.

I had been physically and emotionally uprooted, and I needed to rebuild my sense of home, but still I was not particularly conscious that gardening might play a part in helping me put down roots. I was much more aware as they grew of the garden's significance in our children's lives. They began making dens in the bushes and spent hours inhabiting imaginary worlds of their own making, so the garden was a fantasy place and a real place at the same time.

Tom's creative energy and vision drove our garden making forward. It wasn't until our youngest, Harry, was a toddler that I finally started growing plants myself. I became interested in herbs and devoured books about them. This new area of learning led to experiments in the kitchen and in a little herb garden that by then had become "mine." There were some gardening disasters, unleashing a creeping borage and a tenacious soapwort among them, but eating food flavored with all sorts of home-grown herbs was life-enhancing, and from there it was a short step to growing vegetables. The thrill I felt at this stage was all about produce!

At this point, I was in my mid-thirties, working as a junior psychiatrist in the National Health Service. In giving me something to show for my efforts, gardening provided a counterpoint to my professional life, where I was engaged with the much more intangible properties of the mind. Working on the wards and in clinic rooms was predominantly an indoor life, but the garden pulled me outdoors.

I discovered the pleasure of wandering through the garden with a free-floating attention, registering how the plants were changing, growing, ailing, fruiting. Gradually, the way I thought about "boring" jobs like weeding, hoeing, and watering changed, and I came to see that it is important not so much to get them done, but to be fully involved in doing them. Watering is calming, as long as you are not in a hurry, and strangely, when it is finished, you end up feeling refreshed, like the plants themselves.

The biggest gardening buzz I got back then, and still get now, was from growing things from seed. Seeds give no hint of what is to come, and their size bears no relation to the dormant life within. Beans erupt dramatically, not with much beauty but you can feel their thuggish vigor right from the start. Nicotiana seeds are so fine, like particles of dust, you can't even see where you've sown them. It seems improbable they will ever do anything, let alone give you clouds of scented tobacco plant flowers, and yet they do. I can feel how new life creates an attachment by the way I find myself coming back almost compulsively to check on how my seeds and seedlings are doing; going out to the greenhouse, holding my breath as I enter, not wanting to disrupt anything, the stillness of life just coming into being.

Fundamentally, there is no arguing with the seasons when you are gardening, although you can get away with postponing things a little (I'll sow those seeds or plant out those plugs next weekend). There comes a point when you realize that a delay is about to become a missed opportunity, a lost possibility, and once you have your seedlings tucked up in the soil, you are carried along, as if you have jumped into a flowing river, by the energy of the earthly calendar.

I particularly love gardening in early summer, when the growth force is at its strongest and there is so much to get in the ground. Once I've started, I don't want to stop, and I carry on in the dusk till it's almost too dark to see what I'm doing. As I finish off, the house is glowing with light and its warmth draws me back inside. The next morning when I steal out, there it is—whatever patch I was working on has settled into itself overnight.

Of course, there is no way of gardening without experiencing some disasters and ruined plans—moments when you step outside in anticipation, only to be faced with the sad remains of lovely young lettuces or a line of ruthlessly stripped leaves of kale. It has to be acknowledged that the mindless eating habits of slugs and rabbits can set off bouts of helpless rage, and the persistence and stamina of weeds can be very, very draining.

Not all the satisfaction in tending plants is about creation. The great thing about being destructive in the garden is that it is not only permissible, it is *necessary*, because if you don't do it, you will be overrun. So many acts of garden care are infused with aggression, whether it is wielding the pruning shears, double digging the vegetable patch, slaughtering slugs, killing blackfly, ripping up goosegrass, or rooting out nettles. You can throw yourself into any or all of these in a wholehearted and uncomplicated way because they are a form of destructiveness that's in the service of growth. A long session in the garden like this can leave you feeling dead on your feet but strangely renewed inside, both purged and re-energized, as if you have worked on yourself in the process. It's a kind of gardening catharsis.

Each year, as we come out of winter, the greenhouse takes a hold on me with the lure of its warmth when the world outside is still chilled by the March winds. What is it that is so special about entering a greenhouse full of plants? Is it the level of oxygen in the air or the quality of light and heat? Or simply the proximity to plants with their greenness and their scent? It is as if all the senses are heightened inside this private, protected space.

One overcast spring day last year, I was absorbed in greenhouse tasks—watering, sowing seeds, moving compost, and generally getting things done. Then the sky cleared, and with the sun pouring in, I was transported to a separate world—a world of iridescent green filled with translucent leaves, the light shining through them. Droplets were scattered all over the freshly watered plants, catching the light, sparkling and luscious. Just for a moment I felt an overpowering sense of earthly beneficence, a feeling that I've retained, like a gift in time.

I sowed some sunflowers in the greenhouse that day, and later on when I planted the seedlings out in the garden the best one looked hopeful, but the others suddenly seemed straggly and exposed out of doors. I thought some of them might not make it. I watched with satisfaction their growing upward, and gradually getting stronger. Then their growth took off and my attention moved on to other, more vulnerable seedlings.

I see gardening as a reiteration: I do a bit, then nature does her bit, then I respond to that, and so on, not unlike a conversation. It isn't whispers or shouts or talk of any kind, but in this back-and-forth there is a delayed and sustained dialogue. I have to admit that I am sometimes the slow one to respond, and that I can go a little quiet on it all, so it is good to have plants that can survive some neglect. And if you do take time away, the intrigue on your return is all the greater, like finding out what someone's been up to in your absence.

One day I realized that the whole line of sunflowers was sturdy, independent, and proud, with flowers coming on. When and how did you get so tall? I wondered. Soon that first hopeful seedling, still the tallest and the strongest, was looking down on me from its great height, with the whole wide circumference of its brilliant yellow flower. I felt quite small in its presence, but there was a strangely affirmative sensation in knowing I had set its life in motion.

A month or so later, how changed they were. The bees had cleaned the flowers out, their petals were faded, and the tallest could barely support its bowed-down head. Lately so proud and now so melancholy! I had an impulse to cut the row down, but I knew if I lived with their raggedy sadness for a while, they would bleach and dry in the sun and assume a different kind of stature as they led us toward autumn.

· · ·

To look after a garden involves a kind of *getting to know* that is somehow always in process. It entails refining and developing an understanding of what works and what doesn't. You have to build a relationship with the place in its entirety—its climate, its soil, and the plants that grow within it. These are the realities that have to be contended with, and along the way certain dreams almost always have to be given up. Our rose garden, which we started making when we first carved out some plots from the stony field, was just such a lost dream.

We had filled the beds with the loveliest of old roses, like Belle de Crecy, Cardinal de Richelieu, and Madame Hardy, but it was the delicate, heady, and delicious Fantin-Latour, with its flat petals, scrumpled like pale pink tissue paper, that was my favorite of all. You can nuzzle right into its flower, soft and velvety, and disappear in its scent. Little did we know back then that their time with us would be so brief, but it wasn't long before they began to balk at the conditions they were living in. Our ground did not suit them well, and a lack of ventilation in the wattle enclosures made matters worse. Each season became a battle to stay on top of the black spot and mildew that increasingly assailed them, and unless they were sprayed, they looked sad and sick. We were reluctant to rip them out, but what is the point in gardening against nature? They had to go, but oh how I missed them and miss them still! Even though not a single rose is growing in those beds today, all long since replaced by herbaceous perennial planting, we still call it the rose garden. So the memory remains.

Neither Tom nor I liked the idea of using chemical sprays, but I had a particular antagonism to them; in fact, because of my father's illness, I was afraid of them. It was never entirely clear what had triggered this catastrophe, but among the possible culprits was a long since banned pesticide lurking in the garden shed and an antibiotic prescribed when he had become ill on holiday in Italy the summer before. He nearly died then, but the treatment he received partially reversed the damage, and although he could not be cured, it gave him another fourteen years of life. He was tall and physically strong, so it was possible for all of us to forget at times that he was living with only half-functioning marrow in his bones. The illness was always there in the background though, and when his intermittent life-threatening health crises occurred, all we could do was hope.

In that phase of my childhood, there was a garden that captured my imagination much more vividly than the one at home. My mother would take my brother, me, and any friends in tow to the Isabella Plantation, the woodland gardens in Richmond Park. As soon as we arrived, we would run off and disappear into the massive rhododendrons to enjoy the frisson of exploring and hiding in them. So dense were the bushes that it was possible for a brief time to get lost and feel the panic of separation.

There was another more unsettling element in that garden. In a small clearing, deep in the woodland, we discovered a red-and-yellow painted wooden caravan, which had a sign carved above the door: "Abandon all hope ye who enter here." We used to dare one another to defy the injunction, but the thought of relinquishing hope was not something I could possibly have taken lightly. It felt as if opening that door might release into the world the terrible dread I dared not name. In the end, as with all things unknown, the fantasy proved far more powerful than the reality. One day when we finally tried the door, it revealed a simple yellow painted interior containing a wooden bunk, and of course, nothing terrible happened.

While you are being shaped by experience, you are not aware that it is happening, because whatever is going on is simply your life; there is no other life, and it is all part of who you are. Only much later, when I began to train as a psychoanalytic psychotherapist and embarked on my own analysis, did I recognize how much the structures of my childhood world had been shaken by my father's illness. I came to understand why the injunction above the caravan door had such a hold on my childish imagination and also why, when I was sixteen, the news coverage of a leak from the chemical factory at Seveso in Italy seized my attention. An explosion had released a cloud of toxic gas with devastating consequences, the full extent of which only gradually emerged. The soil was poisoned and the health of local people suffered serious, long-term consequences. The disaster mobilized something in me, and for the first time I became aware of environmental issues and their politics. Such are the workings of the unconscious that I did not see a parallel with whatever unknown chemical had made my father so ill. I only knew I had undergone a powerful environmental awakening.

Turning over the past and revisiting memories like this in the course of my analysis involved a different kind of awakening—to the life of the mind. I came to understand that grief can go underground and that feelings can hide other feelings. Moments of new insight ripple through the psyche, shaking and stirring it up, and although some may be welcome and refreshing, others can be more difficult to assimilate and adjust to. Alongside all this, I was gardening.

A garden gives you a protected physical space, which helps increase your sense of mental space, and it gives you quiet, so you can hear your own thoughts. The more you immerse yourself in working with your hands, the more free you are internally to sort things out and work them through. These days, I turn to gardening as a way of calming and decompressing my mind. Somehow, the jangle of competing thoughts inside my head clears and settles as the weed bucket fills up. Ideas that have been lying dormant come to the surface, and thoughts that are barely formed sometimes come together and unexpectedly take shape. At times like these, it feels as if alongside all the physical activity, I am also gardening my mind.

I have come to understand that deep existential processes can be involved in creating and caring for a garden. So I find myself asking, How does gardening have its effects on us? How can it help us find or re-find our place in the world when we feel we have lost it? At this point in the twenty-first century, with rates of depression and anxiety and other mental disorders seemingly ever on the rise, and with a general way of life that is increasingly urbanized and technology-dependent, it seems more important than ever to understand the many ways in which mind and garden can interact.

Gardens have been recognized as restorative since ancient times. Today, gardening consistently features as one of the top ten most popular hobbies in a range of countries around the world. Quintessentially, caring for a garden is a nurturing activity, and for many people, along with having children and raising a family, the process of tending a plot is one of the most significant things in their lives. There are, of course, people for whom gardening feels like a chore and who would always prefer to do something else, but the combination of outdoor exercise and immersive activity is acknowledged by many as both calming and invigorating. Although other forms of green exercise and other kinds of mindful activity can have these benefits, the relationship that is formed with plants and the earth is unique to gardening. A close contact with nature affects us on different levels; sometimes we are filled with it, fully present and conscious of its effects, but it also works on us slowly and subconsciously in a way that can be particularly helpful for people suffering from trauma, illness, and loss.

The poet William Wordsworth explored perhaps more intensely than anyone else the influence of nature on the inner life of the mind. He was psychologically prescient, and his ability to tune in to the subconscious means he is sometimes regarded as a forerunner of psychoanalytic thinking. In a leap of intuition, which modern neuroscience confirms, he understood that our sense impressions are not passively recorded; instead we construct experience even as we are undergoing it, so that, as he put it, we "half-create" as well as perceive the world around us. Nature animates the mind, and the mind, in turn, animates nature. Wordsworth believed that a living relationship with nature like this is a source of strength that can help foster the healthy growth of the mind. He also understood what it means to be a gardener.

Much as I had felt uprooted, and the creation of our garden was existentially stabilizing for me, the process of making a garden together was an important act of restitution for Wordsworth and his sister, Dorothy. It was a response to the loss of their parents, who had died when they were children, leaving them to endure a lengthy and painful separation from each other. Gardening helped them recover a sense of home. At Dove Cottage they cultivated vegetables, medicinal herbs, and other useful plants, but much of the plot was highly naturalistic and sloped steeply up the hillside. This little "nook of mountain-ground," as Wordsworth referred to it, was full of "gifts" of wildflowers, ferns, and mosses that they collected on their walks and brought back, like offerings to the earth.

Wordsworth frequently worked on his poems in that garden. He described the essence of poetry as "emotion recollected in tranquillity," and it is true for all of us that we need to be in the right kind of setting to enter the calm state of mind needed for processing powerful or turbulent feelings. The Dove Cottage garden, with its sense of safe enclosure and lovely view beyond, gave him just that. He wrote many of his greatest poems while living at the cottage and developed what would be a lifelong habit of pacing out rhythms and chanting verses aloud while striding along garden paths. So the garden was both a physical setting for the house as well as a setting for the mind; one that was all the more significant for having been shaped by his and Dorothy's own hands.

Wordsworth's love of horticulture is a less well-known aspect of his life, but he remained a devoted gardener well into old age. He created a number of different gardens, including a sheltered winter garden for his patron Lady Beaumont. Conceived of as a therapeutic refuge, it was designed to alleviate her attacks of melancholy. The purpose of a garden such as this was, he wrote, "to assist Nature in moving affections." In providing a concentrated dose of the healing effects of nature, gardens influence us primarily through our feelings, but however much they may be set apart as a refuge, we are nevertheless, as Wordsworth described, "in the midst of the realities of things." These realities encompass all the beauties of nature as well as the cycle of life and the passing of the seasons. In other words, however much they can offer us respite, gardens also put us in touch with fundamental aspects of life.

Like a suspension in time, the protected space of a garden allows our inner world and the outer world to coexist free from the pressures of everyday life. Gardens in this sense offer us an *in-between* space which can be a meeting place for our innermost, dream-infused selves and the real physical world. This kind of blurring of boundaries is what Donald Winnicott called a "transitional" area of experience. Transitional processes allow us to imaginatively endow the world and feel part of something larger than ourselves. They are central to children's play, and in adult life they play a role in the creative arts and in religion.

Winnicott was a pediatrician as well as a psychoanalyst, and his understanding of the mind is not an individual psychology; it is always about the child in relation to the family, and the baby in relation to the mother. When you look at a mother and baby from the outside, it is easy to distinguish them as two separate beings, but the subjective experience of each of them is not so clear-cut. The relationship involves an important area of overlap or *in-between* through which the mother feels the baby's feelings as the baby expresses them, and the baby in turn does not yet know where it begins and Mother ends.

Much as there can be no baby without a caregiver, there can be no garden without a gardener. A garden is always the expression of someone's mind and the outcome of someone's care. When we step back from it, how can we tease apart what nature has provided and what we have contributed? Even in the midst of the action itself, it is not necessarily clear. Sometimes when I am fully absorbed in a garden task, a feeling arises within me that I am part of this and it is part of me; nature is running in me and through me.

A garden embodies transitional space by being *in-between* the home and the landscape that lies beyond. Within it, wild nature and cultivated nature overlap, and the gardener's scrabbling about in the earth is not at odds with dreams of paradise or civilized ideals of refinement and beauty. The garden is a place where they can come together, maybe the one place where they can so freely come together.

Winnicott believed that play was psychologically replenishing, but he emphasized that in order to enter an imaginary world, we need to feel safe and free from scrutiny. He employed one of his trademark paradoxes to capture this experience when he wrote of how important it is for a child to develop the ability to be "alone in the presence of the mother." In my gardening, I often recapture a feeling of being absorbed in play—it is as if in the safe curtilage of the garden, I am in the kind of company that allows me to be alone and enter my own world. Both daydreaming and playing are increasingly recognized to contribute to psychological health and these benefits do not stop with the end of childhood.

The emotional and physical investment that working on a place entails means that over time it becomes woven into our sense of identity. As such it can be a protective part of our identity too, one that can help buffer us when the going gets tough. But as the traditional pattern of a rooted relationship to place has been lost, so we have also lost sight of the potentially stabilizing effects of an attachment to place.

The field of attachment theory was pioneered by the psychiatrist and psychoanalyst John Bowlby in the 1960s, and there is now an extensive research base associated with it. Bowlby regarded attachment as the "bedrock" of human psychology. He was also a keen naturalist, and this informed the development of his ideas. He described how birds return to the same place to build their nests year after year, often close to where they were born, and that animals do not roam about at random, as is often thought, but rather occupy a "home" territory, around their lair or burrow. In the same way, he argued, "each man's environment is unique to himself."

Attachment to place and attachment to people share an evolutionary pathway, and a quality of uniqueness is central to both. The feeding of an infant is not enough on its own to trigger bonding, because we are biologically encoded to attach through the specificity of smells, textures, and sounds as well as pleasurable feelings. Places too evoke feelings, and natural places are particularly rich in sensory pleasures. These days we are surrounded by functional places lacking in character and individuality, like supermarkets and shopping malls. While they provide us with food and other useful things, we don't develop affectionate bonds for them, in fact they are often deeply unrestorative. As a result, the notion of place in contemporary life has increasingly been reduced to a backdrop and the interaction, if there is any, tends to be of a transient nature, rather than a living relationship that might be sustaining.

At the heart of Bowlby's thinking is the idea that the mother is the very first place of all. Children seek out her protective arms whenever they are frightened, tired, or upset. This "safe haven" becomes what Bowlby called a "secure base" through repeated small experiences of separation and loss that are followed by reunion and recovery. When a feeling of security has been established, a child becomes more emboldened to explore his or her surroundings, but still keeps half an eye on Mother as a safe place to return to.

It is a sad fact of modern childhood that playing outdoors has become something of a rarity, but traditionally parks and gardens provided the setting for an important kind of imaginative and exploratory play. Creating dens in the bushes as "adult-free" zones is a way of rehearsing future independence, and they have an emotional role too. Research shows that when children are upset, they instinctively use their "special" places as a safe haven in which they can feel protected while their unsettled feelings subside.

Attachment and loss, as Bowlby revealed, go together. We are not primed to dis-attach, we are primed to seek reunion. It is the very strength of our attachment system that makes recovering from loss so painful and difficult. While we have a strong inborn capacity to form bonds, there is nothing in our biology that helps us deal with bonds that get broken, and that means that mourning is something we have to learn through experience.

In order to cope with loss, we need to find or re-find a safe haven and feel the comfort and sympathy of others. For Wordsworth, who had suffered the pain of bereavement as a child, the gentle aspects of the natural world provided a consoling and sympathetic presence. The psychoanalyst Melanie Klein alludes to this in one of her papers on the subject of mourning, where she writes: "The poet tells us that Nature mourns with the mourner." She goes on to show how, in order to emerge from a state of grief, we need to recover a sense of goodness in the world and in ourselves.

When someone very close to us dies, it is as if a part of us dies too. We want to hold on to that closeness and shut down our emotional pain. But at some point the question arises—can we bring ourselves alive again? In tending a plot and nurturing and caring for plants we are constantly faced with disappearance and return. The natural cycles of growth and decay can help us understand and accept that mourning is part of the cycle of life and that when we can't mourn, it is as if a perpetual winter takes hold of us.

We can also be helped by rituals or other forms of symbolic

action that enable us to make sense of the experience. But in the secular and consumerist worlds that many of us now inhabit, we have lost touch with traditional rituals and rites of passage that might help us navigate our way through life. Gardening itself can be a form of ritual. It transforms external reality and gives rise to beauty around us, but it also works within us, through its symbolic meaning. A garden puts us in touch with a set of metaphors that have profoundly shaped the human psyche for thousands of years—metaphors so deep they are almost hidden within our thinking.

Gardening is what happens when two creative energies meet—human creativity and nature's creativity. It is a place of overlap between what is "me" and "not-me," between what we can conceive of and what the environment gives us to work with. So, we bridge the gap between the dreams in our head and the ground under our feet and know that while we cannot stop the forces of death and destruction, we can, at least, defy them.

Somewhere in the recesses of my memory lay hidden a story that I must have heard in childhood which came back to me when I was writing this book. It is a classic fairy tale of the type that involves a king with a lovely daughter and suitors queuing up for her hand. The king decides to get rid of the suitors by setting them an impossible challenge. He decrees that the only person who can marry his daughter is someone who brings him an object so unique and so special that no one in the world has set eyes on it before. His gaze, and his gaze alone, has to be the first to fall on it.

The suitors duly travel to far-flung, exotic locations seeking the prize they hope will guarantee their success, and return bearing unusual and novel gifts that they haven't even glimpsed themselves. Carefully wrapped and extraordinary as their findings are, another human eye has always looked on them before—someone has either made this beautiful object, or found it, or dug it up, like the gem from the deepest diamond mine, which is the rarest and most precious gift of them all.

The palace gardener has a son, who is secretly in love with the princess and interprets the challenge in a different way—one that is informed by his close relationship with the natural world. The trees around the grounds are groaning with nuts, and he presents one to the king, along with a pair of nutcrackers. You could say he calls the king's bluff, for certainly the king is bemused at being given something as ordinary as a nut, but then the young man explains that if the king cracks the nut open, he will see something that no living soul has ever set eyes on before. In the way of all good fairy stories, it is a tale of rags to riches and lovers united. But it is also about how the wonders of nature may be revealed to us if we do not overlook them. More than that, it is a tale about human empowerment, because nature is accessible to us all.

If there were no loss in the world, we would lack the motivation to create. As the psychoanalyst Hanna Segal wrote: "It is when the world within us is destroyed, when it is dead and loveless, when our loved ones are in fragments, and we ourselves in helpless despair— it is then that we must recreate our world anew, reassemble the pieces, infuse life into dead fragments, recreate life." Gardening is about setting life in motion, and seeds, like dead fragments, help us re-create the world anew.

It is just this newness that is so compelling in the garden, life endlessly re-forming and reshaping itself. The garden is a place where we can be in on its beginning and have a hand in its making. Even the humble potato patch offers this opportunity, for when we turn over the mounded-up earth, a cluster of potatoes that no one has set eyes on before is brought into the light.

CHAPTER 2

Green Nature: Human Nature

Snowdrop from the Barn Garden.

Who would have thought my shrivel'd heart
Could have recover'd greenness? It was gone
Quite underground.

George Herbert (1593–1633)

Snowdrops are the first sign of new life in our garden, when winter begins its turn. Their green shoots feel their way up from the dark earth, and their simple white flowers express the purest intention of a fresh start.

Each year in February, before they die back, we divide them up and replant them. For most of the rest of the year they are invisible, though all the while they are growing and replicating themselves underground. While the resident mice feed on other bulbs in the garden, they don't feed on the snowdrops, so they multiply themselves with abandon. It is not only the mass of them that is so compelling, it is the sense of legacy, for the legions of snowdrops that now cover our ground derive from a few buckets of bulbs transplanted from Tom's mother's garden more than thirty years ago.

Renewal and regeneration come so naturally in the plant world, but psychological repair does not come so naturally to us. Although the mind has an intrinsic drive toward growth and development, there are pitfalls in its workings. Many of our automatic responses in the face of trauma and loss, such as avoidance, numbness, isolation, and ruminating on negative thoughts, actually work against the possibility of recovery.

The repetitive patterns of anxious and obsessive thinking that occur in depression set up a vicious circle. This kind of preoccupation is the mind's attempt to make sense of things, but trying to solve an unfathomable problem keeps us stuck in a mental groove and prevents us moving forward. Depression has another inbuilt circularity to it because when we are depressed, we perceive and interpret the world and ourselves much more negatively, and this in turn feeds our low mood and reinforces the urge to isolate ourselves. The truth is that, left to its own devices, the mind easily leads us down a rabbit hole.

I recall a patient from many years ago who long before I started thinking about the therapeutic effects of gardening, sowed a seed in my mind. Kay rented a flat with a small garden and had lived there for a number of years with her two sons. Throughout her life, she had experienced recurrent episodes of depression, some of which had been severe. Her childhood had been marked by violence and neglect. In adult life she struggled to form relationships and had brought her sons up largely on her own. The boys' teenage years were full of conflict, and when both of them left home, in quick succession, Kay became depressed again. For the first time in twenty years she found herself living alone.

It became clear in her therapy that she had internalized a lot of bad feelings about herself, feelings that originated in childhood and which made it hard for her to let good things into her life, because deep down she believed she didn't deserve them. If something good did come along, after a period of time she would start to feel anxious about losing it. As a result, she often sabotaged relationships and other chances to change her life, thereby preempting the disappointments that she thought, and that to some extent life had taught her, would inevitably follow. In this way, depression can become a self-reinforcing state in which it feels safer not to let anything grow, not to risk bringing hope alive, out of fear of being driven by disappointment to even greater depths.

At the back of Kay's flat there was a small garden, which had been trashed by her sons over the years. Now that they were no longer living at home, she decided to reclaim the space, and over the months that followed she acquired the habit of gardening. One day she said to me, "It is the only time I feel I am good." This statement was striking partly because of the conviction with which she uttered it, but also because a sense of her own goodness was so hard for her to come by.

So what did Kay mean by this feeling of goodness? Working in the garden directed her attention outside herself and gave her a place of refuge, both of which were helpful, but above all, gardening provided a real-life confirmation, that the world was not so bad and she was not so bad either. Kay discovered that she could make things grow. Gardening was not a cure for her depression, which after all was longstanding, but it helped to stabilize her and gave her a much needed source of self-worth.

Although gardening is a creative act, it is not always held in high regard. Sometimes it gets trivialized as a "nice" hobby or is pigeon-holed as one of life's luxuries; equally it may be relegated to a form of lowly manual labor. The source of this polarization can be traced back to the Bible. The Garden of Eden is as beautiful as it is abundant, and until Adam and Eve are cast out to toil over hard ground, they live in a state of perfection. If the garden is caught between paradise on the one hand and the curse of expulsion on the other, where is the middle ground? Where can we find garden-ing as meaningful work?

The story of St. Maurilius, who was the bishop of Angers in the early fifth century, goes some way to answering that question. One day while Maurilius was performing Mass, a woman entered the church and pleaded with him to come with her and adminis-ter the holy sacrament to her dying son. Not realizing the urgency of the situation, Maurilius continued with the Mass, and before he was finished, the boy was dead. Consumed by feelings of guilt and unworthiness, the bishop secretly left the city and escaped on a ship to England. During the journey, the keys to the city's cathedral were lost overboard, and he took this as a sign that he was not meant to return. Once in England, he worked as a gardener for an impor-tant nobleman. Meanwhile, the inhabitants of Angers sent out a search party for their beloved bishop. Eventually, after seven years, they found the nobleman's mansion and encountered Maurilius as he emerged from the garden bearing produce for his master. They greeted him warmly and Maurilius was amazed when they handed him the lost keys which they had recovered on their journey.

Realizing that he was now forgiven, Maurilius resumed his life as bishop and was subsequently made a saint. He is depicted in murals at Angers and in a surviving fragment of tapestry digging the English nobleman's garden, surrounded by fruit trees and flowers, and presenting the fruits of his labors to his master.

My interpretation of Maurilius's story is that the regret and self-blame he suffered following the boy's death shattered his sense of identity and triggered a form of depressive breakdown. Over some considerable time he strived to reconcile himself to what he regarded as a failure in his duty of care. Through gardening he found a way to make some kind of reparation for the guilt and unworthiness he felt. In the end he recovered a sense of self-worth (represented in the story by the return of the keys), which enabled him to return to his former role and reconnect with his community.

Following his death, however, Maurilius's seven years of gardening were used within religious teaching as an example of how sins can be expiated by "performing our work in the spirit of penance." But Maurilius's story does not speak of penance or self-punishment to me. He did not take flight to the desert and cultivate hostile ground like the early Christian fathers, nor did he enter a solitary exile like the two patron saints of gardening, St. Phocas and St. Fiacre. Instead, he chose to grow flowers and fruits in a worldly garden. Perhaps through working in the nobleman's garden, he found a relationship with his god that did not demand an excess of self-punishment but, in a more benign way, offered him a second chance, a chance to "make good" and eventually reclaim his role in the world. I like to think it is an early documentation of therapeutic horticulture in action, and I have come to see it as an allegory of the restorative potential of gardening.

In the following century, it was St. Benedict with his *Rule* for monastic living who officially lifted gardening from the realm of penitential toil by asserting the sanctity of manual labor. Benedict's thinking when he first proposed it was revolutionary, not only within the church but also within the wider culture, in which tilling the soil was associated with slave labor and a beleaguered peasant class. For the Benedictines, gardening was an equalizer, and nobody within the monastery was too grand or too learned to work in the garden for a part of each day. This was a culture of care and reverence in which the gardener's tools were to be treated with the same level of respect as the vessels of the altar. It was a way of life in which the body, mind, and spirit were held in balance, and in which the virtuous life was an expression of our interconnectedness with the natural world.

In the aftermath of the fall of Rome, dark times descended on Europe and the land was badly in need of regeneration. The Roman Empire had seen the growth of large estates, or *latifundia*, which were run on slave labor and which exploited the land to the point of exhaustion. As the Benedictines grew in size and influence, they took on some of these abandoned and ruined estates and set about replenishing the land and developing them as monasteries. The reparative work that the Benedictines undertook was every bit as material as it was spiritual, in fact the two were inextricably linked, because of St. Benedict's belief that the life of the spirit needed to be grounded in a relationship with the earth.

A typical monastery had vineyards and orchards as well as plots in which the monks cultivated vegetables, flowers, and medicinal herbs, while their enclosed gardens provided tranquil spaces for meditation and recovery from illness. St. Bernard's account of the hospice gardens at Clairvaux Abbey in France dates from the eleventh century and is one of the earliest descriptions of a therapeutic garden. He writes of how "the sick man sits upon the green lawn. . . . For the comfort of his pain all kinds of grass are fragrant in his nostrils. The lovely green of herb and tree nourishes his eyes . . . the choir of painted birds caresses his ears . . . the earth breathes with fruitfulness, and the invalid himself with eyes, ears, and nostrils, drinks in the delights of colors, songs and perfumes." It is a strikingly sensuous account of drawing strength from the goodness of the earth.

The remarkable twelfth-century abbess St. Hildegard von Bingen was a composer and a theologian as well as a medicinal herbalist. She took the Benedictine teachings further and developed her own philosophy based on the connection between the human spirit and the growth force of the earth which she called *viriditas*. The word combines the Latin for green and truth, and like the source of a river, *viriditas* is the font of energy on which all other life forms ultimately depend. It is the origin of goodness and health, in contrast to *ariditas*, or dryness, which Hildegard regarded as its life-defying opposite.

The greening power of *viriditas* is both literal and symbolic. It refers to the flourishing of nature as well as the vibrancy of the human spirit. By placing "greenness" at the heart of her thinking, Hildegard recognized that people can only thrive when the natural world thrives. She understood that there is an inescapable link between the health of the planet and human physical and spiritual health, which is why she is increasingly regarded as a forerunner of the modern ecological movement.

In a garden filled with light and suffused with the energy of new growth, the green pulse of life can be felt at its strongest. Whether we conceive of the natural growth force in terms of God, Mother Earth, biology, or a mixture of these, there is a living relationship at work. Gardening is an interchange through which nature gives life to our reparative wishes, be it turning waste into nutritious compost, helping pollinators thrive, or beautifying the earth. Gardening involves striving to keep pests and weeds at bay so that there is nourishment in all its various forms, greenness and shade, color and beauty and all the fruits of the earth.

The emotional significance of reparation tends to be overlooked in the world we live in today, but it plays an important role in our mental health. Unlike religious absolution, the psychoanalytic view of reparation is not black-and-white, instead the view is that, like a constant gardener, we need to rework various forms of emotional restoration and repair throughout life. Melanie Klein first recognized the significance of this through her observations of small children at play. She was struck by how often their drawings and imaginary games involved expressing or testing out destructive impulses that were then followed by acts of restoration in which they displayed feelings of love and concern, and that this whole cycle was intensely charged with meaning.

Klein illustrated her thinking through a discussion of a Ravel opera called *L'Enfant et les Sortilèges* ("The Child and the Spells"). The plot, based on a story by Colette, starts when the central character, a little boy, is sent to his room by his mother for refusing to do his homework. In his banishment he embarks on a rampage of fury, reveling in destruction as he trashes his room and attacks his toys and pet animals. Suddenly, the room comes to life and he feels threatened and anxious.

Two cats appear and take the boy out to the garden, where a tree is groaning in pain from a wound he inflicted on its bark the day before. As he starts to feel pity and lays his cheek against the tree trunk, a dragonfly whose mate he recently caught and killed confronts him. It dawns on him that the insects and animals in the garden love one another. Then a fight breaks out when some of the animals he has previously hurt start to retaliate by biting him. A squirrel is injured in the fray and the boy instinctively takes off his scarf to bind its wounded paw. With this act of care, the world around him is transformed. The garden ceases to be a hostile place, and the animals sing to him of his goodness as they help him back to the house to be reunited with his mother. As Klein described: "He is restored to the human world of helping."

Children need to see positive confirmation of themselves in the world around them, and they need to believe in their capacity to love. Adults are no different. But when we get into a spiral of anger and resentment, as the little boy did with his mother, it can feel hard to let grievances go, especially if pride is at stake. What eventually allows these feelings to shift, and bring a return to more caring feelings, is something of a mystery, and sometimes it happens indirectly. For the little boy, it was the vulnerability of nature in the garden and the interconnectedness of life within it that awakened his feelings of love and protection. Feelings like these set up a "benign" or virtuous circle which gives rise to hopefulness in place of despair and depression. This aspect of our psychology is the mind's counterpart to the cycle of life in nature through which destruction and decay are followed by regrowth and renewal.

Plants are so much less frightening and challenging than people that a garden may be a more accessible way of reconnecting with life-giving impulses. For my patient Kay, gardening was a way of expressing nurturing feelings that was not caught up in the unpredictability and complexity of human relationships. In a garden the level of background noise falls away and you can escape from other people's thoughts and judgments about you, so that within a garden there is, perhaps, more freedom to feel good about yourself. This relief from the interpersonal realm of life can, paradoxically, be a way of reconnecting with our humanity.

Just as in bringing up children, in the garden we are never fully in control. Beyond providing the conditions for growth, there is only so much a gardener can do; the rest is down to the life force of plants, and they will grow in their own time and in their own way. That is not to say the gardener can be laissez-faire, because care requires a particular form of attention, a *tuning in* that is about noticing the smaller details. Plants are highly sensitive to their environment and there are many variables at play—temperature, wind, rain, sun, and pests. Many plants tough it out regardless, but to garden a plot well means looking out for them, noticing the first signs of ailing, and working out what they need in order to thrive.

As we cultivate the earth, we cultivate an attitude of care, but a caring stance is not something that is actively promoted in contemporary life. The "replace" rather than "repair" culture, combined with fragmented social networks and the fast pace of urban living, has given rise to a set of values that devalues care. In fact, we have moved so far from placing care at the center of our lives that it has become, as the environmentalist and social activist Naomi Klein recently observed, a "radical idea."

This is not only about values—there are realities to the world that many of us live in that work against these impulses. Our machines have become far too complex for most of us even to think about repairing them, and we have become used to all the immediate "likes" we get through our smart phones and other devices. There is a devaluing of the slower rhythms of natural time, the natural time not only of plants, but of our bodies and minds. These rhythms often don't fit in with the "quick fix" mentality that has come to dominate so much of modern life.

These pressures express themselves as a demand for treatment packages and programs that promise quick results, as if it were possible to speed-dial mental health. While identifying faulty thinking or misplaced feelings can help us to understand a problem so that it immediately becomes less troubling, it will still take months to lay down the neural pathways that accompany lasting change. In situations that are more complex, we not only have to wait for things to grow, we have to first reach the point where we really want things to grow, because the prospect of change, however much we might think we want it, almost always makes us very anxious.

The most popular metaphor in use for the brain these days is the computer, which only encourages the idea that there is a fix to be had. The physical structure of the brain is likened to hardware, the mind to its software, and terms such as "program," "module," and "app" are applied to its functioning. The undeveloped infant brain is even sometimes likened to a database waiting for data to be keyed in. This brain-as-computer metaphor is woefully misleading, not least in the idea that it is possible to separate our hardware from our software. The two are in fact so intimately related as to be effectively indivisible. Our experiences, thoughts, and feelings are constantly giving shape to our neural networks, and they in turn are influencing how we think and feel. But the real problem with the brain-as-computer is that it renders us unnatural.

The idea that we can cultivate the soul or the self like a garden goes back to ancient times and is beginning to be applied to the brain in contemporary science. It is, of course, replacing one metaphor with another, but we cannot think in any sophisticated way without metaphors. Furthermore, this one is more accurate. The cells that create our neural networks have a branching structure and were named *dendrites*, after the Latin word for tree, because of their striking resemblance to one. This resemblance, it has recently been discovered, reflects the fact that neuronal arbors and plants grow according to the operation of the same three mathematical laws. A deeper similarity can be found in the active process of pruning and weeding that maintains the health of our neural networks and is carried out by a group of cells that function as the brain's resident gardeners.

At the very beginning of life, the brain is a tangled wilderness of more than 500 billion neurons. In order to develop into a mature brain, 80 percent of these cells need to be cleared away to provide space for the remaining cells to create connections and establish complex networks. This process gives rise to the unique pattern of connectivity that makes us who we are. The brain grows in early life according to how it is nurtured, through the love, care, and attention a baby receives. As the brain's neurons fire in response to experience, the links between neighboring neurons are either strengthened or weakened. These points of connection, known as *synapses*, involve a tiny gap across which the brain chemicals known as *neurotransmitters* travel in order to connect with receptors on the other side. Over time, synapses that are not being used are pruned away so that the ones in regular use become better established and have room to grow.

The neural networks in our brains are shaped and reworked throughout the entire life cycle. The ability of neuronal connections to change like this is known as *plasticity*, a term that derives from the Greek word for "to mold," but these days it carries an unfortunate connotation of something unnatural. When plasticity was first discovered in the 1950s, no one had any idea how the shaping of our networks came about, and it remained a mystery until the role of *microglial cells* was revealed. These cells, which are part of the immune system, account for one in ten cells in the brain, and it was previously thought they were passive unless activated by infection or injury. It is now known that they appear in the embryo only a few days after conception, and that they are involved in how the brain grows and repairs itself from the very beginning.

These specialist cells are highly mobile, and as they crawl in among our neural networks, they weed and root out weak connections and damaged cells. Most of this activity happens while we sleep, when the brain shrinks and gives the microglia room to go about their work using their finger-like projections to remove toxins, reduce inflammation, and prune redundant synapses and cells.

Recent developments in imaging techniques have made it possible to observe them in action, and it appears that each one has its own patch of neural territory that it tends and that, like true gardeners, they don't only weed and clear, they also help the brain's neurons and synapses grow. This process, which is known as *neurogenesis*, is facilitated by a protein that they and other cells release, called *brain-derived neurotrophic factor*, or BDNF. The effects of this on neuronal cells is something like a fertilizer, which has earned it a reputation as the brain's "Miracle-Gro." Low levels of BDNF lead to depleted neural networks and are increasingly thought to be implicated in depression. BDNF levels can be boosted through various forms of stimulation, which include exercise, play, and social interaction.

A constant process of being weeded, pruned, and fertilized keeps the brain healthy at a cellular level. The activity of the microglia exemplifies one of the fundamental laws that govern life—that health is not a passive process. What is taking place on a microscopic scale also needs to happen on a larger canvas. The mind needs to be gardened too. Our emotional lives are complex and need constant tending and reworking. The form this takes will be different for each one of us, but fundamentally, in order to counteract negative and self-destructive forces, we need to cultivate a caring and creative attitude. Above all, we need to recognize what nourishes us.

We are a grassland species that emerged in the savannah landscapes of Africa, and over the course of evolution, our nervous and immune systems have been primed to function best in response to various aspects of the natural world. This includes how much sunlight we get, the kind of microbes we are exposed to, the amount of green vegetation around us, and the type of exercise we take. The significance of these things will become clearer in the course of this book, but Hildegard's intuition that there is a link between the way plants thrive in nature and human thriving turns out to have been right. When we work with nature outside us, we work with nature inside us. It is why people feel more fully alive and energized in the natural world, why gardeners report feeling calmer and more vigorous, and why spending time in nature awakens the connection-seeking aspects of our human nature.

When I began visiting therapeutic gardening groups as part of my research, I got a strong sense of all these benefits. On one of those visits I encountered a woman called Grace who suffered from anxiety and had been attending a small horticulture project for nearly a year. About ten years previously, when she was in her twenties, she had experienced an unfortunate and distressing chain of events which had culminated in the death of a close friend. Following this she developed depression and began to experience panic attacks. Although the medication she was prescribed reduced some of her symptoms, her life became increasingly restricted. Her anxiety prevented her going out to the corner store on her own, and she spent most of her time indoors, trapped in a cycle of low self-esteem, feeling that nothing was going to change.

Grace had never done any gardening before, and when her psychiatrist first suggested the project, she found it hard to imagine it would be helpful. Although she was uncertain whether or not to attend, once she did, she instantly took to the peacefulness of the garden: "There is no hustle and bustle," she said. "It just calms me down being here."

She liked the fact there was no compulsion to do lots of gardening; it was possible just to sit and unwind if that was how she felt. Grace soon discovered, however, that when she did join in, the impetus of the group carried her along. Shared tasks help group bonding, but natural surroundings play a part too, because people connect more easily when they are in nature together. It means that the psychological, social, and physical benefits of gardening go hand in hand.

The feeling that other people in the group who had been attending for longer were supportive of her made a huge difference to Grace. She also liked the fact that the horticultural therapist took care to show her exactly what she needed to do, and this gave her confidence. On one level, a demonstration like this is simply about practical skills, but for someone as stuck in her life as Grace, a crucial message is also being unconsciously imparted—that change and renewal are possible and that she can help something grow.

When, in time, the plants grow—and, of course, they do grow—then seeing is believing. And eating is believing too. For when you cook and share the produce, you taste it for real, and you know, *really* know, that something good has happened. As Grace said, "It makes a huge difference to see things from start to finish and know that you put the effort in to make it grow." Preparing and sharing food collectively was a new experience for her, as was the taste of freshly grown produce. The first thing she sampled was some sweetcorn, and she was overwhelmed by how full of flavor and succulent it was. She recalled how, one time, when they were tidying up after sharing some soup together, the entire group started singing and dancing in a spontaneous outburst of joy.

Grace was surprised at how involved she became with the plants she looked after, and how much pleasure and satisfaction she derived from seeing them thrive. The contemporary emphasis on self-improvement and self-investment can make care seem like a depleting activity because it requires putting in effort for something other than ourselves, but the neurochemistry of care is not like that. For obvious evolutionary reasons, care has inbuilt neurochemical rewards. The feelings of calm and contentment that accompany nurture have benefits for giver and receiver alike, and there are obvious evolutionary reasons why this should be so. The antistress and antidepressant effect of these pleasurable feelings arises through the action of the bonding hormone oxytocin and release of beta-endorphins, the brain's natural opioids. "It helps me so much," Grace told me. "It's a whole new feeling—while I'm there, I'm in another world."

This "other world" is not only associated with the experience of care and nurture but also the soothing effects of being immersed in nature and the stimulation of sociable activities such as planting, harvesting, and sharing food. A project like this to some extent replicates the kind of simple collaborative living, close to the land, that has typified our species for most of its existence. Grace attends the project once a week and the good feeling she experiences there stays with her for a few days afterward. If she starts to feel anxious when she is at home, just thinking about the garden is helpful: "It's like I have a calm place in my mind now," she said. These days, as a result, she can get to the store on her own and is beginning to get out and do other things as well. When I spoke with her, she had just completed one year and signed up for another, and there was no question in her mind how much the project helped her: "It's eleven out of ten," she told me, even though I hadn't asked her to rate it.

The idea that gardens and nature can help people recover from mental illness first became prominent in the eighteenth century. This is when reformers like the British physician William Tuke campaigned against the appalling conditions and brutal treatments that such patients were being subjected to. Tuke believed that the environment itself could be curative, and in 1796 he built an asylum known as the Retreat, in the countryside near York. Instead of being restrained, his patients were allowed to wander freely in the grounds, and there were opportunities for various forms of meaningful work, including gardening. Conceived of as "a quiet haven in which the shattered bark might find the means of reparation, or of safety," the approach to treatment here was based on kindness, dignity, and respect. There followed an era in which asylums were built in parkland settings with gardens and greenhouses in which patients could spend part of the day growing flowers and vegetables.

In 1812, on the other side of the Atlantic, Benjamin Rush, an American physician who was one of the founding fathers of the United States, published the first manual for the treatment of mental illness. In it, he observed that mental health patients who worked in the asylum grounds because they needed to pay for their care by cutting wood, making fires, and digging in the garden often made the best recoveries. In contrast, those of higher social status were more likely to "languish away their lives within the walls of the hospital."

Well into the twentieth century, many asylums continued to have large greenhouses and walled gardens in which flowers, fruit, and vegetables were cultivated by patients for use in the hospital. In the 1950s, the treatment of mental illness was radically changed by the introduction of new and powerful drugs. The main focus of care shifted to medication, and the role of the environment diminished in significance so that the next generation of hospitals that were built often had little in the way of outdoor green space.

We are beginning to come full circle. Levels of depression and anxiety have increased, and drug costs are rising. This, coupled with a growing body of evidence on nature's beneficial effects on us, is giving gardening, green exercise, and various other forms of green care a new impetus. "Social prescribing" schemes are a recent initiative which allow GPs to prescribe a course of gardening or green exercise instead of, or alongside, medication. The current policy in England is for this kind of community-based initiative to become more common. The GP William Bird, who edited the recently published *Oxford Textbook of Nature and Public Health*, is a strong advocate for green care. He has estimated that for every £1 ($1.31) the National Health Service might spend on setting up a gardening project, £5 ($6.56) could be saved through reduced health costs. As he puts it: "People are living in a state of disconnection from nature and from each other."

Therapeutic horticulture is usually based on principles of organic cultivation. The focus is on environmental sustainability as well as the psychological sustainability that comes from providing people with what they need in order to grow. When the UK charity Mind carried out a large-scale survey of people's experiences of taking part in a range of green activities including green gyms and gardening, they found that 94 percent said that it had benefited their mental health.

One of the strongest findings in research across the last few decades has been the extent to which gardening boosts mood and self-esteem and helps alleviate depression and anxiety. These studies invariably involve people who have chosen to garden, which means that they do not reach the highest standard for clinical trials, in which patients are randomly allocated to a treatment. A group of Danish researchers, however, has recently achieved this. Their study involved assigning patients diagnosed with stress disorders to two different groups. One received a well-proven ten-week course of cognitive behavioral therapy (CBT), a structured program for managing stress, and the other was assigned to a gardening program of the same length. Ten weeks of gardening a few hours a week is not that much, but even for this brief period horticulture provided a similar level of benefit as the evidence-based CBT program. The study, which was published in the *British Journal of Psychiatry* in 2018, was the first horticultural therapy trial to be included in the journal, and its inclusion is an indication that gardening is gaining credibility in the medical mainstream.

Important as they are, trials like this cannot capture the full range of benefits that therapeutic horticulture can offer. Gardening is unusual in the extent to which it encompasses the emotional, physical, social, vocational, and spiritual aspects of life. This, of course, is its strength, but it also makes it hard for research to do it justice. In addition, scientific studies are necessarily brief, and for many people, like Grace, a longer period is likely to be needed. Indeed, for any of us to benefit from seeing things grow, we need to experience the growth cycle through the seasons

One of the longest running and most successful horticulture projects in the UK is Bridewell Gardens in Oxfordshire, where people can stay for up to two years. The gardeners who attend the project—for they are called gardeners, not patients—are typically people who have serious mental health problems, many of them long-term. They are often socially disconnected and have become identified with their illness. In any one year, the team here work with about seventy or eighty people, most of whom attend twice a week.

Gardening is an ordinary activity that is not associated with hospitals or clinics, let alone being ill, and that in itself is normalizing. Working with the natural growth force is about nourishing the good. Through developing an understanding of this, the gardeners at Bridewell realize they can do the same thing in their own lives and that it is not necessary to take all the bad things forward. The follow-up figures show that after completing the program, around 60 percent of participants take up some form of work, either paid or voluntary, or enter training, and a large proportion of the others make different positive steps in their lives, such as beginning a new activity or joining a community group. Given where they started from, these changes are considerable.

Bridewell is set within a large walled garden in the Cotswold countryside. Like the Benedictine monastic gardens, it contains a mixture of productive working areas and areas that have been designed to offer peace and sanctuary. Staff have observed that sessions with the blacksmith can be particularly helpful for people who may have experienced violence and abuse earlier in their lives. This kind of catharsis involves working through emotions and conflicts that cannot readily be put into words. Since one of the strongest determinants of our mental health is how we manage our negative feelings and experiences, this effect is therapeutically important. Sigmund Freud referred to it as *sublimation*, and it can arise through any kind of transformative and creative work. In physical chemistry, a sublimation reaction involves a leap from one state to another, like solid to gas without becoming liquid in between. The artist, Freud argued, does something similar by taking raw instincts and powerful emotions and turning them into creations with aesthetic value.

There are many ways in which anger, grief, and frustration can be sublimated or channeled creatively, and gardening is one of them. Digging the soil, cutting back vegetation, and ripping up weeds are all forms of care in which destructiveness can be put to use in the service of growth. In discharging quantities of aggression and working off anxieties, tilling the earth works on the inner landscape as well as the outer; quintessentially, it is a transformative action.

Only through facing the sadness of loss are we able to recover from it, but the pain involved means we sometimes resort to other solutions. Miss Havisham, in Charles Dickens's *Great Expectations*, refuses to mourn and cultivates grievances instead. When she is jilted on her wedding day, she stops the clocks, shuts out the daylight, and confines herself indoors. Satis House becomes a mausoleum to her broken dreams. Her wedding cake remains like a rotting corpse on the table, with a black fungus inhabited by speckled-legged spiders growing out of it.

It is a peculiarity of human nature that people are able to turn something good into something bad and then relish it. The young girl, Estella, whom Miss Havisham brings up, has not been nurtured by her but formed, as Pip discovers, "to wreak Miss Havisham's revenge on man." In place of love and compassion, contempt and indifference have been planted in Estella's impressionable heart.

The garden at Satis House has turned into a "wilderness overgrown with tangled weeds." But Dickens makes it clear that this is no ordinary reversion to the wild. When Pip wanders through the "desolate and neglected" garden, he encounters "a rank ruin of cabbage stalks" and then something more grotesque—some old melon frames and cucumber frames that "seemed in their decline to have produced a spontaneous growth of weak attempts at pieces of old hats and boots, with now and then a weedy offshoot into the likeness of a battered saucepan." The natural growth force in the garden, as in the mind of its owner, has been perverted, and decay is taking place without renewal.

On his last visit to Satis House, Pip recognizes the extent to which years of reclusive brooding led Miss Havisham's "spurned affection, and wounded pride" to develop into a "monster mania." He also realizes that "in shutting out the light of day, she had shut out infinitely more; that, in seclusion, she had secluded herself from a thousand natural and healing influences." If only she had got the pruning shears out, all that vengeance could have gone into transforming her garden. Instead her grievance consumes her, she goes up in flames, and Satis House is burned to the ground. At the end of the novel, Pip and Estella meet by chance on the site where Satis House once stood. Among the rubble, Pip notices that "some of the old ivy had struck root anew, and was growing green in the low quiet mounds of ruin." With this small sign of nature's renewal, we sense that Pip and Estella's lives may not be so ruined after all.

CHAPTER 3

Seeds and Self-Belief

Insight Garden flower garden at San Quentin
State Prison, San Quentin, California.

Many things grow in the garden that were never sown
there.

Thomas Fuller (1654–1734)

When it comes to making things grow, the rewards that follow
from small interventions can be disproportionately large. I feel
almost ridiculously identified with our asparagus bed, because it
started life in my hands as a very small seed packet. For the same
reason I experience a thrill when my auriculas pop into flower
each spring. Auriculas are so mouthwateringly delicious, with

45

their boiled candy colors and their confectioners' sugar farina, that they always give a sense of delight, but the feeling is intensified by knowing that I had a hand in their making, and it is a form of magic that came home from the Chelsea Flower Show in a brown envelope.

Asparagus and auriculas, it is true, require patience and persistence, but sow some sunflower seeds in spring, and a few months later you will be looking up at a row of giant sunflowers. Sow a handful of pumpkin seeds, and more likely than not, in autumn those seeds will yield more than you can possibly eat. Nowhere in our garden is the marvel of nature's powers of alteration more evident than in the crop of pumpkins that our compost heap yields each year, and it all comes from a few seeds and a pile of waste.

Gardening is more accessible than other creative endeavors, such as painting and music, because you are halfway there before you start; the seed has all its potential within it—the gardener simply helps unlock it. The psychological significance of this came home to me on a visit to a prison gardening project when I interviewed a man called Samuel. He had been in and out of jail for much of the last thirty years, mainly for drug-related offenses. With his thin gray hair and heavily creased cheeks, he looked defeated by life, and when he spoke of his family, I could see that his sense of shame and failure was crippling. Samuel knew he had let them down again and again, and he felt that they had lost all faith in his capacity to stay clean and turn his life around.

This time in jail had been different from his previous spells. There was a horticulture project within the grounds, and having never gardened before, Samuel decided he would try something new. He told me about a phone conversation with his eighty-year-old mother that had taken place a few days earlier, soon after harvesting the squash he had helped grow in the garden. For the first time in decades, he had something good to tell her—something he was proud of. His mother reminisced with him about her own gardening days, and they made a connection over the squash flowers that she'd always loved: "It was a joy for her to hear and not be worried about me."

Talking to Samuel, it seemed that everything about his past was stacked up against him, but the squash harvest was the first piece of tangible evidence he'd had that something in him might be able to change. As he put it: "If nothing changes, nothing changes; something's got to give. But here, I've connected." The newfound sense of possibility he had discovered within the garden meant he had put his name down for a horticultural internship which he planned to start as soon as he was released.

Anyone new to gardening is invariably anxious about whether their plants will thrive. But when new life takes off and we witness a surge of growth, how empowered we feel! At the heart of this experience and how affirmed we can feel by it, there is, I think, a kind of illusion that hooks people into growing things.

If you are an experienced gardener, it is easy to forget the magic of surprise that forms the basis of the illusion, but I don't think it ever entirely wears off. I caught a glimpse of it recently in my husband, Tom, when, just as he was about to give up on them, some tree peony seedlings sprouted from a tray he had sowed nearly three years before. With a grin on his face, as if he had done something really clever, he said, "It just shows, it's always worth waiting."

In Michael Pollan's book *Second Nature*, he recounts a childhood memory in which you can see the illusion in action. Pollan is four years old and he is in the family garden, hiding in the bushes, possibly from his sister. As he pokes around, he catches sight of a "stippled green football sitting in a tangle of vines and broad leaves." It is a watermelon. The feeling, Pollan writes, "is one of finding treasure," but it is more than that, as he explains:

Then I make the big connection between this melon and a seed I planted, or at least spat out and buried, months before:

"I made this happen."

For a moment I'm torn between leaving the melon to ripen and the surging desire to publicise my achievement:

"Mom has got to see this."

So I break the cord attaching the melon to the vine, cradle it in my arms and run for the house, screaming my head off the whole way.

The watermelon "weighs a ton," and what happens next feels like one of life's minor tragedies. Just as he reaches the back doorstep, Pollan loses his balance, and as the melon hits the ground, it explodes.

The words that stood out to me when I read this passage were *I made this happen*. Pollan's boyish conviction and surge of pride is striking and is something we can, if we are lucky, all feel. Such precious moments matter in adult life as well as in childhood, and that feeling is present in the little boy Pollan, racing toward the house, just as it is in Samuel's phone call to his mother. Importantly, in terms of how influential these kind of moments can be, Pollan believes the thrill he felt on discovering that he had inadvertently grown a watermelon has motivated much of his subsequent gardening life.

The psychoanalyst Marion Milner discovered the creative power of illusion when she was teaching herself to paint, a process she wrote about in a book entitled *On Not Being Able to Paint*. Donald Winnicott, who believed in the importance of creativity throughout life, developed Milner's thinking further. In his own imaginative leap of understanding, he came to the conclusion that not only is a baby the center of its own world, it also feels it has created its own world. So when a mother responds to a baby in the very same moment or soon after the feeling of wanting Mother arises, the baby may fleetingly feel that he or she has created the mother, rather than the other way around—such is the scope of infantile omnipotence!

Although we can never access the subjective experience of this earliest phase of life to confirm this idea or not, we can observe how much small children like to believe they are more powerful than they actually are. This illusion needs to be shattered very gently because it forms the basis of self-belief. Too much too soon is not a good thing, because the child's sense of smallness and vulnerability can then be crushing. That doesn't mean the illusion needs to be overtly encouraged either, just fostered a little. We see it in action in the imaginary games children play that offset their feelings of powerlessness and allow them to experience "the joy in being a cause." None of this is restricted to childhood. Winnicott and Milner's insight was that many of our most enriching and inspiring experiences throughout life involve a similar sense of creative illusion.

In the husbandry of seeds and the interaction between mind and nature that is involved, we can experience something of this illusion. Making things grow has a kind of mystery to it, and we can claim some of that mystery for ourselves. We even have a name for the illusion that I am describing: a "green thumb." This illusion is, I think, central to the vital connection between people and plants and contributes to the enormous satisfaction we derive from making things happen and the joy we can feel in being a cause.

The role of what Winnicott called the "good enough mother" is to foster illusion just enough. Through not being entirely perfect (e.g., always available), the mother allows the baby to experience small frustrations which are accompanied by a dawning awareness that magical control over reality does not exist: "The mother's eventual task is gradually to disillusion the infant, but she has no hope of success unless at first she has been able to give sufficient opportunity for illusion."

This "facilitating" process, as Winnicott called it, provides an environment in which a child can grow into him- or herself without being prematurely judged or pressured to be something that someone else wants the child to be. Winnicott understood the task of therapy in a similar way, and once used a gardening analogy to illustrate it. In objecting to the heavy-handed work of a particular psychoanalytic colleague, he wrote: "One felt that if he were growing a daffodil, he would think he was making the daffodil out of a bulb instead of enabling the bulb to develop into a daffodil by good enough nurture."

Winnicott believed that children who do not have enough opportunity to experience illusion find disillusionment much harder to bear and are therefore more easily discouraged or plunged into despair. In other words, the experience of illusion helps underpin our subsequent capacity to bear the disappointments and harshness of reality and provides us with a source of self-belief and hope. In the garden too for all the generosity Mother Nature bestows on us, like a "good enough mother," she never fails to remind us of the limits of our human powers. I like to think that these painful reminders, of our place in the overall scheme of things, mean that although feelings of pride are certainly part of the gardener's emotional lexicon, hubris may be a weed that is not so commonly encountered in the mind of a gardener.

Shaping a bit of reality is empowering, but crucially in the garden, we are never completely in control. The general rule in life is that we thrive best in situations where we have some control but not complete control. A total lack of control is stressful, and too much control is unstimulating, because life becomes boring and predictable. It is why, paradoxically, experiencing both illusion and disillusion, empowerment and disempowerment, doesn't make us give up—it only spurs us on. Which is why Michael Pollan can honestly credit finding that watermelon in the bushes with motivating much of his subsequent gardening life.

When it comes to the business of growing things, the mysterious world of plants can feel intimidating to newcomers, who inevitably fear they might discover they don't have a green thumb. The power of the illusion means that if your first foray into the world of seeds isn't successful, it can be more than disheartening or deflating, even confirming fears like "nothing ever works for me," or "everything I touch is doomed." This is why it is so important for children and for beginners to start gardening with something truly dependable like sunflowers or radishes. Because, in truth, all of us can make plants grow given the right context in which to make the discovery.

We want to feel the thrill of the illusion again, and that, in itself, is compelling. Which is why Michael Pollan can honestly credit finding that watermelon in the bushes with motivating much of his subsequent gardening life.

The transformative power of a garden is seen most clearly in situations where other sources of self-esteem are hard to come by. Over the last ten years, the Royal Horticultural Society (RHS) has been running a campaign to make gardening available in schools and recently commissioned research into the impact of the projects they have been supporting within a number of primary schools, mainly in deprived parts of large cities. There were many benefits that emerged from the study, not least that the garden itself provided a calming environment and that growing vegetables and flowers and activities such as making compost brought aspects of the curriculum alive and helped them assume a new relevance. It was also observed to be a good equalizer because, within the garden, the academic pecking order was quickly forgotten. Among individual children, the beneficial effects were most noticeable in those who were unmotivated or had special needs or behavioral problems.

One thing that really caught my attention was the researchers' findings of a Halloween project in a school near Luton. Most of the children attending this school live in the high-rise blocks that surround it, with little access to green space. There is a large incidence of learning disabilities, and a large number of pupils there function well below the national average. For this group of seven-year-olds, growing their own Halloween pumpkins turned out to be much more than an exciting novelty. For many, it marked a transformation in their confidence as well as their motivation, changes that reached far beyond the project itself. An exercise like growing pumpkins is, on one level, a way of offering factual learning in an entertaining way, but for children with low self-esteem, it can also provide a newfound sense of agency and interest.

It may seem like a large leap from children with learning and behavioral problems to prisoners like Samuel, but the reality is that most prisons are full of people who have fallen by the wayside in the educational system, and the incidence of learning disabilities in the prison population is very high. In addition, many prisoners have acquired deeply ingrained negative self-beliefs that make it hard for them to believe in the possibility of change. However, the experience of making something grow can be a first step in discovering a sense of identity that is not vested in hustling the system or in cheating or stealing, and can provide a source of self-esteem that is not derived from violence or intimidation.

Samuel was serving time as a prisoner at Rikers Island, one of the largest penal colonies in the world. He was attending a program that the Horticultural Society of New York, also known as the Hort, runs in collaboration with the New York City Department of Correction. The GreenHouse project, as it is known, gives four hundred men and women the chance each year to learn how to grow and care for plants, and in doing so provides them with a source of hope and motivation that might help them stay out of jail.

One of the most innovative aspects of the GreenHouse project is that it offers internships with the Hort's Green Team in the community after release. Ex-offenders work on hundreds of different garden and park spaces around the city, contributing to the greening of the city and creating links with the community.

This is the program that Samuel had enrolled in, and it has helped many ex-offenders develop the skills that they first learned on Rikers. Finding legitimate employment after serving time inside can be extremely difficult. There is a vulnerable transition period to get through, and repeat offending in those who leave Rikers is high. More than 65 percent of ex-prisoners are back inside within three years of release, but the re-offending rate for those who attend the Hort's program is only 10 to 15 percent.

Crossing over the bridge to Rikers in the early morning light, I looked back at a sweeping panorama of the Manhattan skyline, which rises only a few miles away across Flushing Bay, while in the other direction, the runways of La Guardia Airport lie across an even shorter stretch of water. Rikers has long been notorious as a dark and dangerous place, a reputation that has intensified in recent years following a series of scandals.

There are eight separate jails on the island, which together house about eight thousand men and women. Ninety percent are African American or Latino, and 40 percent have been diagnosed with mental illnesses. A large number are detainees rather than prisoners: they are awaiting trial. The majority of convictions are for drug possession, shoplifting, and prostitution.

It is said that the island itself is unwholesome, that it emits methane gases. In the 1930s, the site was expanded from its original size of eighty-seven acres to its current four hundred acres with landfill—some of it toxic. Not a place where you would naturally think of making a garden, yet this is what the Hort achieved as long ago as 1986, when they first set up the GreenHouse program on the island. James Jiler, then director, built a greenhouse and oversaw the conversion of a 2.5-acre empty lot into a productive garden. Since 2008, when Hilda Krus took over the running of the program, seven more garden spaces have been created on the island. She, and a team of twelve horticultural therapists and teachers, provide gardening sessions six days a week.

The annual produce, all eighteen thousand pounds of it, is shared so that prisoners, staff, and ex-prisoners working on the Green Team can benefit from it. The participating prisoners also grow perennials for the Parks Department, and some of the cutting flowers are used for Rikers staff lunches. This last may seem like a minor detail, but, as Hilda Krus, the current director of the project, explained to me, it is important that staff as well as participants can benefit from what the garden has to offer. I saw this in action while going through security with Hilda, when one of the corrections officers greeted her with the words "Hey Hilda! Still doing that green thumb!"

The GreenHouse curriculum combines elements of horticultural therapy, vocational training, and ecological awareness. At the end of every session, tools and other implements are checked and counted and then locked away. Although violent outbreaks occur incessantly inside the jails, there has never been an outbreak of violence within the garden itself.

The gardens may be enclosed within high razor-wire fencing, but once inside, you could be in a garden anywhere. That feeling is only disrupted by the regulation orange-and-white striped overalls that the prisoners wear as their work clothes. When I asked if this was their first experience of gardening, quick as flash, one prisoner responded: "Yes—except for growing weed in my closet!" The group working in the garden that morning were all serving time for drug-related offenses. What they valued about the garden varied—some were keen to grow vegetables afterward, others to teach their children how to grow things, and one young man spoke of how he imagined taking a girl for a walk in Central Park and being able to impress her with his newly acquired knowledge of plants.

"You don't see much character here," one man told me, and when I asked what this meant, everyone started chipping in, trying to explain. "In the dorms we rarely talk. It's so closed in, sixty guys in a small place and too much testosterone in there. Here you can take the mask off." Another added, "No one wants to intimidate the flowers or each other," and another: "Everybody is the same here, this cuts through the crap" and "if there's a problem we talk it out. You stop relating to people inside." What I came to understand, and have heard about subsequently in other prison settings, is that gardens have a powerful leveling effect; they offer an environment in which social pecking orders and racial divides become much less relevant. Children taking part in school gardening projects benefit from this effect too. Working with the earth seems to foster an authentic connection between people, free from the posturing and prejudice that characterizes so much human-to-human relating.

In contrast to the grimness and monotony of the rest of Rikers Island, brightly colored cutting flowers such as chrysanthemums were in bloom when I was there, and kale, chard, and peppers were growing in the vegetable beds. When they were walking me around, the men insisted that we take a detour to look at some fully grown maize plants that had sprouted from birdseed someone had spilled on the ground earlier in the year. Not only were they looking forward to eating the corn, the fact that it had grown from something that, for all intents and purposes, had been discarded, held a powerful resonance for them.

Of all the men in the group, I noticed that Martin, a tall mixed-race man who had a gentle manner, seemed to be one of the keenest. When we spoke later on, however, he told me that he hadn't chosen to enroll; he had, as he put it, been "chosen," his name put forward by one of the officers in charge of his dorm. An earlier chance to join had passed him by because he had assumed that gardening could not possibly have anything to offer him. Once he started, he became hooked, and looking back he realizes he had "a closed mind" before: "Everything out here is natural; nothing is forced or coerced or manipulated. It is better. I've learned to appreciate it, embrace it." The sense of physical freedom in the garden is accompanied by an inner sense of freedom in which the possibility of a different way of life can be glimpsed.

Tomatoes, Martin told me, were the biggest revelation—to watch them growing and then experience the incredible difference in taste. He thought his wife could not understand his obsession with the garden, but he wanted to convince her and teach his kids about it too. There was, in fact, an urban farm just around the corner from his home which he used to walk straight by; now he was keen to be part of it. Until coming to the Rikers garden, he'd thought supermarket fruit and vegetables were the best you could get: "I used to think it should be perfect, better than anything, because it's in a package."

Apart from the boost he experienced through growing produce, the other aspect Martin spoke of was the tranquillity and fresh air in the garden: "Here you speak a different language. Inside it's all negativity, commotion, and violence. Out here you can find yourself again. It's a good piece of sanity in an island of insanity." And then as we were finishing our conversation, almost as if he felt he might not have convinced me, he tapped his head and said: "If you have a small gap in there, you can really get something out of this." Just at that point, one of the officers shouted loudly, "Time's up!" "That's his Corrections voice," Martin told me. "It always changes when it's time."

Some of the participants have childhood memories of grandparents or parents tending a plot, but others have had so little contact with nature before that they are afraid of touching the soil. They have never put their hands in the earth. Martin had no concept whatsoever of what gardening involved, and he only got the chance to find out through the enlightened intervention of one of the officers. That "small gap" in his mind, through which a seed of possibility had been sown, enabled him to speak with such eloquence and feeling about it to me.

Later on, I met some of the women detainees and offenders who worked in the garden. I was there to hear about their experiences on the project, but their past lives spilled out in the interviews with me; it was the only way they could explain what the opportunity of being there meant to them. They spoke of violent relationships, abusive pimps, stillbirths, the death of siblings, and parents who died when they were children. Their stories revealed how little care they had experienced in the course of their lives and how the majority of their relationships had caused heartbreak or ended violently.

Vivian told me that she had reached a point where she stopped wanting to live, and that now, thanks to "all the living things in the garden," she does. She became hooked soon after she started working on the project—the place, she said, "blew me away"—and talking to her, I sensed the importance for her of caring for something outside herself, as well as the peace and quiet in the garden. "It's a relief here; all the stress goes away. My favorite place is the greenhouse and learning about all the desert plants, how the plants take in what we breathe out. Sometimes I speak to the plants; they get to share our secrets."

For Carol, like Martin, gardening had been a revelation and was something she wanted to carry on: "I've learned a lot here—how to make your own seeds and see them grow. I never knew how a strawberry is made; it grows a flower first of all. I've got really interesting things to tell my husband now, and I say to him, 'I'll be planting these things.' I want to share it with my kids, show them how to grow things. It's cheaper and it tastes and smells good!"

· · ·

How many people's love of gardening starts with the buzz experienced in the transformation of a handful of seeds to a harvest? This group was no exception, and they too were fascinated by the hidden power of seeds. Some weeks before, Hilda had brought in a coconut to show them just how large a seed can be, and it was sitting in a bucket of water in the middle of the garden with a two foot high shoot growing out of it. A coconut palm was launching itself into the world, and they were mesmerized by watching it happen.

Plants have an inward quality, and interacting with them is a calming and nonjudgmental experience. We can all benefit from this feeling, but there may be another dimension to it inside a prison. The birds and insects come and go, but, rooted as they are, the plants cannot. There is perhaps a kind of sympathy at work in a shared captive state. The convicted prisoners know how much time they have to serve, but the detainees have to live with uncertainty. Gardening can help them cope with this. Setbacks like trial delays can be devastating, and they sometimes happen repeatedly, as in Alberto's case. He told me that whenever he got bad news, he came out to the garden and it would calm him down: "It gets your mind to another place, temporarily."

Another detainee, Dino, was a very shy man who spoke to me about the changes he had seen in himself and others: "It has brought a lot of good things out of us. I'm not a talker, I like doing things." He took pride in making the garden more beautiful, but there were pitfalls in that for him too, and it seemed that he was learning all sorts of life lessons, especially about how to share and collaborate with others. He told me how prone he was to being possessive about things he had worked on: "It's not good to love something too much. I have to hold back from being overprotective—it spoils it for others. This is for everybody to enjoy. That's how much I love it; I want to keep people off it sometimes, but I have to remember I'm not doing this for myself, it's for all of us."

Jaro seemed to be the youngest in the group, and he wanted to show me his favorite flower. He led me across the garden toward a bed that contained some deep red snapdragons: "I'll show you something," he said, and as he picked one, I recalled the fun I had as a child playing with these flowers, just as he was about to do now, manipulating the snapdragon's "mouth" so it looked like a little puppet.

Next, he took me over to see another favorite—the Tiger's Eye Sumac tree. He invited me to stroke the soft hair on its stem. "It's like a tiger skin," he said, stroking it himself. I was struck by his boyishness and how the garden for him was a safe place in which to express such tenderness; feelings that could not ever be allowed to emerge in the threatening environment inside.

When they join the project, Hilda shows the participants how to be gentle in their handling of plants and what kind of things to look out for. She believes the relationship they develop with the plants that they look after is an important part of the therapeutic effect because it allows them to open themselves up in an unthreatening relationship. The fact that plants don't immediately react or respond to us, that they don't flinch or smile or feel pain, certainly not in any way we can recognize, is central to this. If you haven't received much care in early life, if what you've experienced is the opposite of care, then learning how to care later on in life is fraught with difficulties. Not only is the inner template lacking, but vulnerability in others can bring out the worst in you. This is why abuse often gets unwittingly repeated. A plant's vulnerability is different from that of a small animal or vulnerable adult or child—all of these can trigger cruel or even sadistic impulses in those who have been victims of these things themselves, but the fact that you can't inflict pain on a plant means that it doesn't invite cruelty. Working with plants becomes a safe way to learn about care and tenderness—there isn't much of any consequence that can go wrong.

Something about Martin, Samuel, and some of the others I spoke to at Rikers resonated with my years of clinical experience in the NHS. There, I worked with patients who had grown up in deprived parts of the county surrounded by varying degrees of violence, alcoholism, and law breaking. Such intergenerational cycles are difficult to address and mean that therapy treatments sometimes never get off the ground or, if they do, are at risk of being broken off prematurely. There were always some patients, though, who were able to make a lot of a little, and through coming once a week, for a bit less than a year, managed to shift their lives to a different trajectory.

In a world that is dominated by material culture, it can seem that everything has a price, and if you are poor and living in a city, you are inevitably excluded from many of the things that surround you. Working with nature is a different kind of experience. This comes across in something that James Jiler, Hilda's predecessor, observed. Rikers is on the flight path for a number of migratory birds, and one day, a little red cardinal appeared in the garden. The prisoner that Jiler was working with that day noticed it and asked how much a bird like that cost. The idea that nature has riches that don't come at a price and can be enjoyed for free is revelatory for most of the prisoners and gives rise to an entirely new relationship with their surroundings.

Like most things, gardening is not so much about what you do but how you do it. Garden making throughout history has often been about controlling and dominating nature, and it has to be said, even damaging it. There are gardeners who consume excessive water on immaculate lawns in unsuitable climates and who pollute the soil with countless chemicals. But therapeutic gardening is necessarily about gardening sustainably and working with, not against, the vital forces of nature. Working on a program like the

GreenHouse project involves learning about the basics of ecology and offers an awakening to the wider issue of how our food is produced and the whole question of how we live on this planet.

There is not a lot of opportunity within a prison to feel that you've made something good happen, and if you enter and leave prison with a belief that you are incapable of doing anything worthwhile, how can there be any hope of change? Such negative self-convictions are a life sentence in themselves.

This is borne out in a piece of research conducted in Liverpool by the criminologist Shadd Maruna. Through a series of in-depth interviews he investigated the question of what helps repeat offenders turn away from crime. He discovered that offenders who continued relentlessly on a criminal path characteristically had what he called a "condemnation" script of their lives. In contrast, those who changed their lives managed to adopt a new, more "generative" narrative in which past mistakes could be integrated into a more hopeful story.

Vocational training can help increase an offender's prospects of employment, but it needs to be accompanied by other psychological changes like the ones that Maruna describes, because crime and gang involvement will always be more lucrative than any first-level re-entry job. Maruna also observed that some of the ex-offenders' hopeful narratives had an element of defiance incorporated into them. Gardening is, of course, an intrinsically hopeful act and it is a reparative act, but particularly in the world today, it can also be a defiant act. Urban farms, like the one that Martin wanted to get involved in, are part of an expanding counterculture that is focused on growing nutritious food in a sustainable way as an alternative to a highly industrialized food system. In this way gardening can provide a bigger story within which people can locate themselves.

The effect on prisoners of acquiring a larger narrative is demonstrated by findings of research that was carried out on a gardening intervention at San Quentin, California's oldest prison. The Insight

Garden Program here was started by Beth Waitkus in 2002. An evaluation of the program that she has developed showed that the higher the level of eco-literacy a prisoner acquired, the greater the shift in his personal values. In other words, while the permaculture and ecology course that she runs within the prison is educational, it is also a powerful therapeutic tool for change, giving the prisoners a different context in which to understand their lives. As Beth explained to me, the principles of sustainable gardening can become a code for living. By getting their hands into the earth, the prisoners take on board our need "to live with the environment, not against it, and that it is the same for living with people."

The Insight Garden Program has expanded and now operates in eight other prisons in California. Restorative justice, Beth argues, is cost-effective, and she makes the point that the entire program in San Quentin costs less to run each year than keeping one prisoner in jail for the same amount of time. As with the Hort's program, the re-offending rates are very low, and like the Hort, part of the program's success lies in having established strong connections with horticulture projects in the community, such as Planting for Justice, a landscape and gardening practice that is willing to work with ex-offenders. Beth described how transformation happens when people are able to "move from me to we," and remarked that again and again she has observed how growing and caring for plants gives people a different attitude to life. They start to value it.

Gardening has the power to counteract low self-worth in a way that can be particularly valuable for young people who are at risk of offending. Interacting with the natural world has a calming effect, and working with the growth force of plants enables them to achieve something constructive. But most children these days are growing up in a state of disconnection from nature. They do not even get outdoors much. In fact, recent figures show that the average child spends less time outside each week than a maximum security prisoner.

The largest gardening charity in the UK, Thrive, operates in London, the Midlands, and Reading. They run therapeutic and educational programs for people with a range of social and health needs. Their Growing Options project works with fourteen- to sixteen-year-olds who have been excluded from school. Most of them struggle with the basics of math and English and have had little chance previously to do any hands-on activities. Alongside acquiring negative self-beliefs, many have adopted attitudes of opposition and defiance.

The young people attend all day, one day a week, and each has his or her own small plot to look after so the young person can take ownership of it. The beds are located in an open field and protected by a low fence of rabbit netting, which gives the participants a sense of security in the large expanse around them, but at the same time does not hem them in. Running a project like this is challenging work, especially at the start of each intake. It requires resilience and patience on the part of the staff and volunteers to manage difficult behaviors, but simply being outdoors is helpful because the students can take themselves off if they need to let off steam.

Donald Winnicott, who was an adviser to the young offenders' service, did not indulge in a sentimental view of antisocial behavior and delinquency, but he did believe in the importance of recognizing the various forms of deprivation that give rise to it. He coined the phrase "delinquency as a sign of hope" to make the point that young people who are causing trouble are seeking something that they do not know how to get and are going about it in the wrong way. What is important, he emphasized, is that they have not yet despaired of getting it. Behind their destructiveness lies a wish for some kind of recognition, and any hope for their future rests in working with this.

Over time, the participants on the Growing Options project

come to feel affirmed by seeing the plants they grow thrive and produce. One of the girls I heard about who had attended the previous year announced right at the start: "I've never been given rules." It was hard going for the staff, as she did not even want to put her boots on. But, by the end of the year, the same girl gave a talk about discovering how much you can get out of something, even when you think you don't want to do it. Tilling the earth and growing produce can give rise to a sense of effectiveness in a world in which it seems to be getting harder and harder for young people to feel they can be effective at anything. As a result, like many others who attend the project, this girl's self-esteem improved. She went on to higher education afterward, an accomplishment that was not remotely on the horizon when she started.

Although the Growing Options project involves completing modules toward a basic horticulture training, the aim is not to prepare the young people for a future in gardening; rather the project aims to give them "transferable skills" that will help them in the next stage of life, whatever field they choose to pursue, and when it comes to "transferable skills," a sense of self-belief is the most important of them all.

The feeling of "joy in being a cause" is an intense but transient moment in time. It can be highly charged and motivating, but gardening has other, slower effects. The process of internalizing a different set of attitudes is something that takes place gradually, through repetition. In her book about learning to paint, Marion Milner described feeling that through repeatedly performing an activity, she was able to "knit" new concepts into the structure of her being. I think something similar happens in the garden, where "doing" is a way of learning, not only about nature but about ourselves and what we are capable of.

Working with the hands and the body in the garden involves what one of the founding psychologists of child development, Jean Piaget, called sensori-motor learning. This kind of experiential learning is somewhat neglected in education these days, which tends to favor conceptual learning, but Piaget believed it underpins our cognitive development. Only through interacting with the world can we build internal models of it in our minds. "Learning by doing" integrates the motor, sensory, emotional, and cognitive aspects of our functioning, and therein lies its power. As Milner pointed out, this is how things come to be "knitted" into our being and acquire a sense of personal relevance.

Children have a natural impulse to explore and manipulate their surroundings, but increasingly in contemporary life this impulse is suppressed. Much of the time, this lack of opportunity is not even recognized as deprivation, because children are easily distracted by the latest technology, and in staying indoors there is a perception that they are being kept "safe." With its various gadgets and gizmos, technology delivers a wealth of preprogrammed play, but for all their variety and ingenuity, such manufactured illusions keep us in a state of dependence—they could not be further from the kind of creative and empowering illusions that Winnicott and Milner wrote about. As children, and let us not forget it, as adults too, we need to dream, we need to do, and we need to have an impact on our environment. These things give rise to a sense of optimism about our capacity to shape our own lives.

The flush of pride that Michael Pollan felt as a small boy on discovering his watermelon in the bushes meant that as a teenager, he took up gardening in earnest. He developed his cultivation skills through growing not only melons but peppers, cucumbers, tomatoes, and a whole range of other produce. Like the acquisition of special powers, he approached the gardener's craft as "a form of alchemy, a quasi-magical system for transforming seeds and soil and water and sunlight into things of value."

If we put energy into cultivating the earth, we are given something back. There is magic in it and there is hard work in it, but the fruits and flowers of the earth are a form of goodness that is real; they are worth believing in and are not out of reach. When we sow a seed, we plant a narrative of future possibility. It is an action of hope. Not all the seeds we sow will germinate, but there is a sense of security that comes from knowing you have seeds in the ground.

CHAPTER 4

Safe Green Space

Hammocks hanging in the Barn Garden.

Peace comes from the inner space.
Erik Erikson (1902–1994)

Each year, as spring moves into summer, I rush to put the hammocks up between the chestnut and zelkova trees that grow in our garden. Lying in the shelter of the trees' shade, I can feel their tenacity. The first time I hung the hammocks here I wondered if the branches would be strong enough to take my weight, but now with many years' growth behind them, there is no question they can safely hold me. My mind drifts while I gaze into the shifting patterns against the sky until the whispering of leaves and wind brings my thoughts alive.

If I quantified the time that I get to spend in a hammock here, it would seem pathetically brief compared to how much this little grove means to me. But I think it is the potential for access that matters—just knowing that I can take myself there if I want to is enough, as long as I actually do it occasionally.

All gardens exist on two levels—the real garden on the one hand and the imagined or remembered one on the other. This grove has a life all of its own in my imagination, and I can turn to it at any time of year. For the trees in my mind are evergreen, unaffected by the passing of the seasons, unlike the leafless trees that populate the grove in winter. Perhaps this place signifies so much to me because Tom and I lived for ten years or so with a wide-open field around us. The lack of shade in summer was oppressive and the winter winds made us feel exposed. We watched and waited while the saplings that had gone into the ground, not much more than knee-high, put down their roots and slowly started to grow.

Trees give structure and a sense of enduring life to a place. They make us feel safe and protected. Their size and beauty contribute to how easily we develop strong attachments to them. They provide a habitat for birds, insects, and all sorts of other creatures, and for us too—if not physically, then emotionally. Maybe there is something primal in this, because trees, after all, were our ancestral home. Our hominid forebears created nests and platforms high above the forest floor where they were safely hidden from predators below. With their branches and their crowns trees evoke the human form, and more than any other plant life, we invest them with human qualities like endurance, wisdom, and strength.

From high in a tree it is possible to have a vantage point over the landscape, and anyone who climbs trees knows how the branches can cradle you like the crook of an arm. The best kind of holding is protective and open at the same time, so that you feel safe but not trapped. Likewise, most babies past the newborn stage feel happiest when held in familiar arms but able to look outward and survey the world.

The American psychiatrist and psychoanalyst Harold Searles observed that patients who had experienced a breakdown would often gaze at trees for hours at a time and in them find "a companionship which they were not getting from other human beings." He believed this reflected a deep and ancient emotional connection to nature which, in much of everyday life, we are too busy to experience.

There is a striking example of this kind of companionship in the autobiography of the writer and academic Goronwy Rees, who was admitted to a hospital in the late 1950s, following a life-threatening accident. From his bed he had a view into a small garden which he contemplated intensely. "So completely did I become a part of it that when from time to time I fell asleep it was as if the trees stretched their long green fingers into the ward and took me up and enfolded me until I woke refreshed by the cool touch of their leaves." All through his waking hours the garden soothed and calmed him. In contrast, at nightfall, when he could no longer see into the garden, panic overwhelmed him. Left alone with his memories and the terrible pain of his injuries, all he could do was wait for dawn to come.

Rees felt held and cared for through the enfolding of the tree, in a way that not even the most consistent and attentive nurse could provide, and besides, like many patients, he was reluctant to make demands. Being on the receiving end of care is complicated when we are ill. We can worry about being an imposition or feel that we are indebted, but if we open ourselves to nature, she will give her care freely.

In Donald Winnicott's model of the development of the mind, the early sensation of being held plays a central role. "The infant falls to pieces unless held together and physical care is psychological care at these stages," he wrote. The body and the mind are not differentiated at the start of life, so that physical holding is also an emotional holding. Our earliest experience of being held and soothed establishes a template in our minds which helps us re-create that feeling when, later on, we need to "hold" ourselves together in the face of shock and distress.

Nowhere is the feeling of being unheld more intense than following the experience of a severe trauma. Winnicott witnessed this firsthand as a medical student, working with shell-shocked servicemen during the First World War, and it had a profound effect on him. Later on he illustrated what happens when holding fails through the popular nursery rhyme that starts with a large egglike character called "Humpty Dumpty," sitting on a wall. When Humpty has a great fall, "all the king's horses and all the king's men couldn't put Humpty together again." Winnicott thought the reason for the rhyme's universal appeal was that it resonated with a psychological truth that we prefer not to acknowledge to ourselves—that given a severe enough knock, we can all fall apart.

The geographer Jay Appleton developed a psychology of landscape in the 1970s known as "habitat theory," based on our need to regulate the extent to which we can see and not be seen. He believed that we have an innate preference for environments that combine elements of "prospect" with elements of "refuge." According to his "habitat theory," we automatically assess our physical surroundings in terms of possible hazards and scope for protection. A preference for parklike or savannah-type landscapes that offer both prospect and refuge is found across different cultures. Appleton believed that this was because in the course of evolution features that were advantageous to survival such as grasslands with trees came to be symbolized in a way that is aesthetically pleasing. Gardens that have vistas as well as protected spaces within them satisfy our need for prospect and refuge. Much as physical or emotional holding can be protective and open at the same time, so a garden can offer a feeling of safe enclosure without entrapment.

Throughout the ages in both Western and Eastern cultures,

enclosed gardens have offered sanctuary from the turbulence of the world as well as the turbulence of the mind. On entering into a walled garden, you immediately feel you are in a warmer place. The heat of the sun radiates from the walls, and you are protected from the winds and the noises of the world outside. Such settings are particularly helpful for people recovering from post-traumatic stress disorder (PTSD), because the combination of enclosure and openness within it generates strong feelings of safety and calm. Fundamentally, a garden is a space that is free from fear.

Unless you have lived through a serious trauma or worked with people suffering from trauma, it is easy to underestimate the enduring destructive effects it can have, but we all know how quickly the body reacts when we feel threatened and get the shakes and butterflies along with a pounding heart. This fight-or-flight reaction is triggered by the brain's alarm center, known as the amygdala, which lies deep within the brain and is under control of the autonomic nervous system.

We live with our evolutionary past, or rather it lives through us. In terms of the brain, nothing has been lost over the course of evolution, and the structure is, as the neuroscientist Jaak Panksepp described, a "nested hierarchy." The brain's layers are folded on top of one another, with the higher cortical parts enclosing the more ancient mammalian and reptilian structures. These communicate with one another through a myriad of neural networks enabling us to integrate memories, sensations, thoughts, and feelings. Under normal circumstances, the brain is a wonder of connectivity, but trauma profoundly disrupts this state of integration because the activation of the amygdala disables connections to the higher-thinking levels of the cortex. In survival terms this makes sense because why stop to think when a tiger is chasing you? But when it happens in other situations, it is as if we have been hijacked by fear—our thoughts are frozen, our memory fails, and it is hard to speak with any coherency.

When someone suffers from PTSD, this feeling of being hijacked by fear becomes part of everyday life. The activation of the amygdala also changes the way memory is laid down, so that it is not so much recalled but relived. Traumatic memories replay themselves as flashbacks in which it feels like the experience is taking place all over again. It means that the trauma cannot be integrated or laid to rest. The repeated reexperiencing of a trauma in this way, as well as in nightmares, progressively undermines a sense of inner security. The world feels more and more unsafe, and a constant state of alertness about possible sources of threat arises. This condition is known as hypervigilance and is very draining, leaving little in the way of resources for recovery. All sorts of safety habits develop aimed at creating a basic sense of security, such as needing to sit with one's back against a wall.

Living life in such a constant state of fear and arousal, with adrenaline inappropriately pumping around the body, means that it is all too easy for someone suffering from PTSD to be labeled as difficult, manipulative, or aggressive. Other people are busy getting on with their lives in their own safe bubbles and can't see the cause of the fear and agitation in a person who unexpectedly flips and shouts out. After a time, many families reach the end of their tether because they feel they are permanently walking on eggshells.

The first step of any trauma treatment is what the American psychiatrist and trauma expert Judith Herman calls "regaining a sense of safety." The other stages of treatment that she outlined involve more active interventions, but this initial stage is fundamental. She writes, "No therapeutic work can possibly succeed if safety has not been adequately secured." Establishing a sense of trust and physical safety lessens the need to be constantly hypervigilant and on the defensive. It is an extreme version of something that applies for all of us, because it is only when we feel safe that we are able let our defenses down, and it is only when our defenses are down that we can allow new experiences in. Without this, the mind cannot grow and change. This means that in horticultural therapy, the safe enclosure of the garden is a therapeutic tool in its own right.

When you enter through the wrought iron gate of the garden at Headley Court in Surrey, you are instantly transported into a world that feels far away from the Defence Medical Rehabilitation Centre that is right next door. The sense of safe enclosure combined with clear sight lines along its paths provides a spatial experience in which someone who is traumatized can relax the need to be vigilant. The charity HighGround, which was set up by the horticultural therapist Anna Baker Cresswell, runs the gardening program here. Having proved its value, it is moving to a larger walled garden at the newly built Defence Medical Rehabilitation Centre (DMRC) at Stanford Hall in Nottinghamshire.

The garden at Headley Court is surrounded by high yew hedges. With a large pond and fountain at its center, it descends in a series of terraces and vegetable beds beyond which lies an orchard. The overall sensation on the late summer day when I visited was of abundance. The flower borders were bursting with color—tall spikes of blue and pink larkspur and masses of cornflower and cosmos were set against a restful framework of green.

Many of the men who attend the HighGround program are recovering from head injuries or amputations, and they inevitably suffer from PTSD as well. Most of the patients need a series of surgical or medical interventions, and the typical pattern is a sequence of hospital admissions in between which they go home on leave. Carol Sales, the horticultural therapist at Headley Court, tailors an individual program for each person she treats. She plans the person's activities so he can see something through from sowing to harvesting, and have vegetables and flowers to take home to his partner. Hearing Carol speak, it is impossible not to feel the warmth of her personality and her deep commitment to her work.

It is very common for people suffering from PTSD to experience olfactory triggers, specific smells that relate to their trauma and set off flashbacks. The smell of diesel or anything burning are common triggers for men who have seen combat, but there is no risk of encountering these odors in a therapy garden. By contrast, the scented flowers and plants that Carol grows at Headley Court have a calming and uplifting effect. Within minutes of passing through the wrought iron gates, her patients tell her that their heart rates have slowed down.

Gardens are particularly effective at bringing the body to a lower level of physiological arousal in this way. Plants may sometimes be spiky or poisonous, but they will never make sudden movements or jump out at you, so you don't have to be on your guard or watch your back when you are working in their company. Other calming effects include the gentle sound of wind rustling through the trees, which helps in filtering out other potentially distracting and intrusive noises. In addition, the color green strikes the eye in such a way as to require no adjustment. Along with blue, it automatically takes us to a lower level of arousal. Esther Sternberg, a physician who writes about the properties of healing spaces, calls the color green "the default mode for our brains." She explains that "the photoreceptor pigment gene that emerged first in evolutionary history is the one most sensitive to the spectral distribution of sunlight and to the wavelengths of light reflected from green plants." It is not surprising therefore that the amount of greenery in a garden is directly related to how restorative it is.

Roger Ulrich, professor of architecture at Chalmers University in Sweden, has pioneered research into the beneficial effects of nature on the human stress response, using heart, skin, and muscle readings. His findings, over the last three decades, have consistently shown that nature's restorative effects on the cardiovascular system are demonstrable in the body within a few minutes. The instantly soothing effect of a garden is testament to the speed and sensitivity with which the brain processes our sensory experience and adjusts our physiological responses. Activity in the sympathetic branch of the autonomic system that is responsible for our fight-or-flight response is reduced in a garden, while the parasympathetic system, which gives rise to a state of restfulness needed for digestion of food and recovery of energy, is activated. There is undeniably a survival advantage in feeling pleasantly relaxed and disinclined to move on in surroundings that are flourishing and able to sustain life. It is thought that these autonomic responses helped our remote ancestors select environments in which they were more likely to thrive.

Whilst changes in heart rate and blood pressure can be detected within minutes of exposure to natural surroundings, levels of the stress hormone cortisol take a little longer to reduce, typically dropping after twenty to thirty minutes. Cortisol has insidiously damaging effects when levels are raised over long periods of time, because it suppresses the immune system and disrupts the metabolism of glucose and lipids. It also impairs memory through its destructive effect on neurons in the hippocampus and inhibits production of the brain's "fertilizer," brain-derived neurotrophic factor (BDNF), which promotes healthy growth and repair. In this way, enduring stress is toxic to the brain. These effects not only make new learning harder but contribute to life losing its richness and meaning.

In providing a concentrated dose of flourishing nature, an enclosed garden like Headley Court can have strong anti-stress effects. According to Carol, the greenhouse in the center of the garden is where the men feel most safe. Filled with the scent of flowers such as rose geraniums and sweet-smelling cyclamen, it is a calming and productive place. This strong sense of protected space means that the men's attention, which otherwise would have been scanning their surroundings, can be directed to the task at hand. One of the men was working in the greenhouse when I visited, and I was struck by how absorbed he was in picking tomatoes while soaking up the heat of the sun. Most of us take for granted the basic ability to focus on whatever we are doing, but for people who are traumatized it is a huge step forward and helps them feel they are regaining some control over their minds.

Caring for plants is intrinsically a mindful activity, whereas care that is carried out in an inattentive or mindless way is not true care. To practice true care means becoming receptive to another as we tune in and focus on the needs of someone or something outside ourselves. This kind of immersion is something that Carol helps the patients at Headley Court develop. At the start, they often find it hard to focus on what they are doing but, given practice, any task can be done mindfully. Carol calls it "therapy by stealth."

Trauma disrupts the way the mind processes experiences in time because the past is constantly invading the present. Practicing mindfulness can help reverse this because it involves focusing on the present moment. When thoughts, feelings, or memories disrupt this, they are not pursued or evaluated, they are simply acknowledged, and attention is returned to the present. So if Carol is digging up carrots with one of her patients, as they wash and eat them, she will ask her patient to notice his sensations and discuss the flavor and texture of the carrots with her. When they are weeding or planting out seedlings, she deliberately slows things down, so there is a chance to take in the colors of the flowers and the insects searching for pollen and nectar. All the while, she is trying to keep the patient in the moment. When the mind is operating on red alert, it is difficult to open up to experience in a relaxed and receptive way, but recovering this ability is important because it helps put the past in its place. Studies show that states of mindful awareness decrease signals to the amygdala and help restore a more integrated state of neural activity within the brain.

Carol told me about a serviceman called Rob who had always loved outdoor pursuits but, having lost both his legs in an explosion, found it hard to see any kind of future for himself. He had been in the hospital for some time before his curiosity took him to the garden. Carol started him off working in the greenhouse. Then, after a few sessions, he opted to try some digging outside. There was "a lightbulb moment," she told me, when he realized that even with his prosthetic limbs, he could actually do it. Once he made this discovery, he came to the garden as often as he could, and when he was discharged Carol sent him home with a supply of plants for him to continue looking after in his own garden.

Finding ways of motivating men like Rob to carry on gardening afterward is important because the patients can only attend HighGround for the relatively short duration of their rehabilitation treatment. Unless they have something to take them outdoors once they are back home, many stay indoors and depend on the television and internet for external stimulation. Carol says the men often try to normalize it as a form of "man-caving," but it is much more problematic than that, involving as it does an almost total withdrawal from life.

The differentiation between a retreat on the one hand and a refuge on the other is important because they have different psychological implications. A retreat is a defensive move, generally in a backward direction. A refuge is a stopping point, a place of respite from which we can reemerge feeling strengthened. Refuge is better suited to helping us get back to life. When Jay Appleton identified that a "universal characteristic of primitive man, transmitted innately to his modern descendants, is the desire to see without being seen," he was pointing to a voyeuristic tendency that is ingrained in our basic psychology. The internet plays into this desire par excellence, and it can become a retreat that takes people further and further from real life because it gives an illusion of prospect. It provides a vantage point on the world while being in retreat from it, so that it is possible to be completely sedentary while exploring a whole other world. The garden as refuge, however, maintains a link with all sorts of realities of life at the same time as providing respite from the world; importantly it also involves getting out of doors.

One of the most basic benefits of spending time outdoors is the exposure to daylight. We easily forget that light is a form of nourishment. Our bodies create vitamin D from sunlight on our skin, and in addition, the blue light in the sun's rays sets our circadian rhythm, our sleep-wake cycle, and regulates the rate at which serotonin is produced in the brain. Serotonin provides a background sense of well-being, helps to regulate mood, and promotes empathy. It also has an important effect on how we think and react because it reduces aggression, encourages reflective thinking, and makes us less impulsive. There is mounting evidence that PTSD involves a dysfunction of the serotonin system in which a vicious circle is set up. When serotonin is deficient, the threshold for activation of the amygdala is lowered, with the result that the body's stress response is triggered more and more easily.

All the serotonin in the brain is derived from two bundles of neurons located deep in the brainstem, known as the serotonin raphe. Professor David Nutt, a psychiatrist who is an expert on the serotonin system, likes to point out that in evolutionary terms, the human brain evolved exceedingly fast, and that while the cortical expansion of the brain led to an eightfold increase in size, the serotonin raphe stayed the same. From this point of view, we are constitutionally vulnerable to serotonin depletion, a situation that was resolved for our ancient forebears through ample sunlight, exercise, and contact with the soil, all of which help boost serotonin levels.

Exercise has mood-elevating effects through increasing levels of neurotransmitters like endorphins and dopamine as well as serotonin. It also promotes release of BDNF and can help set in motion an upward spiral in which serotonin and BDNF enhance the action of each other. In addition, physical exercise has a direct integrating effect on the brain that can help reverse the abnormally low levels of activity in the prefrontal cortex that are found in PTSD.

Recently another beneficial effect of exercise has been discovered. Persistent states of stress are linked with raised levels of a metabolite called kynurenine, which is associated with inflammatory changes in the brain. When we use the large muscles in our legs, we activate a gene that reduces the circulation of kynurenine. Exercise has long been recognized to promote brain health, but this finding shows that muscle metabolism can have a specific anti-stress effect.

An element of turning "passive to active" makes gardening fundamentally empowering. Robert Sapolsky, professor of neuroscience at Stanford University, has studied stress in primates and found that without some form of physical outlet, the effects of stress are liable to be internalized in a much more damaging way. Most forms of exercise help mitigate stress, but the more pleasurable or absorbing it is, the stronger the effect. Exercising outdoors is better still. It has been shown that green exercise, as it is often called, is more effective at lowering stress levels and improving mood and self-esteem than going to the gym. The garden gets you going, and while you might count the minutes on an exercise machine, no one counts minutes in the garden. It is not exercise time, it is gardening time.

Part of the pleasure of digging in the garden is the smell of wet earth. The aroma, known as *geosmin*, is released through the activity of soil bacteria called *actinomycetes*, and it has a pleasing and soothing effect on most people. The human olfactory center is remarkably sensitive to it, presumably because it helped our prehistoric forebears detect vital sources of life. Some people can even detect it at concentrations as low as five parts per trillion.

Apart from boosting mood through exercise and smell, digging in the garden may help regulate serotonin through directing the action of other bacteria in the soil. About ten years ago, the neuroscientist Christopher Lowry discovered that small amounts of a bacterium commonly found in soil can boost serotonin levels and help regulate the immune system. *Mycobacterium vaccae* thrives in ground that has been enriched through manure and composting, and when weeding and digging the earth, we inhale and ingest it.

We co-evolved with a range of symbiotic bacteria, including *M. vaccae*, that have recently been acknowledged to be "old friends" because of their ability to regulate the immune system. Lowry's experiments have demonstrated that mice exposed to *M. vaccae* exhibit lower levels of inflammation and an increased resilience to stress. Other studies have found that mice that consume *M. vaccae* are able to complete a maze test in half the time of other mice. Further research has revealed that these bacteria, through unknown mechanisms, activate the brain's resident gardeners, the microglia cells, so that inflammation in the brain is reduced. They also act directly on the part of the serotonin system that supplies the prefrontal cortex and the hippocampus with serotonin, which may account for why the mice in these experiments also showed signs of better mood regulation and why their cognitive function and memory improved.

The magnitude of the effect of *M. vaccae* in humans is not yet clear, and it may prove hard to measure in a garden environment, not least because there are so many other physical and psychological benefits at work, but the findings left the research team wondering if we shouldn't all be spending much more time playing in the dirt.

In addition to *M. vaccae* there are likely to be other strains of bacteria commonly found in the soil that will enhance mental health. A single teaspoon of garden soil contains something in the region of a billion microbes, so perhaps it's not surprising that gardeners have been found to have a more varied and therefore healthier range of gut bacteria. The picture that is emerging from different research studies is that various bacterial metabolites produced in the gut help activate the vagus nerve, which is part of our rest-and-digest parasympathetic system, and that other metabolites engage in a kind of "cross talk" with the brain's microglia cells, thereby shifting the brain to a more anti-inflammatory state.

Sunlight, exercise, and contact with the soil play central roles in gardening's restorative effect on the nervous system. At the same time, when a great deal of loss has to be faced, the metaphorical level of meaning in a garden is also an important part of the therapy. The mind's capacity to symbolize is impaired in a traumatized state, but a garden offers a ready-made set of symbols that can be a psychological lifeline. Carol gave me a memorable example of this in relation to the ancient pollarded sweet chestnut trees in the orchard at Headley Court. The trees consistently fascinate her patients, and they sometimes speak of wanting to clamber up onto their broad stumps, where they imagine sitting encircled in the branches that have regrown. Pollards are a living symbol of survival. They have been chopped and set back, yet have found a way to carry on growing, as these injured soldiers must also find a way to do.

In Dorthe Poulsen and Ulrika Stiggsdotter's research at a veterans project in Denmark, they describe how much security the veterans derive from the presence of trees, and how they become a primary focus for their reattachment to life. The setting is the Hørsholm Arboretum to the north of Copenhagen, and deep within it, like an enclave in the forest, is a garden called Nacadia. To reach the garden, you walk along a wide path lined with magnolias and rhododendrons. The conifers, some of them rare and very old, ascend toward the sky, and birdsong fills the air. A wooden gate leads through a pergola into the garden. Within its two acres there is a greenhouse, a lake, and a stream. There are places to rest, with recliners, as well as hammocks between trees, and productive vegetable beds.

Poulsen and Stiggsdotter observed that when they first arrived, most of the veterans sought out a tree or found a den that became their own special place of safety. Some used the tree platforms that have been built in the garden, while others spent time sitting under the great mammoth tree, which with its low branches creates a strong feeling of protection.

One veteran spoke of how he gained relief by simply being with a tree: "There is a tree, and I am sitting here, no expectations, no questions, no nothing." Another said that for the first time he felt safe enough to close his eyes. The mammoth tree is like a gentle giant of the plant world, and one veteran who was particularly drawn to it described a strong tactile relationship with it: "When you touch it, it's almost porous, and feels snug. It has such a thick bark to protect itself. It gives me peace here; it has quite a majestic feel about it, such an old tree."

The kind of attachment we can form to trees is the reverse of the attachment we might form toward tiny seedlings. A seedling is so much smaller than we are, and we provide it with care and protection, but in the shelter of a tree, it is we who are the small one and we can lean on its great strength. There is something powerfully preverbal in all of this because we all long at times to communicate our deepest feelings without words. It is perhaps a natural impulse to take distress and suffering that is hard to articulate and bring it to a form of life that has no need of words. In James Frazer's classic account of mythology and religion, *The Golden Bough*, he gives examples of ancient rites involved in tree worship from around the world that suggest that this impulse lies deep within the psyche. Some of the rituals involve a symbolic transfer of illness, grief, or guilt onto a tree, reflecting a belief that a tree can bear the weight of human suffering. It is as if in its mute and reassuring presence, a tree can accept us along with whatever ails us and will not flinch from our loneliness, our sorrow, or our pain.

• • •

Everything that happens in a garden takes place in slow time; the flowers, shrubs, and trees simply get on with growing quietly at their own pace, and so it is with people. Recovery from severe trauma is necessarily slow. Take the example of Eddie, an ex-serviceman in his forties whom I met when he was working on a gardening project run by the charity Thrive. He had been participating for nearly two years and was close to gaining a horticultural qualification.

When he first started working in the garden, Eddie felt full of shame. He was jumpy and suspicious and needed to regulate his proximity to other people. Horticultural therapists are used to this pattern, and part of their skill is in recognizing when someone is ready to start working alongside other people. Eddie nearly dropped out several times during the first couple of months, but gradually his suspicion subsided and he began to feel less jumpy, although given a choice, he still preferred to work on his own.

Trauma is an intensely isolating experience. While other forms of relationship may feel too threatening at the start, nature can help alleviate this disconnected state. I witnessed this, when during a circuit of the grounds Eddie paused by a eucalyptus tree: "I never walk by without doing this," he said as he picked a couple of leaves, crushed them, and inhaled the aroma. Handing me some leaves and inviting me to do the same, he explained, "It always gives me a mental buzz." I felt it too, for the smell of eucalyptus is uplifting. It struck me that this interaction with the tree had become a ritual for him, a kind of formalized greeting he enacted each time he walked by. For all intents and purposes, Eddie had befriended that tree. It was his point of connection, and it became clear how much, especially in the early months, it had helped to steady him.

Until that moment by the eucalyptus, Eddie had not made eye contact with me. The tree somehow made it safe to do so. I took in his face, which had retained a boyish look in spite of his age, and he then fixed me with his gray eyes as I listened to his story.

He had signed up for the army at the age of eighteen, but the first sign of his problems appeared in his late twenties when he started waking in the night with a jolt and shouting out. Whenever he came home from duty, he was always "jumpy" and "on guard." He spoke of how hard it is when you can't see your enemy and "you're always thinking, What's that person up to? Is that car going to blow up?" He started self-medicating with alcohol, and although he was managing to hold his life together, he gradually underwent a personality change, losing his former "happy go lucky" and "chatty" self, although he occasionally gave me a glimpse of it as he told me more about his life.

His problems finally came to a head when his drinking escalated and his marriage broke up. For a short time he took to living in his car. Soon afterward, he was admitted to the hospital, where he received some cognitive behavioral therapy and attended an anger management group. Eddie's story is not unusual; on average it takes eleven to thirteen years for a veteran with PTSD to seek help. By the time the veteran does, his or her life has often disintegrated. Many end up, as Eddie did, losing their marriages, their jobs, and their homes too, with alcohol dependence affecting about 75 percent of them. It is difficult in the armed forces to reveal that you are not coping. Eddie felt that he spent "years trying to battle this madness on my own." "It's pride isn't it?" he said to me, "just not wanting to admit it." In spite of that, he missed the army life and spoke nostalgically about the camaraderie.

Feeling ashamed is a big barrier not only to seeking help but also to making use of help once it is available. Eddie told me how suspicious he was of others when he first started working in the garden, adding, "Dare I say it—I was judgmental. It was like— what am I doing here with people with mental health problems?" By contrast, the natural world offers an environment in which people can feel accepted just as they are. Eddie was conflicted about receiving help from other people, but the uplifting smell of the eucalyptus tree was a free gift of nature, and what possible shame could there be in getting a boost from a tree?

It is significant that the first connection Eddie experienced in the Thrive garden was that tree's cleansing and uplifting scent. It is hard to open yourself up to new experiences if your mind is full of toxic feelings, but smell cuts through that effect. It is the most powerful and primitive of our senses because the nose is in direct communication with the amygdala and the centers for emotion and memory deep within the brain. These parts of the brain evolved together out of the olfactory system, which is why feelings, memory, and scent are all so closely connected.

For veterans like Eddie, who have been traumatized, the process of opening up to life again is a gradual one because it takes time for the kind of brain changes that occur in PTSD to begin to recover. This is why the building up of repeated experiences of existential safety is so important and strengthens the life-affirming feelings that have been disconnected or weakened by trauma.

Eddie spoke with passion about how his relationship to the garden had developed. "You see so many beautiful things," he said, which makes him feel "there is a God and it's bigger than me." This sense of being part of something larger was striking: "In nature everything is intertwined, everything has a purpose—the bees pollinating, the pests and the other things that eat them. The flowers and the plants, why do they grow?" He did not answer his own question, nor did he expect me to, but he sat back and held my gaze intensely as he exclaimed: "Wow! The color it just lifts you!"

Within the safe enclosure of this garden, Eddie had rediscovered his love of nature and his sense of religious faith. This sense of communion with nature went back to his childhood. He remembered going to the park as a boy. "I used to walk for miles there down to the river," and he recalled "finding little secret places tucked away like little oases. It was unspoiled nature."

The internalization of a place like this forms a landscape in the mind—an inner resource that can be replenishing. I felt in Eddie recollecting and telling me all this that the garden had helped him reconnect with something undamaged by trauma. The way he was able to link back to his childhood memories of nature through his current experience in the garden was a sign that he was regaining a more integrated sense of self and recovering his sense of identity. As he said, in nature everything is "intertwined." Through working with plants and the soil, he had recovered the ability to experience inner peace.

When the eminent American psychiatrist Karl Menninger began working with traumatized veterans in Kansas after the Second World War, he was impressed by the extent to which working with plants helped his patients open themselves up to life again. Eddie's experience is in keeping with this observation. Menninger promoted horticultural therapy as a valuable adjunct to psychiatric treatment throughout his career. In doing so, he described gardening as an activity "that brings the individual close to the soil and close to Mother Nature, close to beauty, close to the inscrutable mystery of growth and development." He recognized that an important kind of intimacy can be experienced in the garden, and it is an intimacy that is not about other people.

There was a newly made bed that Eddie had worked on largely on his own, planting it with flowers and grasses. Seeing what had been "waste ground turned into something beautiful" gave him a great deal of satisfaction. The soil had been compacted, and it had taken hard physical work to achieve the transformation, the kind of exertion that is good at detoxifying feelings of anger and frustration. As he was telling me how much he loved the feeling it gave him, he stopped in his tracks and pointed: "That's it," he exclaimed, "that little bed over there. That was me!" Eddie's words betrayed the extent of his identification, as if in transforming that patch of earth, he had reclaimed himself from the waste ground too.

CHAPTER 5

Bringing Nature to the City

Central Park in June.

The enjoyment of the choicest natural scenes in the country and the means of recreation connected with them is thus a monopoly, in a very peculiar manner, of a very few very rich people. The great mass of society, including those to whom it would be of the greatest benefit, is excluded from it.

Frederick Law Olmsted (1822–1903)

There is a corner of my vegetable garden where some lupines grow. Although their roots are embedded in Hertfordshire soil, each summer when they come into flower, they transport me back to a valley deep in the heart of the island of Crete.

This little patch of lupines holds within it a memory of traveling with Tom to look at wildflowers. We were staying in a remote taverna where the owner had offered to be our guide for the day. The three of us set off walking and talking, occasionally stopping to look at plants or sample the tender wild asparagus that was growing in abundance. At some point, Tom and Lambros made a diversion to look at a tree, but I was enjoying my walking rhythm and strode onward following the winding route.

As I turned a corner, I saw a grove of olives entirely surrounded in blue. We had seen some lupines earlier that morning, but this was a meadow full of them, and on such an impressive scale—it was irresistible. I left the path and clambered up, picking my way through the host of flowers.

From the look of the trees, it was an ancient place. With a feeling that I had stumbled on something almost secret, I came to a halt. How long I stood basking in blue with the sun beating down from clear skies overhead, I cannot say. Time seemed not to be passing but stretching, and a profound stillness entered into me. The spell was only broken when I heard a familiar voice calling my name. Then I savored a last solitary moment before summoning the others to join me.

As soon as we were back at home, I searched for wild lupines seeds, filled with a desire to reconnect with that moment in the Cretan meadow. Seeds of that strain are hard to come by, and in the end I settled for a different wild form—the *Lupinus perennis*. The lupines that I grew that year, and still grow now, are taller and their color does not match the brilliance of that original blue. Yet this patch of lupines has remained for me an incarnation of another place. Each summer as they come into flower, a gateway opens in my mind through which I can retrace my Cretan steps.

Like other artistic endeavors, garden making can be a response to loss. Creating a garden can be as much a re-creation as a creation; an idea of paradise, something that reconnects us with a landscape we have loved and which compensates us for our separation from nature. Way back in ancient history, the fabled hanging gardens of the city of Babylon were intended to do exactly that. King Nebuchadnezzar II built them in order to alleviate his wife's pining for the lush green mountains of the homeland she'd left behind. In constructing a pyramid with elevated walkways, he gave her the next best thing to a green mountain on which she could stroll and ease her homesick heart.

Long before this, the ancient Sumerians had started building cities, and when they did so, they brought nature into them. The idea of greening the city is not a modern one: urban parks and gardens are in fact as old as cities themselves. Plans of Uruk, one of the very first cities of all, built in about 4000 BC and located in what is known today as Iraq, show that it was one-third garden or park, one-third field, and one-third dwellings. The ancient Romans had a name for it: *rus in urbe*, literally "bringing the countryside to the city." *Rus in urbe* compensated people for living in a state of separation from nature and made it possible to have the best of both.

Throughout history, even the best of cities have been noisy, crowded, and smelly. The great seventeenth-century essayist and gardener John Evelyn drew on the idea of *rus in urbe* when he proposed a series of parks and gardens around London to relieve the city of its noxious smog. His choice of plants included honeysuckle, jasmine, lilac, rosemary, lavender, juniper, and musk rose. These highly scented bushes and trees would, he thought, through "innocent magic" "perfume the adjacent places by their breaths" and help counteract the sulphurous sea-coal smoke that filled the air. Nature's riches would bring other benefits for Londoners too, such as improved health, the enjoyment of beauty, and opportunities for relaxation.

Evelyn's bold plans were never realized, but he thoroughly understood the garden's power to transport and bring respite from the city's excesses. Trees filter noise, and plants clean the air, but Evelyn's "innocent magic" lies in the way that gardens gently soothe and stimulate all five of our senses at the same time, so that we are carried away by the sensuality of it all. Even a little pocket of garden can create an island of peace that helps to counteract the wear and tear of city life and feed our longing for contact with the natural world. With carefully selected flowers and trees, and maybe flowing water, such spaces can transport us far from the confines of the city, without us ever having to leave it.

Green land is life-sustaining land, its greenness signifying abundant food and a local source of water or skies that produce reliable rain. There is no escaping the fact that it is green leaves that support life on this planet, from the air that we breathe to the food that we eat, but it is easy to forget this elemental truth in the cities of today with their landscape of metal, glass, and concrete, and the twenty-first-century food that comes in a can or plastic tub, along with so much of the other artifice that surrounds us. The Old Testament saying "all flesh is grass" sounds almost creepy to our modern ears, so far removed are we from the basic facts of life.

When we are surrounded by streets and high-rise apartment buildings, nature can feel like something that happens in faraway places, and plants slip into the background of life's necessities. And yet the green pulse of life still calls to us. The urban concrete and tarmac is hard on us, literally hard, and the noise and pollution speaks of the desert and the dust bowl. The taps may have running water in them, but still we are primed to respond to green. However much we are distracted by the neon lights and drawn to the city's humming, thumping energy, somewhere in the deep ancestral recesses of our minds an alarm bell rings, signaling to us this is not a good place to be. Sometimes all it needs is a suggestion: some flowers on the windowsill, the sound of wind in the trees, the warmth of the sun, or the gentle flowing of water. Nature's riches are different to those that the city peddles and promotes.

You only have to observe office workers on their lunch breaks to see how people gravitate toward green space and sunlight. The tree-filled London squares, the park benches and deck chairs, the edges of fountains, all offer places where people can let the city slip by, sidestep it for a while, and reinvigorate themselves. Spending time in nature, and not necessarily very much time, twenty minutes can suffice, restores our mental energy and strengthens the brain's ability to focus. This unconscious interaction between mind and nature has far-reaching effects, with important implications for our mental and physical health.

One of the best descriptions of the benefits people experience in green nature was written in the middle of the nineteenth century by the American landscape designer and creator of New York's Central Park, Frederick Law Olmsted. Beautiful natural scenery, he wrote, "employs the mind without fatigue and yet exercises it; tranquillises it and yet enlivens it; and thus, through the influence of the mind over the body, gives the effect of refreshing rest and re-invigoration to the whole system."

City dwellers, Olmsted noted, suffered from a range of afflictions such as "nervous tension, over anxiety, hasteful disposition, impatience [and] irritability." They had, he also observed, a tendency toward "melancholy," a term that was widely used in the nineteenth century for depression. Olmsted believed that the benefits of green space needed to be available to everyone, especially those, like the city laborers, who had few opportunities to travel beyond the city. The fact that such space was woefully lacking gave rise to cemeteries being used for recreation, a social phenomenon that infuriated Olmsted. Cities were failing to meet people's needs.

When he visited England, Olmsted was inspired by Birkenhead Park in the city of Liverpool. This beautiful place was, he declared, a "People's Garden," which he wanted to re-create in America. In the parks he designed, there were no beds of bright, showy flowers and no formal geometry. He worked in the pastoral and picturesque styles, using native vegetation to evoke natural landscapes. Scenery like this was, in his view, "a prophylactic and therapeutic agent of value." He thought that by visiting his parks people could get well and stay well.

The rapid expansion of metropolitan living during this era gave rise to the idea that city living was responsible for undermining people's health. In fact a new disease was invented to account for it: *neurasthenia*. George Miller Beard, the American physician who first described it in 1869, declared it a "disease of civilisation." Sufferers were afflicted by a disabling lack of both mental and physical energy, often in combination with other symptoms, such as insomnia, anxiety, and irritability. The illness was said to stem from overstimulation, overexertion, and overindulgence, blamed variously on the city's cut-and-thrust business culture, the demands of intellectual life, and the vices and luxuries that went with metropolitan living.

Olmsted's city laborers were unlikely to be diagnosed with it, for it rapidly became an illness of the well-to-do and the intelligentsia. The cure was "Rest" or "Go West." Women were invariably confined to bed, while men were advised to leave the city and immerse themselves in the great outdoors. Walt Whitman and Theodore Roosevelt were among the many famous sufferers who took the nature cure.

The growth of the cities around the modern world had only just begun when Olmsted and Beard were writing. At the start of the nineteenth century, globally only 3 percent of people lived in urban areas; now more than 50 percent do. The proportion of the world's population living in urban environments is projected to rise to 70 percent within the next thirty years, and this has already been exceeded in the US, where 80 percent of the population are living in cities. As urban centers have expanded, so has the contribution of mental illnesses to the global burden of disease.

The diagnosis of neurasthenia may have disappeared from the medical lexicon, but the phenomenon that Beard described has not gone away. We classify these symptoms now as anxiety and depression, and compared to rural areas, rates of both of these are higher in urban settings. Depression is around 40 percent higher, anxiety disorders are 20 percent higher, and increased levels of violent crime in cities unsurprisingly result in higher rates of PTSD. A recent UK study found that the risk of experiencing psychosis is about 40 percent higher for young people growing up in poorer neighborhoods where there are high levels of crime. Separating out cause and effect is not straightforward though, because illness and other social stressors can lead people to migrate to urban centers. This is particularly the case for psychotic illnesses, which also have an association with social deprivation.

For all that cities provide as economic engines and cultural hubs, it seems we pay a price for city living, and we pay it with our mental health. The urban environment drip-feeds its inhabitants with small amounts of stress; day in, day out, people are exposed to noisy, crowded, polluted streets. Health surveys of commuters reveal what anyone who has spent a lot of time commuting already knows, that the journey to work leaves many people struggling with frustration, fatigue, anxiety, and feelings of hostility.

Social inequality and social isolation, along with intense competition for housing and jobs, are the norm in most cities. In addition, city dwellers tend to have more unhealthy, sedentary lifestyles, have less control over their environment, and experience greater fears of crime than people living in rural areas. For each individual, the mix of these stressful ingredients will be different, but cumulatively they take their toll.

The vulnerability of city dwellers to mental health problems is compounded by a relative lack of "protective factors" in their lives. City living makes it harder for people to maintain the kind of strong links with family and friends that are known to reduce susceptibility to mental illness. It also makes it harder for them to have regular contact with nature. As cities have grown larger, people have become more isolated from the natural world. Some of the large cities of today contain extended areas of high-density housing with little in the way of green life around them. The real-estate value of land and the huge demand for it means that remaining pockets of urban green space are constantly under threat.

These days there are research teams in universities all around the world investigating the health benefits of nature—indeed, it is a rapidly growing field of inquiry. While the positive effects of city parks and gardens on mental health are not of the same magnitude as those conferred by strong social bonds; they nonetheless operate quietly, helping to shift people's tolerance of stress. Proximity to green space has been shown to reduce aggression and anxiety, improve mood, and reduce mental fatigue. It also changes the way people behave, encouraging them to take more exercise and to interact with their neighbors. But in spite of the evidence that has accumulated for all these effects, we are in many ways only beginning to understand the complexity of the ways our minds and bodies respond to the natural environment.

The idea of "green nature" can be taken to suggest that a patch of lawn will suffice, but complexity and variety are important in terms of nature's restorative effects. A study led by the ecologist Richard Fuller in the city of Sheffield in the UK found a clear relationship between the benefits people derived from visiting parks and the amount of biodiversity in the vegetation. These findings show that the ancient concept of *rus in urbe* bears weight. When it comes to urban parks and gardens, the more full of life and naturalistic they are, the better.

If increasing the amount of green space in cities is to gain credibility as a public health intervention, the beneficial effects need to be quantified on a population level, which is not easy to achieve. Recent research carried out by Fuller in Brisbane, Australia, has attempted to do this by looking at how often people visited the city parks in relation to the state of their health. One of the problems in carrying out research on the effects of the urban environment is that people who are healthier and wealthier can choose to live in greener areas, and generally, they do. In order to correct for this, Fuller and his team carried out a series of computations on the mass of data they obtained, which helped them take into account the other main social and economic factors known to influence health. The outcome suggested that if everyone in Brisbane visited an urban park every week there would be 7 percent fewer cases of depression and 9 percent fewer cases of high blood pressure. It is a study of just one city, and Fuller hopes that someone will repeat it soon in another part of the world.

There is an inescapable relationship between health and income. Hence, the most socially deprived inhabitants of a city are consistently found to have the poorest mental health. A complex range of factors contributes to this but increasingly it looks as if lack of access to green space is one of them. This is strongly suggested by the findings of a study carried out at the Centre for Research on Environment, Society and Health (CRESH), based at the Universities of Glasgow and Edinburgh. The team, led by Richard Mitchell, looked at social, economic, and health disparities in relation to neighborhood provision of amenities in a large-scale study of cities across Europe. The researchers analyzed the provision of shops, public transport, and cultural facilities, as well as access to green space. The only one of these variables to show a significant effect was the presence of neighborhood parks and gardens. The team calculated that the inequalities in mental health that are associated with low income could be reduced through proximity to green space by as much as 40 percent. This impressive figure surprised the researchers. Olmsted was right to think his parks could make a difference to the health of low-paid city workers.

The presence of street trees can be enough to make a difference, as they have been found to have a significant impact on how people feel about their lives. A team led by Marc Berman from the Environmental Neuroscience Lab at the University of Chicago studied the distribution of trees on residential streets in the city of Toronto. They combined this information with a survey in which inhabitants were asked to rate their own health. After making adjustments for income, education, and employment, the team calculated that having just ten more trees on a city block was associated with lower levels of mental distress of the same magnitude that an extra $10, 000 of income would be expected to bring. It is a staggering figure to put on nature's riches although most people, given a choice, would probably opt for the money rather than the trees.

As well as promoting better mental health, having access to greenery and trees helps to lower levels of both neighborhood and domestic violence. The environmental scientists Frances Kuo and William Sullivan, from the University of Illinois, published a number of influential studies demonstrating these effects around the turn of the millennium. Their research showed that people living in deprived social housing communities in Chicago who had greenery around them felt more hopeful and less helpless about their circumstances in life than people living in similar housing with little access to green space. They also reported lower levels of aggression in the home.

In a different study, Kuo and Sullivan analyzed rates of theft and violent crime and found that around buildings with trees and gardens nearby, the rates were lower. From their findings, they calculated that introducing green space where it is lacking could reduce crime by as much as 7 percent. Gardens can help make neighborhoods safer because they draw people outside. They function as intermediate spaces, where residents can gather and connect with one another, barriers get broken down, and new friendships spring up. Kuo and Sullivan found that people living in social housing with gardens knew more of their neighbors and were more likely to feel they had supportive networks around them. Within a city, the impact of transforming neglected and alienating places through greening them is not to be underestimated.

Cities are crowded, and our minds are crowded too, but a visit to a park can help expand our sense of mental space. We are able to take a step back, think more clearly, and return from our excursion feeling freer and less constrained by whatever was impinging on us before. This effect is associated with changes in the brain that have been measured in research led by Gregory Bratman from the University of Washington College of the Environment. The volunteers in the study were randomly assigned to a ninety-minute solitary walk, either in a park or along a highway. Those who walked in the park showed improvements in their mental health scores; in particular they were found to be dwelling much less on anxious or negative thoughts. Ruminating on negative thoughts is associated with activity in the subgenual prefrontal cortex, and the fMRI brain scans (functional magnetic resonance imaging) that the research team carried out showed that blood flow to this area had been reduced in the park walkers, in keeping with the calming effect that the participants reported. When our hunter-gatherer forebears moved through the landscape, their safety depended on them being fully present to their surroundings in a receptive and attentive way. There are evolutionary reasons why being in nature might switch off anxious thoughts and promote a feeling of relaxed alertness in us—to be lost in a recursive loop of rumination is not a good survival strategy.

• • •

In terms of evolutionary time, people have been inhabiting large, densely built-up cities for a very short time—only six generations or so. In contrast, environmental scientist and professor at Essex University Jules Pretty has calculated that for 350,000 generations people lived in close proximity to nature: "Put human history into one week, starting Monday, and this modern world emerges about three seconds before midnight on the Sunday." Many of the negative effects of city living stem from a fundamental mismatch: the human brain evolved in the context of the natural world, yet we expect it to function optimally in the unnatural urban surroundings that many people inhabit today.

States of relaxed and immersive attention helped our remote ancestors survive in the wild. Successful hunting and gathering depends on this kind of attention, and in being relatively effortless, it can be sustained for long periods of time. By contrast, contemporary lifestyles rely more heavily on a narrow, focused form of attention. The significance of the two different kinds of attention was demonstrated in a series of experiments carried out in the 1980s, by the psychologists Stephen and Rachel Kaplan. Their influential theory of "Attention Restoration" is based on the finding that natural settings are a highly effective way of giving our task-focused thinking a rest and restoring our mental energy. When we overuse our conscious cognitive processing skills, we are susceptible to what they called "attention fatigue." By taking time out in nature, we can experience what they called "attention restoration." There are many studies that demonstrate this effect. One, for example, found that students who walked 45 minutes in an arboretum performed 20 percent better in subsequent tests than a similar group who walked along busy urban streets. The Kaplans' work substantiates Olmsted's observation that spending time in nature simultaneously calms and enlivens us.

Attention is, however, much more than a cognitive function. The psychiatrist Iain McGilchrist argues that we make an error if we reduce it to this, because attention is, as he puts it, "the main medium by which we enact our relationship with the world." Having spent the last twenty years researching the relationship between the right and left hemispheres of the brain, McGilchrist has concluded that they specialize in different forms of attention. The left hemisphere gives rise to a narrow, focused attention, while the right hemisphere's functioning is characterized by a broad and open attention to our surroundings. This same hemispheric specialization for processing incoming information is found in other animals and is thought to have evolved because it was necessary for survival. Animals and birds need to direct their attention on killing and catching their prey while simultaneously staying alert to the wider terrain.

This model is necessarily simplistic when applied to the human brain, which is complex and highly integrated. McGilchrist acknowledges that our hemispheres communicate all the time and contribute to everything we do. However, we can overuse certain processing skills and neglect others so that we feel disconnected from our feelings, our surroundings, and other people. As he explains, the reality of contemporary life, and the prevalence of screens and computers, means we are dependent on the left hemisphere's mode of attention processing about 80 percent of the time.

McGilchrist believes that this imbalance is linked to the rise of anxiety and depression, as well as contributing to more generalized feelings of emptiness and mistrust. This is because the left hemisphere prioritizes everything functional and specializes in categorizing experience. Its focus on "getting" and "using" does not bring much meaning or depth to life. The right hemisphere, by contrast, specializes in connection rather than categorization. It brings us the richness of life through being better connected to the body and the senses. Our capacity for empathy and our deepest humanity comes to us through the right hemisphere, as well as our feelings of connection to nature. According to McGilchrist, the right hemisphere puts us in touch with the freshness and aliveness of the world.

To feel a sense of emotional connection with other forms of

life and be in touch with aliveness is linked to what E. O. Wilson, the eminent Harvard biologist, called *biophilia*. With his biophilia hypothesis, he put forward the idea that there is an innate "emotional affiliation of human beings to other living organisms." Since he first proposed his biophilia hypothesis in 1984, biophilia has become a buzzword within environmental psychology. Wilson's hypothesis is based on the fact that the natural world was the main influence on the evolution of our cognitive and emotional functioning. People who were most attuned to nature and most predisposed to learn about plants and animals would have survived better. Because we no longer commune with the natural world on a daily basis, we don't develop the same level of attunement, but still it lies latent in all of us.

Being out and about on busy city streets means having to process a lot of auditory as well as visual information, and it disrupts our ability to focus. Horns, sirens, alarms are all intended to put people on alert and keep them safe, but they drain our energy in trying to filter them. Navigating a tide of people on a busy pavement is exhausting at the best of times. Everyone is going at a different pace. Both our physical and mental space is under threat in different ways in the city environment. For people suffering from psychotic illnesses the sheer number of people and the sensory overload involved in negotiating the streets can make it extremely challenging. Two research studies at the Institute of Psychiatry in South London have found that for patients with a psychotic illness, just a ten-minute excursion to buy some milk, using a route along a busy pavement, was enough to cause a marked increase in symptoms, especially in their anxiety and paranoid thinking.

When I met Francis, a young man with a psychotic illness, on a mental health project based in a community garden, I could see these factors in operation. His pale blue eyes struck me with their sensitivity, and I thought that in another era, he might have turned up at the monastery gate seeking a place of refuge. He first became unwell five years before and had been admitted to the hospital on several occasions. He had been diagnosed with schizophrenia and knew that he needed to take medication for the long term.

Once someone becomes unwell, the city environment can make it more difficult for them to recover. Francis told me about his most recent breakdown, which had taken place two years previously, at a point in his life when he was living on his own. He felt his surroundings had contributed to his relapse by exacerbating feelings that the world was unsafe. His flat was on a busy road congested with buses, cars, and trucks. Pedestrians walked up and down outside his window, and he found it increasingly hard to ignore the footsteps of the people in the flat above. Indoors, he felt constantly on edge. Outdoors was no better; if anything his anxiety and paranoid thinking were worse. The sensory overload he experienced when walking along the street made him feel open and vulnerable to other people, as if he had lost his psychic skin. It seemed he could find no peace.

This sense of crowding and disturbance Francis experienced in the outside world was mirrored by a feeling of crowding inside his mind. It reached a point where every thought seemed to be challenged by a voice telling him that he was in the wrong. He took to staying in bed and listening to music with headphones on, regardless of whether it was day or night. A community mental health team became involved in his care, and in spite of daily visits to his flat, he was admitted to the hospital again. He eventually improved enough to move to his parents' house. Over the next few months, he completed a course of cognitive behavioral therapy, which helped him manage some of his conflicting thoughts, but he was unable to regain his sense of motivation.

Loss of motivation is a common symptom of schizophrenia and can also be a side effect of some antipsychotic medication. This was the case for Francis. A dysregulation of the dopamine system in the brain underlies much of this effect. The neurotransmitter dopamine is one of the basic chemicals of life, and we share it with other mammals. It triggers the kinds of exploratory or seeking behaviors needed for survival and plays a crucial role in the brain's "reward" system—which is in fact more like a seeking system, because it is driven by the anticipation of a reward more than the reward itself. This gave our hunter-gatherer ancestors the get-up-and-go to explore their surrounding terrain—if they had waited until they were hungry, they would have lacked energy to traverse the ground and collect food. As a result, the brain evolved to reward us for learning about our environment.

Most of our dopamine arises from two tiny clumps of cells deep within the ancient layers of the brain. Long nerve fibers convey it to the farther-flung reaches, including the cortex, which means that in humans the urge to explore that it engenders is intellectual as well as physical. Dopamine generates a sense of purpose and a state of optimistic expectation, and it boosts connectivity and communication throughout the brain so that if our dopamine levels are low, we feel that we have lost our "mojo."

When a friend of the family told Francis about a local community project that he was eligible to attend, he decided to give it a go. The garden was on the edge of a large housing estate very close to a main road. Nestling, as it did, behind some trees, it was a haven of green, in stark contrast with its surroundings, which were, as he put it "too concreted up." He had always enjoyed being out in nature, but his body was weak after spending so much time in bed in the preceding months.

At the beginning, he found the physical work of planting, watering, and weeding extremely challenging but he stuck at it. The project organizers in the garden were experienced in dealing with mental health problems, and some of the other participants were similarly vulnerable. Francis didn't interact with them much, but he felt secure in the work they were doing together. Gradually, his ability to concentrate on what he was doing began to improve, and with no sources of threat around him, his sense of focus began to shift. Being immersed in nature helped his anxious ruminations become less troubling. He started noticing variations in the weather and picking up on changes in the plants. He began to tune in to "how each day is subtly different from another day." Gradually, through working in the garden, he was able to open himself up to the world outside.

During the first year that Francis worked on the project, contact with other people continued to be problematic for him. Every social encounter was complicated by a feeling that he was responsible for the other person's happiness. By contrast, dealing with plants was more straightforward—there were no confusing or anxiety-provoking signals from them and no feelings to take into account. "I trust nature," he told me. Paranoia and trust are the opposites of each other, and when anxiety is running high, all sorts of things can trigger paranoia. Working with plants gave him a feeling of calm because, as he put it: "There is something more honest about plants compared to people."

Unlike the veterans' attraction to the resilience and strength of trees, this nonthreatening relationship was about vulnerability. Looking after plants, the "delicate plants" as Francis called them, put his own vulnerabilities in a different context. He identified with the plants and could therefore learn from them: "They are vulnerable but they seem to be positive, they go through the seasons. They stay here and they're pretty successful." He regarded the plants in the garden as his "gentle guides" because they showed him a different way of being. From this, he had come to understand that vulnerability need not be a disaster.

Francis described how he used to try to "hold on to things too much," and when they were gone, he would get angry with himself. Through gardening, he had come to what he called a "deeper understanding" of life and had grown accustomed "to the fact that things come and go." He also stopped getting so angry with himself. He had always been rather messy and disorganized, but he behaved differently in the garden: "You can't do that here—gardening is all about being organized. If you don't look after the plants, they will perish and die." Francis had not once been bored by gardening, although he had often felt bored by other things.

Tending the garden had given him a newfound sense of purpose and motivation. The project was a resource for the local community, and as a result he felt he was doing something "relevant." He still found concentrating difficult at times, but his memory had improved. After eighteen months, he thought he was almost ready to start on a horticultural training and hoped eventually to find employment as a gardener. Something he said to me toward the end of the interview seemed to sum it all up: "I am more aware of life now—out of the shock of it."

Projects such as the community garden that Francis worked on can have many different therapeutic aspects to them, from the beneficial effects of the garden setting on stress levels, to the relationships that participants can form with plants as well as people. Above all, for someone who has become withdrawn like Francis, gardening provides the kind of complex environmental stimulation that the brain thrives on.

Decades of research on laboratory rats (whose neural circuitry is similar to ours) have shown that when they are raised in what neuroscientists call enriched environments they are healthier, more resilient to stress, and better at learning than rats that have not been. Their brains show evidence of increased neurogenesis and raised levels of BDNF, with twice as many neurons in the dentate gyrus of the hippocampus, which plays a critical role in learning and memory.

An enriched environment cage typically contains a wheel, a

ball, a tunnel, a ladder, and a small pool—the rat equivalent of a playground. The different forms of stimulation within it trigger seeking and exploring activity. The comparison rats are reared in standard cages containing only food and water. Laboratory work on the effects of environmental enrichment on brain development has had little to do with natural forms of enrichment. Kelly Lambert, professor of behavioral neuroscience at the University of Richmond in Virginia, decided to include a third type of cage—one that contained soil and plant material, including sticks, stumps, and a hollowed-out log, in place of the plastic and metal toys.

Rats are nocturnal, so their behavior was monitored under a form of red light that is not detected by them. When Lambert looked at the footage the next day, as predicted the rats in the empty cages were in her words "behaving like zombies," barely interacting with one another, and the rats in the standard enriched cages were much more active and sociable. But when she looked at the rats in the natural environments, she could not believe what she was seeing. She was so surprised that she called over her assistant to watch with her. For generations back, none of these laboratory-bred rats had been anywhere near nature, and you might have expected them to prefer their toys to sticks and dirt. But surrounded by the little bit of nature in their cages, they were the most excited and active lab rats the research team had ever seen. They were playing and digging and clearly enjoying themselves. More than that, they were connecting and interacting with one another in a much more sociable way.

The findings were so striking that Lambert and her team ran a second set of experiments, this time for a longer period of sixteen weeks; again, the "city rats" and the "country rats," as Lambert calls them, were compared to each other, as well as to the rats reared in standard cages. The results of the biochemistry tests on the city and country rats were largely similar, with both being superior to the unstimulated rats, although the ratio of the hormone DHEA to corticosterone was healthier in the country rats. But it was when it came to the analysis of their behavioral patterns that the country rats definitely had the edge. Compared to the city rats, they were more resilient when they were exposed to stress, they explored for longer and showed more persistence in tests, and they were more sociable with other rats.

Although Lambert calls them "city rats" and "country rats," what she gave her country rats was not countryside (that would have involved setting them free); it was more like giving them a garden to play in. What's amazing about this is that in all the decades of research on enriched environments, the difference between natural and artificial stimuli had been so little investigated before. It seems that contact with natural elements stimulates the nervous system in a more powerful way than artificial elements can. The rats certainly recognized the difference; they were demonstrating the rat equivalent of biophilia.

The enrichment effect is one of the reasons that the nineteenth-century "Go West" cure was much more successful than the "Rest" cure for neurasthenia. Today we are living in an era of separation from nature that in the history of our species has never been more extreme. Not only has the growth of our cities distanced us from nature, but our technology, with its ubiquitous screen culture, separates us too. In some parts of the world people barely go outdoors anymore. It has been reported that Americans, for example, on average spend 93 percent of their time either in an indoor environment or sitting in an enclosed vehicle.

Common sense suggests that fresh air, daylight, exercise, and access to green, quiet places are going to be good for people's health in cities. We have, though, reached such a point of remove from these elements that we need scientific evidence to demonstrate their effects to us. There is, however, one benefit of green space that the science demonstrates and that common sense might not predict so well, and that is what's called its "pro social" effect.

Lambert discovered this in her experiments when the country rats groomed one another and interacted with one another in a more sociable way. Frances Kuo and William Sullivan observed it in the Chicago housing studies that showed a strengthening of social networks when trees and gardens were nearby. In terms of city living, this may be one of nature's most profound effects on us. Put simply, people behave better and connect with one another more when they are in the presence of plants and trees.

The sociability effect of green vegetation on people has been measured in the laboratory. One study found that being in the presence of indoor plants or looking at scenes of nature (as opposed to urban scenes) prompted people to make decisions that showed higher levels of generosity and trust. The more immersed people were in the natural scenery, the stronger the effect. A different study carried out in Korea using fMRI brain scans found that pleasing natural scenery activated parts of the brain involved in generating empathy. The researchers followed the scans with psychological tests and found increased generosity too. These experiments suggest that we become more trusting and giving when we feel enriched by nature.

City living confronts us with a mass of other people, which challenges our ability to trust and undermines our capacity for empathy. The urban environment skews us toward indifference and suspicion. The instincts that promote survival of the self come to the fore, and our thinking follows suit. The presence of nature, on the other hand, helps us to feel more connected to the world around us. Rather like putting on a different pair of spectacles, we see the world differently, and it's not confined to the trees and the greenery; we see people differently too. Trees, parks, and gardens work on us imperceptibly, softening our gaze. Everyone shifts a little bit closer toward empathy and human connection.

CHAPTER 6

Roots

Carrot harvest.

Shall I not have intelligence with the earth? Am I not
partly leaves and vegetable mold myself?

Henry David Thoreau (1817–1862)

The first fruits of the vegetable patch are without doubt best savored
in situ. No carrot is tastier than one casually rinsed under the garden
tap, no radish more softly spicy than one that's still warm from the
earth. Tender new arugula leaves are all the more succulent if you eat
them while you work at thinning a row, and baby broad beans are
almost impossible to resist—why wait to cook them when, untimely
ripped, they can be sampled fresh from their downy pods?

There is a patch of sorrel by the gate into our vegetable garden which I planted many years ago in a stony corner of a raised bed. In early summer I used to find our children crouched round it in a huddle, grazing like rabbits, excited by its taste. Young sorrel leaves are as good as any sherbet; their lemon zing bursts in your mouth and gets you salivating like nothing else. A few times a year I harvest some leaves for soups and sauces, but more often than not, I too stop as I pass through the gate to get a sorrel "fix."

Even weeds have their rewards. Each spring I pick the first flush of nettles to make soup and gather red orach leaves to add to our salads. Then there are the self-sowers like nasturtiums and calendula that I planted many years ago and which have seeded themselves freely in our vegetable beds. Throughout the summer I collect their edible red and orange petals and use them to adorn all sorts of dishes.

Of all the garden foraging possibilities, my favorite is the wild strawberry. These little alpine fruits never make it into the kitchen, let alone onto a plate. In summer when I am working in the garden, I seek them out, feeling in the foliage for their deep red jewel-like berries. It is the delicious complex of flavors that makes them so compelling; sweet and sharp, flowery and fruity, fresh and musty, all at the same time.

There are many possibilities for the kind of environment we can create for ourselves through gardening, and one of them is a homey foraging ground. When we go out to gather fruits, flowers, and other garden produce, our anticipation of reward stimulates an energizing dopamine release much as it propelled our Paleolithic ancestors out of their caves.

It may seem like a contradiction to talk of foraging in your own garden, but little bits of wilderness constantly creep into any garden, and even on a small patch, the pleasures of wandering and finding feel more like gathering than harvesting. When it comes to the question of how our remote ancestors first started cultivating the earth, the overlap between foraging and gardening takes us back to how it must have all begun. What might exploring this phase of our prehistory tell us about the origins of gardening in the human mind?

Humankind's first attempts at gardening are a part of our prehistory that is inevitably hard to trace. Unlike tools, carvings, and other artifacts, virtually nothing has survived, most of it lost to the recycling and regenerating powers of nature—although recent advances in soil and plant analysis are beginning to reveal intriguing clues. By contrast, the origins of farming have been much more fully mapped out. The genetic changes involved in the domestication of Neolithic crops show that farming began to be practiced around twelve thousand years ago in the Fertile Crescent, a large area which now includes the Middle and the Near East. It used to be thought that like a new invention, agriculture had spread outward from the Fertile Crescent, but we now know that farming developed independently in at least ten other regions, including China and Central America.

This period of our prehistory has come to be known as the "Neolithic Revolution." The influential archaeologist V. Gordon Childe gave it this name almost a hundred years ago because the practice of farming ushered in such profound social and economic changes. The trigger for this transformation was believed to have been diminishing food supplies caused by climate change, and the assumption was that hunter-gatherers gained little experience of seed propagation until necessity prompted them to start cultivating the earth. This focus on staple crops gave rise to the idea that the farm came before the garden and that nonessential cultivation developed later. However, the skills involved in propagating plants could not have developed in fields. Hunter-gatherers must have learned to till the earth in small plots, and given the delay from seed to fruition, as well as the modest scale of people's first efforts, it seems unlikely they were motivated by survival needs.

Childe wrote the popular book *Man Makes Himself* in which he portrayed cultivation as a scientific-like breakthrough that enabled people to take control of nature. Although he acknowledged that small-scale garden cultivation would have preceded farming, he regarded this as an "incidental" activity. Unlike agriculture, it was invariably the women's domain, while the men, as he put it, got on with "the really serious business of the chase." Gardening would have taken place alongside other female occupations such as child-rearing, gathering, and food preparation. The main foraging tool, the digging stick, was used for unearthing roots and tubers as well as for tilling the earth. But small as they may have been, these gardens were far from "incidental"—they signified a major shift in the relationship between plants and people.

Rather than being a revolution, it has become increasingly clear that what took place at the start of the Neolithic was the result of a slowly evolving relationship between plants and people. As Dorian Fuller, professor of archaeobotany at University College London describes, the first farmers were drawing on "a collective memory and deep cultural traditions of plant tending that developed in the later Paleolithic." Even when hunter-gatherers were not practicing cultivation, according to Fuller, the ethnographic evidence suggests that they were fully aware of how plants reproduce themselves.

Fuller specializes in the origins of cultivation in China and explains that the earliest gardens were not devoted to subsistence foods but "high-value foods," which he thinks were intended for feasts or special occasions. In other words, the motivation behind the gardens may have been bound up with social rituals and social status. By contrast with the monocrops grown in fields, pre-agricultural gardens were characterized by diversity, and plants were cultivated for use at different times of the year.

112

Inevitably, different plants were grown in different parts of the world, but generally the first plants that people grew were highly desirable or scarce. Various non-food plants come into this category, including medicines and hallucinogens as well as herbs, spices, dyes, and fibers. The bottle gourd, for example, is known to have been widely cultivated for use both as a container and a musical instrument, and, along with the fig, it was one of the first plants to have been domesticated. This pattern of growing life-enhancing plants long before staples is particularly well documented in Mexico. Here the chili pepper, the avocado, the bean, several species of squash, and a number of fruit trees, such as cosahuico and chupandilla, were domesticated several thousand years before such staples as maize, millet, and amaranth.

The archaeologist Andrew Sherratt has come up with a particularly neat reversal of the conventional narrative about cultivation, by characterizing the path that people took from gardening to farming as one that started with growing luxuries and ended with growing commodities. The focus on growing life-enhancing plants means that from the very beginning, gardening was an expression of culture.

Evidence is also mounting that many hunter-gatherer tribes were not as nomadic as previously thought. In addition, seeds are readily portable. Simple gardening based on fast-germinating annuals would have been compatible with moving between seasonal camps. When foraging grounds were abundant enough, hunter-gatherers sometimes settled for longer. Increasingly, it looks as if it was plentiful food rather than scarcity of food that created the conditions for small-scale cultivation to begin. Settlement sites by lakes, marshes, or rivers that provided water and fertile ground, with a stable warm climate and surroundings rich in natural resources, gave people the time and opportunity to experiment with plants.

The prehistoric hunter-gatherer camp known as Ohalo II is on just such a site. Located on the Sea of Galilee, the remains have been remarkably well preserved under the water. Around 23000 BC a small group lived here in a collection of six huts by the shore. Traces of more than 140 wild plants collected from the surrounding terrain show that they were actively foraging. Further analysis carried out by a team of Israeli archaeologists has revealed evidence that the inhabitants were also growing a range of foods including peas, lentils, figs, grapes, almonds, olives, and emmer wheat. These findings are unusually early, some eleven thousand years before other evidence in the Fertile Crescent.

This mixed lifestyle could more properly be called hunting-gathering-cultivating. Not only did foraging and tending plants take place side by side, but in some instances the two activities blended into each other. Rather than simply collecting food, when resources were available, hunter-gatherers began to practice various forms of proactive foraging or "managed foraging" as it is sometimes known. They started to weed out undesirable plants, create spaces around the ones they wanted to see flourish, and clear areas of ground. There is, in fact, no neat dividing line between foraging and cultivation. Instead, as the American anthropologist Bruce D. Smith writes, there is a "vast and diverse middle ground."

The earliest forms of gardening on the planet are now thought to have emerged in the tropical forests of Southeast Asia. Analysis of the soil and patterns of rainfall in the forests of Borneo reveal that fifty-three thousand years ago, during the last ice age, inhabitants were harnessing the power of fire to fertilize the ground and let in the light. At some point in the course of evolution, the human mind became receptive to nature's patterns and people started imitating them. The forest-dwellers would have observed how the burned ground that followed lightning strikes gave rise to a tender flush of new vegetation. Nature created the first "gardens" and, in doing so, provided the model. As forest gardening became more established, people began to shape the environment in other

ways, through diverting water, weeding, fertilizing, and transplanting saplings. To cultivate is to humanize the wilderness and promote the life-enhancing aspects of the environment. You could say
that it marks the very origins of culture. The word "culture," after
all, is derived from working the soil and the growing and tending
of plants.

We tend to think of nature as dominated by predatory relationships, but there are plenty of partnerships to be found in the natural world, some of which look remarkably like cultivation. All
species construct what ecologists call a "niche" in their environment. Every organism has to do this in order to live, and its niche
can have a destructive or constructive effect on other organisms
around it. Mutually beneficial or symbiotic relationships between
two different species emerge through a reciprocal form of evolution, known as co-evolution.

Take the example of the long-spined limpets that inhabit the
rock pools of South Africa's Western Cape. Unlike most other
limpets, these manage their foraging grounds. Each limpet tends
its own "garden" of brown *Ralfsia verrucosa* algae. So how does a
limpet set about gardening? First, it clears the ground. This means
stripping an area of rock using its powerful rasp-like tongue, and
then, as the *Ralfsia* algae start to colonize it, the limpet weeds out
other more vigorous and less desirable species of algae. Before long
it has its very own patch of tender and nutritious turf. The limpet's
excretions act as a fertilizer and the water it stores and releases
from under its shell stops the algae from drying out at low tide.
All this maintenance combined with continued weeding keeps the
garden in top condition. Crucially, the limpet consumes the algae
no faster than it can regrow. This is what biologists call "prudent
grazing," and the limpet does this by "mowing" its lawn in strips.

There ought to be a sign saying "Keep Off the Lawn," for no

other limpet is allowed to stray onto, let alone sample, another limpet's *Ralfsia*. Most other limpet species survive through free-range foraging, and if one of these dares to trespass, it will be barged into retreat. The *Ralfsia* doesn't last long without the limpet's protection; it is either eaten into oblivion by other foraging limpets or is swamped out by more vigorous algae.

Ants are particularly good at forming symbiotic relationships, many of which are believed to be millions of years old. With their large workforces, cultivating ants are engaged in an activity that resembles farming. There is the leaf-cutter ant, which creates underground fungal gardens, and the Fijian ant, which has recently been discovered to plant seeds of Squamellaria and cultivate its fruits.

In addition to "farming" ants and "gardening" limpets, there are also species of termite and beetle that "cultivate," and there is even a seed-planting worm. When it comes to mammals, however, *Homo sapiens* stands out as the only example: we are the gardening ape.

Whatever role human culture may have played in kick-starting cultivation, nature also played a part. As the archaeologist Kent Flannery wrote, the origins of cultivation "involved both human intentionality and a set of underlying ecological and evolutionary principles." Flannery, who was based at the University of Chicago and specialized in the prehistory of Mexico, was drawing attention to the role that plants themselves played in the plant-people relationship, particularly through their ability to respond to human interventions by mutating and hybridizing.

Two very different ideas have been put forward about how the garden might have developed from the ecological niches that hunter-gatherers inhabited. While one links the emergence of the garden to waste disposal, the other suggests it may have been an unintended consequence of ritual.

The "dump heap" theory was proposed in the 1950s by the American ethnobotanist Edgar Anderson, who hypothesized that when hunter-gatherers were able to stay in one place long enough, they would have benefited from plants that sprouted up in the dunghill, which, after all, is the perfect location for the alchemy that turns seeds and manure into food. Anderson was struck that plants such as gourds, squash, amaranth, and beans, all of which readily grow in trash heaps, were the first plants to be cultivated in many parts of the world. In his view, the role these plants played in the development of cultivation had been underestimated because, in contrast to wheat and rice, they tended to be perceived as somewhat "humble."

Cleared areas of ground also lend themselves to plant colonization. Some of the self-seeders in hunter-gatherer camps are thought to have been those with psychoactive properties. Tobacco, henbane, and poppy are all of this type and may well have achieved a closer relationship with humans in this way. Furthermore, many of the "inadvertent" gardens that arose in trash heaps would have included a range of plants that do not naturally grow together. As a result Anderson thought they provided a crucible for hybridization and plant-breeding. Whatever kind of plants cropped up, it would have been the most desirable that received protection—giving rise to the first domestic gardens, or "doorstep gardens," as they are sometimes called.

Anderson's theory about the origins of the garden is widely accepted and makes biological sense. There is a less well-known proposition suggested by Charles Heiser, another twentieth-century American ethnobotanist, that concerns the origin of a different kind of garden.

The coming of the first fruits each year serves as a reminder of how dependent we are on the earth to nourish us. Traditionally, their appearance, or rather reappearance, has been a cause for celebration and sacrifice. Rituals associated with the first fruits are some of the earliest customs to have been recorded and can be found in most cultures around the world. Their universality led Heiser to wonder if they could be far older than we realize.

According to ethnographic records, there are hunter-gatherer tribes that leave the first fruits on the plant as an offering to the gods, in some cases returning a sample of seed to the earth and marking the spot with stones. Heiser speculated that when such rituals were enacted in prehistory, the scattered or buried seed would have given rise to inadvertent gardens. In this way, he thought it was possible that "the first planting and the first sacred garden could have come into existence at the same time."

Heiser's theory takes us into the hunter-gatherer mind and reminds us that an environment can be a spiritual as well as a physical home. Certainly, it is true that as far back as we can trace, gardens feature strongly in religion and mythology, and records from antiquity show that every temple had its own garden. It is usually assumed that garden cultivation came first and that the beliefs and rituals associated with planting came later, but Heiser's thinking turns this sequence on its head. He put forward his idea in the 1980s, and since then the part that ritual practice played in the evolution of human culture has assumed a more central place in our understanding of prehistory. If rituals are now thought to have made a significant contribution to the origins of art, why not to the origins of cultivation too? It is, as Heiser himself indicated, something about which we can only speculate.

The hunter-gatherer world is an animate world. Every aspect of nature is alive with its own characteristic energy and spirit; the sacred is part of everyday life, and rituals are a form of symbolic interaction with the spirit world. They honor the earth and try to influence it at the same time. Rituals bring a sense of order to situations that are uncertain or precarious. They can alleviate anxiety, affirm shared values, and enhance group bonding. In terms of our prehistory, it is thought that rituals played an important role within hunter-gatherer culture through maintaining the level of social cohesion that was needed for groups and tribes to function successfully.

One of the defining works on the practice of ritual was produced almost a hundred years ago by the great anthropologist Bronislaw Malinowski. He spent several years during the First World War living on the Trobriand Islands, a remote part of Papua New Guinea, and wrote three books about this vanishing world—one of which, *Coral Gardens and Their Magic*, is devoted entirely to the gardening practices of the Trobriand people.

The islanders had a long tradition of fishing, but Malinowski decided that they were "first and foremost" gardeners. Although it was the men who took the lead, families would garden together, and Malinowski observed the joy they took "in delving into the earth, in turning it up, planting the seed, watching the plant grow, mature, and yield the harvest." Community life revolved around the gardens, which as a collective source of pride and ambition gave rise to "a surprising care for the aesthetics of gardening."

Although the Trobriand people were knowledgeable horticulturalists, no amount of skill was considered enough to ensure that plants would grow well. Magic was essential to a garden's productivity. Each village had a head man, or *Towosi* as he was known, who was also the garden "wizard." The *Towosi* conducted all the key ceremonies in the cultivation calendar. Some of these rituals concerned offerings of food to the spirits; others involved a sacred digging stick with which the wizard would strike the soil. Almost all involved the chanting of magic spells that resembled poems or hymns. "Growth magic," as Malinowski called it, may seem like a world apart from our own, but perhaps we find a residue of it in the way we talk of "green thumbs," for there is always an element of mystery involved in growing plants.

The aesthetic qualities of the garden were an intrinsic part of the Trobriand magic, for it was believed that only if the garden looked right would it grow well. The yam tubers were planted out in grids, and enormous care was taken over the alignment of the beds and the vertical poles up which the yam vines were trained. Malinowski described each garden as "a work of art," and the anthropologist Alfred Gell subsequently developed this idea further. "If we thought of the quadrangular Trobriand garden as an artist's canvas on which forms mysteriously grow, through an occult process which lies partly beyond our intuition, that would not be a bad analogy," Gell observed. He regarded the careful training of vines and tendrils up the poles as being carried out according to principles that were "no less 'aesthetic' than those of the topiaries in the formal gardens of Europe." These observations raise the possibility that the earliest forms of aesthetic gardening may have been intimately bound up with the practice of ritual.

People and plants were closely linked in Trobriand culture. In fact, human reproduction and plant regeneration were held in a kind of equivalence, for the same spirit was believed to be responsible for new life in both. The growth-promoting spell that was chanted to accompany the first yam planting culminated with the lines "The belly of my garden lies down / The belly of my garden swells / The belly of my garden swells as with child." And the garden really did swell in the ensuing months, as an earthy mound rose up over each burgeoning yam. The idea of a symbolic pregnancy has been found in other yam-growing cultures, some of which refer to the planting of the yam as the placing of a "father" tuber into the earth with the understanding that in time, this "mother" place will bring forth yam progeny.

This is not anthropomorphism in the modern human-centric sense. Plants are like people because people are like plants; they are part of one nature with shared qualities that connect them, and it is a way of thinking that was not unique to Papua New Guinea. Among the Achuar tribe of the Upper Amazon, the humanization of cultivated plants is taken even further; an Achuar woman has two sets of offspring, her own children and the plants that she tends. This remote tribe of hunter-gatherers, which has a long tradition of cultivation, was studied during the mid-1970s by anthropologist Philippe Descola, when he and his wife, fellow anthropologist Anne-Christine Taylor, spent several years living among the Achuar. In contrast to the Trobriand gardens, the Achuar gardens are private spaces, and Descola relied on his wife for much of the gardening field work because men were not usually allowed to enter them.

The boundary of each garden is marked with banana trees, and within these enclosures the women cultivate staple foods like manioc, yam, and taro, as well as fruit trees and a wide range of medicinal plants. The Achuar women are skilled horticulturists, and their gardens generally contain about a hundred different species, some domesticated, some wild. The only tools they use to manage their large plots are small machetes and digging sticks, and much as in the Trobriand Islands, the aesthetic presentation of the garden matters. For an Achuar woman, keeping her garden well weeded is a source of personal pride. Descola describes how the plants in the gardens are "set out, according to their affinities, in beds separated one from another by little sandy paths as carefully raked as those in a Japanese garden."

The Achuar also believe in garden magic. To be a good gardener, it is necessary to learn a great number of magical songs known as *anent*. These are an integral part of tilling the soil and are quietly chanted by the women as they work. Many of the songs are addressed to the spirit Nunkui, who, according to Achuar mythology, is the mother of all cultivated plants and is believed to dwell just under the surface of the soil. Although they are demarcated, the garden and the jungle are regarded as if they were in a continuum. For the Achuar, the wild plants that grow deep in the forest are part of a different kind of garden, one that is cared for by Nunkui's brother Shakaim.

Individual plants are attributed with something resembling a soul, and different varieties are endowed with different characters. The cultivation of manioc is heavily ritualized, for unlike the other plants in the garden, it has sinister qualities. Cultivating involves a particular transaction in which "manioc allows itself to be eaten by human beings provided they assume responsibility for ensuring its continued propagation." When the women sing to the plants, they ally themselves with Nunkui's generative powers, as in the song of supplication to the manioc that repeats the line "Being a Nunkui woman, I am always calling nourishment into existence." As Descola describes, the Achuar women's gardening "can be seen as a daily repetition of the act of creation in which Nunkui gave birth to the cultivated plants."

This "horticultural mothering," as Descola calls it, works reciprocally, because the women find a kind of mothering for themselves within the sanctuary of the garden. Among the Achuar, public displays of emotion are discouraged, but within the gardens the women can safely express their grief and suffering as well as their joy. They also take themselves there when it is time for them to give birth. The garden is the place in which new life enters into the world and where it can be protected and nourished. More than that, the women are strengthened by the belief that here in the garden, they can appropriate something of Nunkui's creative powers.

We now think of the social world as limited to the human world, but for hunter-gatherers it is much more all-encompassing. The social, the natural, and the spiritual are not separate domains but part of one world. In his work on the evolution of human consciousness, the psychologist Nicholas Humphrey argues that it was *Homo sapiens*'s social intelligence that was most influential in how our species developed. He makes the case that we are predisposed to fit the "non-social into the social" and that the beginnings of cultivation would have been heavily dependent on this. Caring for plants involves a level of attunement with their needs as they grow and develop. It is a process of give-and-take, based on what he identifies as a "simple social relationship."

The human brain is primed to enter into an intimacy with nature as part of our hunter-gatherer heritage. We can hardly say that gardening is in our DNA, but a link with plants surely is, for our remote ancestors' survival depended on it, hence the deep human affinity that exists with plants and our propensity to develop an understanding of their habits and their properties. The practice of cultivation, as it developed, drew on these skills and combined them with the human instinct for care. Our capacity for care is one of the things that sets us apart as a species, and we are unusual among primates in the extent to which we share food and care for our sick. Accounts of our prehistory, however, tend to focus on advances that signified superior human intelligence and technical mastery. In contrast, something like the role of care, which is associated more with women than men, is not necessarily highlighted, but in all likelihood it was care more than anything else that changed the early human relationship with plants.

The anthropologist Tim Ingold makes the point that we cannot make or manufacture the fruits of the earth, we can only provide the conditions for growth. Hunter-gatherer beliefs, he argues, reflect this reality. Growing plants and raising animals is not that different from bringing up children: "Caring for an environment," he writes, "is like caring for people: it requires a deep, personal, and affectionate involvement, an involvement not just of mind or body but of one's entire undivided being."

Western culture, by contrast, has prioritized ideas about the human domination of nature.

Our colonial past is full of encounters that involved settlers arriving in distant places with ideas about the conquest and mastery of nature and failing to recognize the value of a much older way of relating to the land. One such example took place in 1843 when the British-born explorer James Douglas went ashore on the south side of Vancouver Island. He was employed by the Hudson's Bay Company and had been charged with finding a site for farmland near which a new trading post could be established. In contrast to the surrounding coastline of "dreary wilderness" and dense, inhospitable conifer forests, this place was, as he described it "a perfect Eden." He wandered through meadowlands in which ancient Garry oak trees were rising from a sea of blue flowers and millions of butterflies filled the air. The meadows contained a variety of flowers, including several species of lily, but it was the density of common camas (*Camassia quamash*) and great camas (*Camassia leichtlinii*) flowers that made the place such an astonishing sight.

Douglas was mistaken in thinking this was an untouched "Eden," for it was, in fact, the ancestral home of the Lekwungen tribe of the Coast Salish people of British Columbia, who had hunted and gathered along this coast for thousands of years. The Lekwungen people lived in seasonal camps in the summer and permanent villages in winter, sustained by salmon, roots, and berries. The men would hunt and fish while the women foraged for a wide variety of plants, including horsetail, fern, cow parsnip, and clover. They also collected fruits and nuts and rooted up the edible bulbs of flowering plants such as the camas and the lily. Looking at this landscape with a prospector's eyes, Douglas regarded their foraging grounds as "uncultivated waste."

Earlier travelers had introduced the Lekwungen to potatoes,

which they grew below the camas meadows, where the soil was moist enough for them to thrive. These plots were easily recognizable as cultivation, but the idea that the flourishing meadows, with their beautiful flowers and majestic trees, might have arisen through human intervention did not occur to Douglas. In fact, the meadows were regarded as sacred. Each one was a garden within which Lekwungen families cared for their own plots, these having been passed down over successive generations through the matrilineal line.

Camassias are a type of wild hyacinth, and each year in May and June, when their tall spikes came into flower, families would set up camp. These seasonal gatherings, as ethnographic studies indicate, were an important time of reunion and celebration, full of singing and gossiping—and the beauty of the meadows must have contributed to the joyfulness too. The women spent days turning over the ground using their digging sticks to weed out invasive plants and remove stones. The larger camas bulbs were collected up into baskets while smaller ones were replanted and "wild" camas transplanted to replenish the stocks. But there was one type of bulb that the women assiduously removed, that of the white-flowered death camas. This is a plant of powerful toxicity that is actually from the *Zigadenus* family but resembles the camas so closely that you can only easily tell them apart at flowering time. The bulbs, the leaves, and every part of this plant is poisonous and accidental ingestion is often fatal.

Sometimes the newly dug beds would be covered in seaweed to improve the soil, but the Lekwungen also enriched the ground by setting fires in the autumn. This seasonal burning eliminated the shrubby growth which otherwise would swamp the camas and kept the coniferous trees at bay, allowing the Garry oaks to regenerate, for intense heat helps the acorns of this rare oak to germinate.

The harvested bulbs, which look like small onions, were cooked in large pots for hours and hours, or baked in earth ovens sometimes for days, until they became soft and sweet, resembling chestnuts and tasting, it is said, something like baked pear. Once cooked, bulbs were either eaten or laid out to dry in the sun for winter supplies. If cultivating the camas had been mainly driven by a need for carbohydrate, the Lekwungen might well have abandoned it for the less labor-intensive potato, which provided them with a more reliable source of starch. But the cultivation of the camas meadows was embedded in their culture, and the bulbs were regarded as a delicacy.

Following Douglas's arrival, the settlers banned the burning of the meadows. The human-plant balance within the ecosystem changed, leaving the camas flowers to be choked out by fast-growing shrubs and the Garry oaks to dwindle and decline. Some of the meadowland was plowed up and sown with barley, oats, or wheat; some was used as pasture for cattle, sheep, and pigs; and some of it was built over to create the new Hudson's Bay Company fort at Victoria. Douglas had assumed that the thriving "natural" parklands so full of flowers boded well for the future of farming here, but the luxuriance of the spring growth on these meadows gave little indication of the free-draining soils or how sparsely the summer rains fell. A Mediterranean type of climate prevails along this stretch of coast, and many of the settlers' farms failed to thrive.

The colonialists shipped *Camassia* bulbs to other parts of North America and to England for use in gardens not as edible bulbs but as ornamental plants. We grow them in our garden at home, and each year their flowers bloom for two or three weeks just as spring turns to summer. I always mourn their passing, for their tall, elegant spikes really are a heavenly shade of blue.

Many plants respond to grazing and harvesting with increased vigor and growth; it is part of the reciprocal relationship that exists between animals and plants—an effect unlikely to have been missed by hunter-gatherers, with their keen observation skills. The Salish Lekwungen's meadow gardens would have developed from simple foraging. Rooting up the largest of the bulbs, returning the rest to the ground, and weeding out the toxic death camas all helped the camas to regenerate and thrive.

In 2005, researchers at the University of Victoria set up an experiment to study the effects of traditional Salish cultivation methods. They marked out plots that were left untended to simulate camas growing in the wild, while on other plots they replicated the Coast Salish seasonal cycles of digging, harvesting, transplanting, and burning. After several years, the tended plants were growing much more vigorously and producing larger bulbs, leaving no doubt that Salish practice had been effective at intensifying the camas growth.

The archaeobotanist Glynis Jones uses the phrase "agricultural mindset" to characterize the way that European settlers disregarded the indigenous forms of cultivation they encountered. Jones, who is professor of archaelogy at the University of Sheffield in England, cites the example of how the traditional Maori gardens were dismissed by colonialists as "primitive low-technology agriculture." It is only much more recently that they have been recognized as what she calls "successful intensive gardening."

The Maoris were descended from a long line of gardening people. Their ancestors traveled from Polynesia in small boats and brought plants with them to stock the gardens they would make in their new home. They had to contend with a very different climate in New Zealand and quickly learned to protect their plots from the cold southerly winds within enclosures of reed-and-manuka-brush fencing, seeking out sites that would catch the best of the sun's precious warmth. They had to give up growing bananas, coconut, and breadfruit, but through ingenious use of carefully placed flat stones, which warmed the soil, they managed to carry on growing kumara (sweet potato).

The Maori gardeners kept their soils rich by digging in charcoal and ash, and the heavier loamy soils were mixed with shells, sand, and shingle. Taro, yam, gourds, and sweet potato were all grown to supplement foraging for wild plants, but the gardens contained a variety of other plants with different uses. Cabbage trees for their roots, karaka trees for fruit, the aute paper mulberry for making tapa cloth, and some ornamental shrubs, like the kaka beak (*Clianthus maximus*) and napuka (*Veronica speciosa*), were also grown. These sophisticated horticultural skills were overlooked when the Maori gardens were first documented by European settlers.

The Europeans also failed to recognize the cultural significance of the small, separate plots, the *māra tautāne* in which the Maoris made the first planting of kumara tubers each year. The food that was produced in these sacred gardens was not for human consumption. Much as Charles Heiser described in his account of first fruits rituals, the kumara grown here were set aside as an offering to Rongo, the god of cultivation. This intimate relationship between cultivating the earth and religion would have been anathema to the colonialists. Their places of worship were separate from the land and their concept of paradise was an unearthly one. Tilling the soil for the pioneers was more of a utilitarian exercise, driven by economic profit. Emptied of deeper meaning, the land was simply there to be exploited. The desacralization of the natural world brought with it the idea that humans can control nature, and gave rise to a loss of respect for the earth, a deep misapprehension that continues to plague us today.

There is an ancient Sumerian myth that tells of how the art of gardening was acquired and of how the gardener betrays his sacred relationship with the land. The myth, which dates back five thousand years or so, is one of many stories featuring the goddess Inanna, who in being associated with passion, procreation, and power bears similarity to the later Greek goddesses Aphrodite and Demeter.

The ancient civilization of Sumer was set within the Fertile Crescent on the floodplain between the Tigris and Euphrates rivers, in what is now southern Iraq. This is where the very first cities arose as a consequence of the Sumerians' mastery of farming. They also developed the first written language and recorded the earliest mythologies. One of these, known as "The Gardener's Mortal Sin," features the first documented gardener in literature. The story, as translated by Samuel Noah Kramer, opens with a man called Shukallituda struggling with the elements in his attempts to create a garden. The hot, dry winds blow dust in his face, and although he waters his plants, the harsh rays of the sun burn them till they wither and die. Then one day he lifts his eyes to "the lands below" and "the lands above" and sees that plants flourish when they are sheltered by a tree. He learns by imitating the "divine laws" that are inscribed in nature, and his garden finally flourishes when he plants a set of *sarbatu* trees to provide much needed shade.

One day, the goddess Inanna lies down to rest in Shukallituda's garden. Exhausted by her long travels across the heavens and the earth, she falls fast asleep. Shukallituda spies on her, and unable to control his lust, he rapes her as she slumbers. At dawn, when she awakes, she is horrified to find that she has been defiled and vows to find and punish the mortal who has abused her. But Shukallituda takes flight and goes into hiding in the cities. In her fury, Inanna sends three plagues against the Sumer people. The first turns the water red: "All the wells of the land she filled with blood, all the groves and gardens of the land she sated with blood." The second batters the land with destructive winds and storms, but the third plague, and the tale's ending, is unknown as a crucial part of the ancient tablet is missing.

For the Sumerians tilling the land was symbolically linked with human procreation. They believed that the fertility of their soil depended on an annual ritual marriage between the King of Sumer and the goddess Inanna. The sacred union of the king and goddess is celebrated in other Sumerian poems, also translated by Kramer, where it is portrayed as a loving and tender union. King Dumuzi is Inanna's first husband, and when he makes an advance, she responds enthusiastically: "Plow my vulva, man of my heart." After their lovemaking is over, the poet describes how, as Dumuzi lies resting, "grains rose high by his side" and "gardens flourished luxuriantly by his side."

There is a small, beautifully decorated Sumerian seal that disappeared from the National Museum in Baghdad in 2003, during the Iraq War. As the American tanks rolled in, a wave of looting broke out, and along with many other precious antiquities, the seal was stolen. It may never be seen again, but its depiction of a harvest festival scene survives in photographs of the seal. Delicately carved, four-and-a-half thousand years ago, the seal shows men carrying baskets filled with produce as offerings for a goddess perched on a throne. The Sumerians believed they had a responsibility to serve the gods, and on closer inspection, it is possible to see that the goddess is sitting on a man's back. We are witnessing a first fruits festival, and like all Sumerian festivals, it symbolized a renewal of the people's covenant with the gods.

In spite of their creed, the Sumerians ended up exploiting the land. "The Gardener's Mortal Sin" tells of the rape of the goddess Inanna, and by extension, the rape of the earth. It portrays a destructive shift in the human relationship with nature arising from the betrayal of a respectful gardening ethic. Although the Sumerian people understood that the land needed to rest, much as the tired goddess in the myth needed sleep to recover, still they took and took from the soil, refusing to let fields lie fallow. Their actions gave rise to the world's first ecological disaster and eventually brought about their downfall. The plagues sent by Inanna in the myth bear some resemblance to what took place. A lack of care for the land led to soil erosion. As a consequence, the water courses ran red with a fine tilth, and dust storms became more frequent. The Sumerians also over-irrigated their fields, causing a white saline crust to form on the surface; this, perhaps, the missing third plague.

The myth may have foreshadowed events in Sumerian history, but it is also a fitting myth for later epochs, including our own. You can only force the land for so long. In former times, European settlers used to talk of breaking the land, as if it could be compelled into servitude. But care for the land helps root us. Without care, we are cast adrift, like Shukallituda, who ends up hiding in the cities, having lost his spiritual home. The moral is clear: our gardens, in the widest sense, are not going to flourish unless we follow the "divine laws"—that is the laws of nature. When greed and desire lead us to violate those laws, we do so at our peril.

The natural world is a living continuum, and triumph over nature, as Carl Jung wrote, is "dearly paid for." Jung understood the value of the ancient sense of connection with the land, a connection that was physical and spiritual at the same time. He thought that a malaise of "uprootedness" lay at the heart of much modern life because so many city dwellers had lost this traditional connection. Lacking a relationship with nature, life becomes stale, and "people live as though they were walking in shoes too small for them."

Jung believed that however modern we are, our primitive ancestry lies within us like an untapped resource: "Aren't we the carriers of the entire history of mankind?," he wrote. "When a man is fifty years old, only one part of his being has existed for half a century. The other part, which also lives in his psyche, may be millions of years old. . . . Contemporary man is but the latest ripe fruit on the tree of the human race." We need to reconnect with what he called "the dark maternal, earthy ground of our being," but in seeking to control nature, we have isolated ourselves from her and robbed ourselves of our natural history. The answer, as Jung saw it, lay not in a losing of the self in the wilderness, a form of escape that he observed could be used like a drug, but instead in a direct contact with the soil and its life-giving properties. Growing his own potatoes gave him "a great deal of pleasure," and he believed that "every human should have a plot of land so that their instincts can come to life again."

These same life-promoting instincts have since been differentiated by modern neurobiology. They include the seeking system, which enlivens us in a forward-looking and optimistic way and initiates foraging behavior or other reward based activities. The caring and nurturing instincts undoubtedly find expression in the garden too. The other great life-promoting instinct is the sexual one, which Jung might not have had in mind, for he thought too much was attributed to sublimated sexuality within psychoanalytic theory. However we in ethnographic studies, and ancient literature such as the Sumerian myth, we find that tilling the soil was regarded as a form of procreative intercourse with the earth.

The practice of gardening has not changed much since humans first started to till the earth—after all it has little real need for technology. The human mind hasn't changed much, either. To be in touch with the aliveness of the natural world is deep in our psychological ancestry. Although the rituals associated with cultivation may not be so manifest in our culture today, there is no escaping the structure of the seasons, and we continue to perform the same ancient pattern of tasks throughout the year.

Gardening always involves reckoning with forces larger than ourselves. However much we put our stamp on a place, make it fit to fulfill our needs (in whatever way we might define them), a garden is its own living entity, one that we cannot fully control. It is a relationship of mutual influence, through which we too are shaped— a process that I've come to see as the growth of the gardener's mind.

The idea that in caring for plants something similar to a "simple social relationship" can arise rings true to experience. I feel it in my own gardening, and it is the case for many of the people I interviewed for this book—such as Eddie with his ritual greeting of the eucalyptus tree, Vivian who confessed to sharing her secrets with the greenhouse plants, and Francis who learned about managing vulnerability from his "gentle guides."

While the idea of give-and-take in our relationship with the natural world may be under threat in modern life, the intimacy of the garden means that it is something many gardeners understand. The American garden writer Robert Dash put his finger on it when he wrote that the root of gardening's power "is that of reciprocal behavior. We tend it in exchange for the gift of it." This type of relationship is important because it fosters a sense of respect for the other. We can feel we have earned our rewards and experience gratitude for the fruits of the earth. It is very different from a relationship based on exploitation, which fosters a sense of entitlement, giving rise to the idea that we can take what we like from the earth.

The homey foraging ground is not only for us: we set something in motion, enriching our surroundings with biodiversity, creating environments for the birds and insects to occupy, so that the niche takes on a life of its own. Nowhere else can we get quite this feeling or sense of connection, or one with such ancient origins. Through foraging, harvesting, planting, weeding, and all the other forms of garden giving and taking, we return to our essential relationship with nature.

CHAPTER 7

Flower Power

Flower pollination in action.

*I work at my garden all the time and with love. What I
need most are flowers, always.*

Claude Monet (1840–1926)

There are times when our garden simply stops me in my tracks.
I remember once being brought to a halt by a delphinium. It was
in the midst of a busy time both at work and at home. There were
tasks mounting up in the garden as well: sowing the next batch
of seeds, thinning the salads and herbs, and hoeing the beds. But
that morning, I was focused on getting jobs done before our weekend guests arrived, knowing there would soon be lots of people in

the house to feed. Heading out of the house straight toward the freezer in our shed, I steered a course past the delphiniums that line the path. As I reached the last one, its blue spike hailed me, and one of its iridescent flowers caught my eye. It was a flower on the tallest spike in the stand—the deepest of deep variegated blues—and the light was shining through it. Intense color commands your attention. It says look! Look closely! And you have to. And I did. I stared into the center of that blue flower eye.

With the other flower spikes swaying gently around me, I lost myself, and in that losing was joined by a blackbird singing in the hedge. My thoughts, which had been racing and scattered, went quiet. A sense of space inside my mind shifted out toward the hedge and up toward the skylarks singing high overhead. The birds had been there all the time. How had I been so oblivious, so deaf to their song?

It was a simple pause in a busy morning, and yet it changed the whole day, rescuing my outlook from the frantic swell inside me. And more than that, it is a moment that returns to me, partly in its wonder, and partly in its warning. A reminder to take heed of the beauty that is around me.

The eighteenth-century philosopher Immanuel Kant described how we love flowers "freely and on their own account." Kant used flowers to illustrate his concept of "free" beauty, that is a form of beauty which we respond to regardless of utility or cultural value. Certainly, we know beauty when we see it. We recognize it as if something in us has been lying in wait for it. Beauty holds our gaze and saturates our awareness. Somehow the boundary between our self and the world shifts and we feel more alive in the moment of flourishing that it offers. Although the experience may be fleeting, beauty leaves a trace in the mind that survives its passing.

Flowers introduced Claude Monet to a compelling world of

color and harmony: "I perhaps owe having become a painter to flowers," he wrote. He first cultivated his water lilies with no thought of painting them. For him, gardening and painting were part of the same artistic endeavor. During World War I, he remained in his garden, refusing to be separated from his flowers, even as the enemy troops were approaching.

Sigmund Freud also had a great love of flowers. As a boy, he would roam the woods near Vienna, collecting rare plants and flower specimens. According to his biographer Ernest Jones, Freud developed an "unusual familiarity with flowers," becoming something of an amateur botanist. Natural beauty fed Freud's creative energy, and in adult life he would regularly escape to the mountains to walk and write. During long summer holidays in the Alps, he took care to pass his love of nature on to his children, teaching them to recognize wildflowers, berries, and mushrooms. Freud was fascinated by the hold that beauty can have over us: "The enjoyment of beauty," he wrote, "has a peculiar, mildly intoxicating quality of feeling," and while beauty cannot protect us from suffering, it can, as he put it, "compensate for a great deal."

How do we account for the feeling of intoxication that Freud described? What is the secret of beauty's hold on us? Intuition suggests that it may be linked to our capacity to experience love, and research indicates that this is indeed the case. Semir Zeki, London-based professor of neuroaesthetics, believes that our need for beauty lies deep within our biological makeup. His work has revealed that regardless of the source of it or the sensory stimuli involved in perceiving it, the experience of beauty is consistently accompanied by a unique pattern of brain activation on fMRI scans.

Zeki's first experiments were on people he exposed to music and artworks, including a painting by Monet. Then he decided to broaden his field of inquiry and include an abstract form of beauty. He introduced "beautiful" mathematical equations to a group of mathematicians, a cerebral source of beauty that is unfamiliar to many of us, but exists nonetheless. His participants were given a range of different images, music, and equations to respond to. The experiences they found beautiful all produced the same pattern of activity within their brains, involving the medial orbitofrontal cortex, the anterior cingulate cortex, and the caudate nucleus, brain regions that are part of our pleasure and reward pathways and are associated with romantic love. These pathways also play a role in integrating our thoughts, sensations, feelings, and motivations. They are associated with our dopamine, serotonin, and endogenous opioid systems and damp down our fear and stress responses. Hence, beauty calms and revitalizes us at the same time.

The human aesthetic response includes an affinity for patterns in which regularity and order are combined with variation and repetition. The simple geometries we find in nature are perhaps at their most concentrated and compelling in the beauty of a flower's form. Wildflowers, for example, commonly have five petals arranged in pentagonal symmetry. But no matter how elaborate or simple, the structure of any flower displays proportion, balance, and harmony, and we respond to this much as we respond to rhythm and harmony in music. This reaction may be linked to Zeki's findings on mathematical beauty, for in the evolution of human culture, botanical patterning must surely have played a part in awakening the human mind to the possibilities of abstract beauty and mathematical form.

Flowers first appeared on the planet after the age of the dinosaurs. Tethered to the earth as they are, plants need to recruit others to help them reproduce. The vast array of colors, patterns, and scents they display evolved not to entice or interest us but to attract the insects of the air.

Flowers are the masters and mistresses of biological signaling, summoning the moths, the wasps, the flies, and the bees with promises of sweet nectar to feed on. Scent gives a signal that a flower is ready to be fertilized. It is especially important for night pollinators, like the moths that pilot themselves by following trails of fragrance in the dark. Some of this olfactory communication is honest, some is seduction—smells that act as pheromones, triggering mating behavior—and some is plain deception—the sweet smell of nectar where there is none.

For the most part, however, the insect-flower relationship is based on reciprocity. The insect enacts the flower's bidding and enters the floral bedchamber; the flower gets the assistance it needs with procreation and the insect collects sweet nectar in return. This two-way relationship emerged through a process of co-evolution, and there are benefits for both sides. Sometimes the arrangement resembles exclusive rights: a flower targets one type of insect which remains loyal to that species of flower. The most supreme example of flower-insect co-evolution involves the star-shaped flower of the orchid *Angraecum sesquipedale*. In 1862, Charles Darwin was sent a specimen of this Madagascan flower. At that point no insect was known to exist with a proboscis long enough to reach all twelve inches down the nectary tube to pollinate this plant. Darwin concluded from what he already understood of co-evolution that there had to be an as yet undiscovered insect capable of this long reach. His thinking met with skepticism at the time, but forty years later, the long-tongued sphinx moth was discovered.

What is harder to explain through the theory of co-evolution is the relationship that exists between insects and flowers that practice sexual mimicry. Take the bee orchid, whose striking markings so closely mimic the female bee that they attract male bees to land on them. Darwin believed that some hidden benefit, like a carefully secreted source of nectar, would eventually come to light and explain why these bees were willing to expend so much energy trying to mate with a flower, but this has not turned out to be the case. Instead the explanation lies in a form of neural priming in the bee.

The nervous systems of even the most primitive and simple of creatures rely on dopamine or closely related molecules to initiate seeking behaviors. The human reward pathway may be a more complex version of that found in the bee, but in similar fashion, promise can carry more weight than outcome. The rewards advertised by flowers energize bee foraging through the action of dopamine, and experiments on bumblebees have found that when this neurotransmitter is blocked, bees will cease looking for nectar. This effect helps explain why insects might stay loyal to flowers that don't deliver.

There are flowers, for example, that attract male flies through the pheromones in their scent as well as petal markings that resemble a female fly. So effectively are the fly's mating instincts hijacked by this sexual mimicry, that he ejaculates on the flower, all the while loading himself up with pollen. It is a form of insect "porn" in action. Biologists call a phenomenon like this a supernormal stimulus. It is "super" because the attraction to it is stronger than the real thing. Such stimuli involve the exaggeration of key environmental cues such as patterns and markings, thereby diverting the instinct away from the function for which it was intended. But like humans, not all insects are equally susceptible. There are some types of bee that play it safe, returning mainly to flowers that offer them a reliable source of small amounts of nectar.

Nectar is not the only substance that insects can collect; there are cases in which it is the flower's scent itself. The male euglossine bee, which lives in the tropical rain forests, is an insect parfumier, gathering samples of fragrance from each flower he visits, mixing and storing them in his rear-end perfume pod, and thereby creating his own customized scent. Collectively these bees pollinate more than seven hundred different kinds of orchid that grow in the rain forests. The complexity of floral notes in the bee's individual perfume is thought to signify the extensiveness of his travels and his skills in foraging. Either way, the scents these bees collect are seductive and help them find a mate.

Much like the bees, we get a buzz from flowers. The magnitude of the cut-flower market testifies to this. Flowers speak to our unconscious in a way that is hard to entirely fathom. We respond as if to an invitation that says, "come closer, smell me, pick me, carry me with you." Some excel in purity, some in simplicity, while others are more seductive, even erotic, in their form. They wake us up to beauty, and as with the bees they encourage loyalty in us. Most of us have our favorites.

Freud had a particular love of orchids. Each year, on his birthday, colleagues, friends, and patients would present him with floral gifts. It became such an event that the Viennese florists stocked up in advance. On his seventy-fifth birthday, according to one of his old friends, Hanns Sachs, "orchids in all colours and descriptions came by the cartload." But Freud's favorite orchid was one not to be found in a florist's shop. It was the rare *Nigritella nigra*, an alpine orchid with dark purple-red flowers and a delicious, spicy fragrance of chocolate and vanilla. According to his son Martin Freud, this little flower had "pride of place" in Freud's heart. Its intoxicating scent evoked memories of a time when as newlyweds, he and his wife, Martha, were out walking on the Schneeberg, the nearest mountain to Vienna. They had spotted a group of the orchids, and Freud had climbed a steep, grassy slope to pick a bunch for her.

The American poet Hilda Doolittle, known as H.D., was a patient of Freud's in the early 1930s. She once gave him a gift of narcissi, and their heady scent had such an impact on him that she felt she had unwittingly, as she put it, "bust into his unconscious." Of course, nothing unlocks our unconscious more effectively than our sense of smell. The narcissi's sweet, some would say cloying, fragrance was, Freud told her, "almost my favourite scent." The flowers set him off on a reminiscence about how the "poet's narcissus" had grown wild in the wet meadows around the house at Aussee, near Salzberg, that he and Martha had rented for several years running. It was a favorite place for family holidays when their children were small, and he had thought of it as "a paradise." There was, he continued to tell H.D., only one flower dearer to him than the narcissus, the "incomparably fragrant gardenia," which always put him "in the best of moods." He associated it with a time twenty years earlier when he was staying in Rome and was able to buy a fresh gardenia for his buttonhole each day.

Memories and associations play a part in forming our attachments to flowers, but there is undoubtedly some chemistry going on too. The chemical constituents of various floral scents prime our moods and influence how alert or relaxed we feel. Lavender, long known to have a calming effect on us, has recently been shown to raise levels of serotonin. In contrast, the smell of rosemary is stimulating and boosts levels of both dopamine and acetylcholine. Citrus blossoms are uplifting through the combined effects of serotonin and dopamine. The smell of roses, perhaps the scent we most strongly associate with love, is good at reducing levels of the stress hormone adrenaline, and in one study this was by as much as 30 percent. In addition, through the action of phenylethylamine, the fragrance of the rose reduces the breakdown of our natural opioids (endorphins), creating a feeling of lingering calm.

How did the human love of flowers begin? In *How the Mind Works*, Steven Pinker suggests that humans became attracted to flowers because they indicated future food supplies. Hunter-gatherers who took note of flowers and their locations could return later to collect nuts and fruit, which would have given them a survival edge.

Flowers can also signify an immediate gain, for where there are flowers, there are likely to be bees, and where there are bees, there is likely to be honey. Our remote ancestors were every bit as susceptible to the delights of sugar as we are.

The oldest flowers found in a hunter-gatherer settlement date from twenty-three thousand years ago at the Ohalo II site on the Shores of the Sea of Galilee. An accumulation of flower remains in one of the huts there indicates that whoever lived there had gathered a large number of *Senecio glaucus* flowers. Endemic to this part of the world, their yellow flowers are like small chrysanthemums. There is no known culinary, medicinal, or other use for them, which raises the possibility that they may have been brought back to the camp in preparation for a ritual or other special event.

The earliest known grave that contains flowers is at a Natufian burial ground in Israel and is fourteen thousand years old. These would have been collected from the wild, but humans are thought to have started cultivating flowers surprisingly early—about five thousand years ago. Professor of psychology Jeannette Haviland-Jones and professor of genetics Terry McGuire of Rutgers University, New Jersey, argue that we should not underestimate the evolutionary role of pleasure in motivating our remote ancestors to do this. Many of the flowers that were cultivated early on are ones that appear when ground is disturbed. Haviland-Jones and McGuire conjecture that when flowers self-seeded on land cleared for agriculture, some may have been left to grow because people liked them. Over time, humans began to act as agents for flower seed dispersal and would have selected the most fragrant and attractive ones. The cultivated flower's niche in the ecosystem is therefore a human emotional niche.

Flowers lift our mood and enrich our emotional lives. The Lemon Tree Trust charity discovered the value of this recently when they started setting up gardens in Syrian refugee camps. Although food supplies were sorely needed, about 70 percent of the plants the refugees chose to grow were flowers, so intense was their need to introduce beauty into their surroundings.

Flowers may well have provided our remote ancestors with the first consoling narrative. When self-consciousness emerged in human prehistory, it brought with it an experience of separation and an awareness of mortality. These existential predicaments have been with us ever since, raising age-old questions: How to make sense of life? How to deal with the pain that comes from living? The life of a flower offers us something to hold on to, a form of protection against fears of fragmentation in the face of death. Ephemeral and fragile as flowers are, they are the agents of continuity. For the flower in its beauty is destined to die, that its fruit may live and bring forth more flowers from its seed.

Without doubt, in the early civilizations flowers held deep meaning. The ancient Egyptians, in particular, regarded flowers as divine messengers, and they filled their temples with garlands and bouquets, sometimes on a vast scale. The flowers they grew included jasmine, cornflower, iris, and lily of the valley, but the blue water lily, or lotus, was the holiest flower of all. In ancient Egyptian religion, the lotus was believed to hold the secret of rebirth. Its sweet, heady fragrance was said to transport the mind to a higher plane, like a bridge between the sensual and spiritual realms.

A flower's sole purpose in life is to ensure that procreation takes place. Flowers can be sexy because sex is their business and, to the human eye, there is an erotic quality to some of their forms. We see it in the colorful exuberance of reproductive organs that are on display in certain botanical prints. The modern painter Georgia O'Keeffe did not like attention being drawn to the erotic element in her work; understandably perhaps, for being explicit spoils the effect. As long as the experience stays subliminal, we can have it both ways: sex with beauty and innocence.

Like many lovers before him, Freud kick-started his courtship of the young Martha Bernays by presenting her with a red rose. In the first summer of their engagement, Martha went away for a break and stayed in a house with a beautiful garden. Late one night, Freud wrote her a letter which began by addressing her host:

> Gardener Bünsow, lucky man to be allowed to shelter my darling sweetheart! Why didn't I become a gardener instead of a doctor or writer? Perhaps you need a young chap to work for you in the garden, and I could offer myself so as to bid good morning to the little princess and perhaps even demand a kiss in return for a bunch of flowers.

Freud was twenty-seven when he wrote this, and he was embarking on his medical career. It would be nineteen years before he published the seminal work on dreams that made him famous.

Freud's wish to be a gardener may have been a lover's flight of fancy on a hot summer's night, but he was a great garden lover. Scattered among the pages of *The Interpretation of Dreams* are a large selection of flowers: cyclamen, artichokes, lily of the valley, violets, pinks, carnations, cherry blossom, tulips, and roses. Freud was interested in how images of plant life can both represent and conceal the sexual content of dreams. He described how "the ugliest as well as the most intimate details of sexual life may be thought and dreamt of in seemingly innocent allusions." These symbols, he pointed out, reach back to remote antiquity, and include the maiden's garden in the Song of Solomon.

One of the dreams that Freud interprets reveals a young woman's fears about sexual intercourse. The dream starts with her coming down from a height and climbing over a fence to enter a garden. She is concerned not to tear her dress and keen to remain respectable. She is carrying a large branch covered with lots of red flowers resembling cherry blossoms or possibly camellias. The gardeners are combing tufts of moss-like hair that are hanging down from the trees. The young woman stops to ask how a branch of flowers like the one she is carrying could be transplanted into her own garden. One of the gardeners embraces her, she rebuffs him, and then he offers to take her to her own garden and show her how her branch could be planted. Her longing for the sensuality of love and her confusion about the facts of life are both apparent. There is something rather repellent in the images of the moss being groomed, in contrast to the alluring red flowers she hopes might flourish in her own garden. The dream garden is free from the constraints and conventions of society, a place in which it is safe to be curious about sex.

Flowers are the simplest way to change the atmosphere in a room. With their talent for influencing our moods they prime us to feel relaxed. They carry an intimation of something good and offer a promise of fruitfulness, perhaps promoting a flowering of thought. There was only a small courtyard garden at Freud's home on Berggasse Street in Vienna, and from his study he had a view of the lime and horse chestnut trees that grew there. Martha cultivated flowers in their glazed veranda and brought them home from the market to decorate the house. Many of Freud's patients were surprised on first visiting him to discover that his consulting room was so comfortable and alluring. The flowers of the season— red tulips, narcissi, or orchids—often adorned the table on which his prize antiquities were displayed. Sergei Pankejeff, otherwise known as the Wolf Man, who became a patient of Freud's in 1910, recalled that the plants brought a feeling of life into the room and that "everything here contributed to one's feeling of leaving the haste of modern life behind, of being sheltered from one's daily cares."

Oskar Pfister, a pastor who went on to become a psychoanalyst, wrote a letter to Martha after Freud died, in which he recalled his first visit to their home in 1909: "In your house one felt as in a sunny spring garden, heard the gay larks and blackbirds, saw bright flower-beds, and had a premonition of the rich blessing of summer." The phrase "flowers are restful to look at, they have neither emotions or conflicts" is attributed to Freud, and I suspect he was rather fond of saying this. The simplicity of flowers must have provided a counterpoint to the arduous work of uncovering his patients' conflicts and emotions. They also reminded him of his travels. A basket of orchids in his study, he once wrote, gave him "the illusion of splendour and glowing sunshine."

Belief in the restorative powers of nature was a strong part of Austrian culture at that time, and Freud rarely missed an opportunity to travel to the mountains. He once referred to it as "a medicine," and the effects were on the mind as well as the body. For Freud, an immersion in nature was always invigorating and helped to renew his appetite for life.

A conversation took place on one of Freud's mountain walks in the summer of 1913 when he was accompanied by the poet Rainer Maria Rilke and Rilke's lover, Lou Andreas-Salomé. Afterward, Freud wrote about it in an essay entitled "On Transience." He describes how Rilke admired the beauty of the scenery but could feel no joy in it because it was doomed to extinction when winter came. In nature's loveliness, all Rilke could see was a harbinger of loss. Freud tried to convince his companions to the contrary by arguing that "transience value is scarcity value in time. Limitation in the possibility of an enjoyment raises the value of the enjoyment.... A flower that blossoms only for a single night does not seem to us on that account less lovely." However, neither Rilke nor Andreas-Salomé were persuaded.

Reflecting on the conversation later, Freud decided that a powerful emotional factor must have been at work in the "sensitive minds" of both his friends. Freud points out that the enjoyment of ephemeral beauty entails opening ourselves to the loss of something we value. We are confronted with this not only in the fleeting beauty of the flower but also in the passing of the seasons, so that, he argues, we have to do a little bit of mourning each year as winter approaches. The experience of mourning, which Freud called "love's rebellion against loss," involves pain, and the mind "instinctively recoils from anything that is painful." Freud came to the conclusion that his companions' inability to share his joy that day was because of a "revolt in their minds against mourning."

When we suffer a major loss in life, we immediately recoil in an almost involuntary way. We don't want to—can't—accept the all too painful reality. Mourning can be the hardest emotional work we ever have to do and we need a sympathetic presence, some source of comfort, a thing, a place, or a person that we can hold on to in our distress. But mourning varies in intensity, according to the significance of what we have lost. We encounter losses in so many different ways throughout our lives that it is, Freud writes, as if we are always mourning for something. The cycle of life can help us because in the depths of winter, a belief in the return of spring gives us something to hold on to. "As regards the beauty of Nature," Freud observes, "each time it is destroyed by winter it comes again next year, so that in relation to the length of our lives it can in fact be regarded as eternal."

In living, we are always somewhere on a line that runs between losing and finding. This is the dance of time with its recurrent cycles of loss and restoration and loss again. We can see it in the child running back to the mother that he or she has lost sight of in the park and then running off again. It is there in the games of peekaboo which mesmerize children of a certain age, and there throughout our lives in the patterns of rupture and repair that break and mend our closest attachments. It is about our loves and our hates, our fulfillments and disappointments—and is the paradox that lies at the heart of attaching to and valuing life. Love, which expands the heart so much, also exposes us to loss.

• • •

The walk that Freud recorded in his essay "On Transience" had taken place a year before the First World War broke out. By the time he was writing, two of his sons were fighting on the front lines. While the passing beauty of nature may bring intimations of loss, the war had confronted those affected with losses on a different scale. He describes how the devastation of war had destroyed "the beauty of the countrysides through which it passed," shattering pride in the achievements of civilization and proving "how ephemeral were many things we had regarded as changeless." In nature's powers of recovery, Freud found a source of hope that when the war was over it would be possible to build up again all that had been destroyed. His sons, Ernst and Martin, survived the fighting, but in the Spanish influenza epidemic that swept through Europe after the war, the Freuds lost their daughter Sophie.

Whatever form they take, traumatic and life-altering losses disrupt the emotional landscape that we inhabit, sweeping away much that we have cherished and wished to preserve. At such times of crisis, the world feels permanently changed and we are left uncertain of what can be recovered and what will return. When everything feels so precarious, and nothing, it seems, can be depended upon, where can you put your faith, your love, and your hope? Sometimes this question raises itself with a resounding urgency and then, like a dormant seed that surfaces from deep within us, it is with the promise of spring that nature vouchsafes us an answer.

The war had made it difficult to travel, but in the years that followed, Freud was able to return to the mountains and immerse himself in nature. During this period, he was developing his ideas about the role of the life and death instincts in the psyche. His letters to his daughter Anna tell of his solitary walks and plant collecting. "The rain today didn't stop me from going to a special place and picking the magnificent white orchids (Planthera bifolia) which are so incomparably fragrant," he wrote. Freud was reattaching to life, nourishing the life instinct within him.

The theory of Eros and Thanatos that emerged in this phase of his work was Freud's response to the First World War. He described how the life and death drives operate in and through all living things. To illustrate this, he quoted Goethe's *Faust* in *Civilization and Its Discontents*: "The Devil himself names as his adversary, not what is holy and good, but nature's power to create and multiply life—that is, Eros." The force of Thanatos can express itself through violence and destructiveness, or find expression in a more silent way within the mind, pulling us toward passivity and emotional deadness. Freud's Eros is a much broader concept than sexuality, which it is sometimes taken to mean—it encompasses our creativity and our love of life.

Freud's concept of Eros was reworked in the 1960s by the psychoanalyst and social psychologist Erich Fromm, who used the term "biophilia" to define "the passionate love of life and all that is alive." For Fromm, a healthy mind has a wish to further growth, whether in a person, a plant, an idea, or a social group. He contrasted biophilia with necrophilia, which is anti-growth and involves being drawn to things dying or deathly. As with Freud's life and death drives, the two principles are extremes of a continuum. The strength of our biophilia helps us to "persevere in life." Fromm believed that many modern ills were linked to the loss of our unconscious kinship with the natural world, giving rise to a level of unrecognized separation distress in us: "The soil, the animals, the plants are still man's world," he wrote, and "the more the human race emerges from these primary bonds, the more it separates itself from the natural world, the more intense becomes the need to find new ways of escaping separateness."

The term "biophilia" was used again in the 1980s by E. O. Wilson and, as discussed previously, has since become a cornerstone of environmental psychology. Wilson's evolutionary perspective has led to a much wider acceptance of the idea that we are innately disposed to respond to certain aspects of the natural world.

The human species evolved to be good at forming relationships. We are so good at them that the brain has been called a "relational organ." The botanical world also evolved to be good at forming relationships, so it's not surprising that in the course of our prehistory we formed such a strong affiliation with plants and flowers. The problem in contemporary life, though, is not only a lack of contact with nature but also how we close our minds and fill the gap in our lives. Like the insects that are misled by the mimicry of flowers, we are suckers for a supernormal stimulus. We are easily set off-kilter. All sorts of artificial stimuli grab our attention and hijack the dopamine reward pathways that evolved for hunting and gathering in the natural world.

We forage in the shopping mall, we seek on the net, driven by the same addiction-promoting, primitive reward system that is not about rewards, but keeps us seeking, ever seeking, never satisfied, susceptible to thrills that are big on anticipation but poor on actual delivery. The process drains our pockets and our dopamine reserves along with our optimism and energy. The dopamine system is perilously prone to overstimulation, which sets up a vicious circle in which we seek yet more stimulation. It is so powerful we end up wanting things we don't actually desire or have a use for.

Psychoactive drugs and alcohol work in a similar fashion through overtaking our dopamine reward pathways, eventually creating a state of physical dependence. Addiction involves turning away from reality and ultimately turning away from life. It is hard for the gentle stimuli of nature to compete with this, although the beauty of the natural world, especially the beauty of flowers, can sometimes help awaken or reawaken a love of life.

I encountered a remarkable example of this in a woman called Renata on an Italian drug rehabilitation program based at San

Patrignano, close to the Adriatic coast. She had spent the last two-and-a-half years growing flowers in the nursery that was attached to the therapeutic community there. Before that, having grown up in a troubled and unstable family, she had started using drugs in her late teens. As with many addiction sufferers, what began as a form of self-treatment for mental pain became an illness in itself, so that by her early twenties she had a serious drug habit to feed.

Horticulture is only a small part of the treatment at San Patrignano. There are thirteen hundred residents in the community, and fifty different skills-based units, in which over the course of three to four years each resident learns a new craft or trade. There is also a large vineyard which is one of the main sources of income. The belief is that through learning a new skill, the residents can be helped to build a new life. In order to do this they have to leave their former lives behind, and for most of the first year they are not allowed contact with family or friends.

Most of the residents are in their late twenties, and they live together in family-like groups of about eight. They are encouraged to confront what led them to take drugs in the first place and are offered emotional support to help them do this. The philosophy behind San Patrignano is powerful in its simplicity—that focusing on people's strengths rather than their weaknesses will help them grow. The entire community congregates for lunch in the great hall each day. We ate three courses of home-grown food on long refectory tables, simple but delicious. A thousand people dining together in this vast space felt vibrant and yet monastic at the same time.

The gardens provide food for the community as well as supplying a local restaurant and a local supermarket. On a thirteen-and-a-half-acre site, the men work with the fruits and vegetables while the women tend the flowers. Renata was in her late twenties and had short dark hair, cut in an angular pixie style. Initially she was reserved, but there was an intensity in the way she spoke about her experience of working there. The biggest change, she told me, was that she had realized that she wanted to live.

She needed to finish watering the flowers in the hoophouse that she looked after, so I accompanied her. I had never seen so many massed petunias in a single space and had never thought there was much to like about petunias before this encounter. On one side they were set out in vibrant squares of scarlet, purple, yellow, pink, mauve, and white. An undeniably impressive display, but it was the flowers on the opposite side that held my gaze. Here, the entire length was a showstopper of vivid magenta petunias. I stood with my eyes drinking it in while she finished her watering.

Renata, I discovered, had always loved being outdoors and thought that was why the program organizers had chosen this training for her, but in spite of this, it had taken her a long time to derive any satisfaction from the work. She described how much she had "hated" the job at the beginning and "resented" the plants she was tending. From the time she first arrived until the start of her second summer these toxic feelings dominated her experience.

Like her attitude to the plants, her relationships to people in the community were initially based on resentment and mistrust, and these feelings had been slow to change too. She was unstinting in her analysis of why: "I was very proud and arrogant. Not reaching out to people." Before coming here, she told me, when she was in the grip of her addiction she couldn't bear to wait for anything: "I used to be like a big Godfather wanting everything to be done instantly."

For as long as Renata could remember, there had been something "ugly" inside her from which she was always trying to escape. This feeling had led to her drug habit. As she explained: "When you have a bad emotion you take a drug to get rid of it, and when you have a good emotion you take a drug to make it even better." Through being in the community she had come to recognize that the sense of ugliness she suffered from was linked to how she "used to be so full of hate."

We were walking out of the polytunnel toward the open air

when I noticed some small cacti lined up on wooden shelves in a corner by the entrance. I commented on them, admiring their bright orange and pink flowers. "These are my favorites!" Renata exclaimed. As she spoke of how much those cacti meant to her, I realized I had stumbled on something significant. The cacti had been left behind, abandoned by her predecessor. For nearly a year she hadn't taken any notice, until one of them sprouted a tiny orange flower. It caught her eye, and for the first time it occurred to her that these plants were languishing. So she decided to rescue them.

As she spoke, her sense of affinity with them was apparent. Neglected, as she had once been, spiky and prickly, it was hard to find a way in, somewhat like her. It is difficult to kill a cactus. Deep within the plant, the life-preserving juices are heavily guarded and defended—cacti excel at playing the long game. The life-preserving forces within the human mind may be easier to extinguish, especially when deadly narcotics are involved. Yet something deep in Renata answered to the call of that little flower and the languishing stumps of those cactus plants. They were instrumental in turning things around for her. Now, with so many of them in bloom, they were clearly thriving. Her pleasure in the fact that she had rescued them was infectious. We stood for a time admiring them, connected in our shared sense of joy.

Something like this is a small act of reparation in the context of rebuilding a life, but it is the kind of experience that can foster a belief in the possibility of a new beginning. We change the world through what we do, and in the process we are changed ourselves.

In short-cutting the pleasure and reward pathways, drug addiction trumps all other forms of attachment, including the attachment to life itself. Renata's primary attachment for many years had been to the substances she was dependant on. It can be hard for recovering addicts to let themselves attach to life again, and even harder if past attachments have entailed destructiveness and negativity. The philosophy of the community at San Patrignano is to provide the conditions in which something new can grow. For each individual this will be a different process. You wouldn't pick a group of ailing cacti for their obvious therapeutic effects, but somehow Renata had let herself "adopt" them, and for the first time, she began to glimpse what she called "the serenity of life."

Out in the open, we started to talk about what might come next for her. She knew she was not ready to leave the community yet, but she was beginning to think about the future. The one thing she knew was that she must not return to working in a bar as she had done before. She was acutely aware of how easy it would be to "blow it all in one instant." Recently she had begun to think about training to be a social worker. She realized that she wanted to do something "more giving" with her life, and an idea had started to form that she might work with children in a cancer center.

"Plants are like people" she told me, "they need your help. Without you they don't live." Cultivating flowers, she continued, "means you are always giving something to somebody." These flowers gave pleasure to her and to others working on the site, as well as people back in the community, where they decorated tables and—she was keen to add—gave pleasure to the people who bought them in the supermarket. Her sense of the good feeling that radiated from the flowers had transformed her understanding of what it means to work. She had started to experience the gardener's sense of give-and-take: "If you care for the plants," she told me "they give back to you."

In the turnaround that had taken place within her, in her escape from narcotics, and in her newfound wish to live, Renata's eyes had been opened to a different way of being. As we were about to part, I took one last, long look at the row of deep magenta flowers that had first commanded my attention. Renata's parting words to me encapsulated the journey she had made. Gesturing toward them with a huge grin on her face, she exclaimed: "Don't you see how beautiful they are?"

CHAPTER 8

Radical Solutions

New Roots Community Farm in the Bronx
run by New York Botanical Garden and
the International Rescue Committee.

To forget how to dig the earth and to tend the soil is to
forget ourselves.

Mahatma Gandhi (1869–1948)

There comes a moment in the autumn when I realize that if I don't
attend to my collection of auriculas, it will be too late. By this point
in the year, they have taken on a weary, bedraggled look and have
become clumpy, with new leaves growing at the base of each plant.

These baby plants, or offsets, are a form radical growth, spring-ing as they do from the top of the root, and if left in place they will start to form a crowd. The task of repotting involves delicately separating them from the mother plant and keeping their own small root intact. Some are ready to break away, while others cling, and although there are always casualties, each plant typically yields three or four new plants. And so the collection multiplies itself.

For much of the year on the mountain slopes where auricu-las grow wild, the conditions are relatively dry, which means that once their flowering season is over, they need much less water. It took me a few years to learn just how sparing to be, and as a result some of my plants started ailing. Further inspection revealed signs of root rot, the only remedy for which is to cut the decaying tis-sue away. So, in hope of salvaging them, I equipped myself with a scalpel, some surgical spirit, and a pot of yellow powder called "flowers of sulphur" and set up a clinic on the potting bench. The work of slicing off the rotten tip and coating what remained of the carrot-like root with protective powder was a strangely satisfying process, combining as it did the roles of doctor and gardener.

This exercise in plant surgery would prove to be a one-off because my auriculas began to fare better once I acquired some terra-cotta pots. Three boxes of small pots came up in an online auction, and I bid for them without fully reckoning on the three-hundred-mile round-trip to the north of England that winning them would involve. A week or so later, I was heading up the motorway to Sheffield. When I arrived at the address—a small terraced house on a large modern housing estate on the outskirts of the city—I was met at the front door by a taciturn man.

He and I immediately began loading the dusty wooden crates full of neatly stacked pots into my car. I ventured to ask about their origins. It turned out they had belonged to his father, who'd been a keen gardener and had recently died. He asked me what I would use them for. "Growing auriculas," I answered and then inquired about his father. Auriculas had, he told me, been his father's hobby. He had spent the last two months clearing out his father's belongings. Now it was done. The pots were the last of his father's possessions to go. Then his manner warmed as he said how relieved he'd been to discover I wasn't a dealer, that the pots would not be split up or sold on; that they were "going to a good home." As I drove away, I felt as if I'd been entrusted with a legacy, and I pictured his father, much as I picture my grandfather, cultivating quiet beauty in his greenhouse. A large part of the enduring pleasure I experience in working with these lovely old pots derives from them having been passed down from one generation to another.

Later I learned that there was a long tradition of working men cultivating auriculas in that part of the country. The tradition dates back to the mid-eighteenth century when the Industrial Revolution started in the north of England. Sheffield became a center for the production of ironware and cutlery. The "cutlers," as the factory workers were called, along with the weavers from neighboring manufacturing towns, were renowned for their horticultural skills. In fact, it was the silk weavers who had originally brought their love of flowers with them when they were forced to relinquish their hand looms and move from the countryside to work in the mechanized mills.

The workers' "back-to-back" dwellings were cramped, but the cool shade of their narrow yards suited the auricula rather well. These artisan growers developed new varieties of the exquisitely patterned flowers known as "fancies" and "edges" and achieved velvet-deep reds and purples in the flowers known as "selfs." They also increased the density of the farina, a fine white dust that coats the leaves like flour. In the thin mountain air of their natural setting, it acts like a sunblock, protecting the plant from the harshness of the sun's glare. Paradoxically, this adaptation served a protective purpose in the industrial towns too and helped the plants cope with the thick soot and acrid smoke that plagued the air. There was perhaps a synergism at work in which transplanted flowers were being grown by uprooted people—one providing the other with a symbol of resilience. Mass production had ridden roughshod over the craftsmen's skills, and the shaping and perfecting of flowers provided them with an outlet for self-expression and creativity.

Floristry, as the cultivation of flowers was then known, also provided a focus for social life. The mass migration to the towns had dislocated people from their communities and weakened their social networks. Florist societies brought amateur horticulturalists together in collaboration and in competition. The societies were devoted to a range of different flowers, including tulips, auriculas, carnations, pinks, and pansies. Much as the cutlers and weavers excelled at auricula growing, other trades had different specialties; the cultivation of the pansy, for example, was particularly associated with coal miners. Gooseberry growing was popular too, especially in Lancashire. There were gooseberry clubs in most of the manufacturing towns, and the annual gooseberry growing competition was a fixture in the social calendar. The cool northern climate provided ideal conditions, and as with the auricula, it was possible to grow a prize-winning specimen in a small backyard.

Nature pays no heed to our social structures: flowers bloom and fruits and vegetables grow regardless of an individual's wealth or class. Since plants are largely self-replicating, gardens don't require a constant flow of money, either. But to be able to garden in the first place, you need access to a patch of land. Many of the early manufacturing centers made provision for this in the form of community garden plots (called allotments in England) for food growing, on their outskirts. When the physician and author William Buchan visited Sheffield in 1769, he observed: "There is hardly a journeyman cutler who does not possess a piece of ground which he cultivates as a garden," and he noted that their gardening had "many salutary effects." For low-paid workers it was a valuable source of nutritious food and a form of healthy exercise that brought respite from the loud machinery and monotony of factory work: "The very smell of the earth and fresh herbs revives and cheers the spirits," wrote Buchan, "whilst the perpetual prospect of something coming to maturity delights and entertains the mind." In the face of grinding industrial work, cultivating the land provided a source of pride and dignity.

The study of botany provided another way of sustaining a connection with nature. There were factory workers in Manchester, the largest of the industrial centers, who regularly spent their day off walking out into the countryside to collect specimens, and their botanical expertise was recognized. Meanwhile, as the nineteenth century wore on, industry was turning the urban centers into horticultural deserts. Where nature wasn't absent, it was despoiled in front of people's eyes. The few surviving trees were blasted and blackened with soot. The great Victorian novelist Elizabeth Gaskell lamented in her depiction of Manchester, "Alas! there are no flowers." As manufacturing expanded, overcrowding meant that yards and gardens were filled in. Starved of nature, people found fulfillment in local flower shows, which became a hugely popular form of entertainment. The phenomenon peaked in the 1860s, when Manchester alone held eight a year. A brief immersion in the floral kingdom gave ordinary people access to the revitalizing effects of beauty.

The human need for aesthetic sustenance is often underrated, but as Carl Jung observed, "we all need nourishment for our psyche. It is impossible to find such nourishment in urban tenements without a patch of green or a blossoming tree." With industrialization, the worker's relationship to work became less nourishing as well. Production lines fragmented the process and people were responsible for only a small part of the outcome, whereas in earlier times when the crafts flourished, the worker, Jung wrote, "derived satisfaction from seeing the fruits of his labour. He found adequate self-expression in such work." Two essential sources of grounding and balance had been lost: proximity to nature and fulfilling work. Jung thought this had resulted in a "rootless condition of consciousness," which he believed led to either an "exaggerated self-esteem" or its opposite, an "inferiority complex." "I am fully committed," he wrote, "to the idea that human existence should be rooted in the earth." He was an advocate for gardening as a form of replenishing work: "A captive animal cannot return to freedom. But our workers can return. We see them doing it in the allotment gardens in and around our cities; these gardens are an expression of love for nature and for one's own plot of land."

The urban gardening movement is in the midst of a revival today. Many of the predicaments that Jung described are still with us—a disconnection from nature, desolate urban environments, and a lack of meaningful work. Much as when urban cultivation began, we are living in an era of social and technological change that is accompanied by rising levels of inequality. Today, many of the former centers of industry are languishing and people are turning to the earth to sustain themselves, not so much against industrialization, but against the blight that's been left in its wake.

Take the town of Todmorden, which sits at the confluence of three deep valleys, twenty miles north of Manchester, England. It was once a thriving center for the textile industry, but the factories and mills here have long since closed and unemployment among its fifteen thousand inhabitants has been high for decades. When the financial crash of 2008 hit the town, the number of empty and derelict buildings increased, making it harder than ever to imagine any hope of recovery. The effects of austerity followed soon after. Public services were cut and litter accumulated around the town. A group of friends who were sitting around a kitchen table shared their concerns about the deteriorating conditions they were witnessing. They wanted to create a better future for the next generation. How, they wondered, could they go about building a more sustainable community?

One thing was clear from the start—the focus had to be food, because everyone needs food. The slogan they came up with, "If you eat you're in," reflected the inclusivity they wanted to achieve. They tried to imagine what it would be like if people could live and work in an edible townscape. In the spirit of conducting an experiment, they began sowing runner bean seeds and other vegetables in the grounds of a derelict health center which sat like a scar in the middle of the town. When the produce was ready to be harvested, they put up a large sign painted with the words "Help Yourself." This was the beginning of the movement known as "Incredible Edible" that is led by two women, Pam Warhurst and Mary Clear. When they held a public meeting, they discovered a strong groundswell of support. People started enlisting as volunteers, helping plant vegetables at other sites around the town.

Incredible Edible has introduced greenness into what was a gray, forlorn landscape. Around Todmorden, different plants are being grown according to need. There are strawberries outside the home for the elderly because while many of the residents lack their own teeth, they still enjoy soft fruits. Outside the butcher's shop, there is a bed of rosemary, sage, and thyme, so the butcher can tell his customers to help themselves. Some plants have local history like the gooseberries, or "goosegogs" as they're colloquially known. They are unavailable in the shops, which makes them popular, and people pick them to put in pies. The beds surrounding Todmorden's new health center were prickly shrubs. "What kind of message is that giving?" Incredible Edible asked. "Shouldn't a health center be growing healthy food?" Now there is a small apothecary garden with herbs like chamomile, lavender, and echinacea, and cherry and pear trees outside the entrance.

Altogether, more than seventy food growing plots are scattered around the town, and anyone can help him- or herself to anything.

Everywhere you look, there is a planter or a bed or a small plot with something growing in it that is tended. As I wandered along the edible towpath, over the canal bridge, past the huge, brightly colored Incredible Edible mural, taking in the health center with its fruit trees, the butcher's shop with its herbs, and the police station with its planted boxes, and ending up at the street Incredible Edible persuaded the council to rename Pollination Street, I was struck by the extent to which the movement had taken community gardening outside the enclosure of the garden. Todmorden is a radical experiment in urban foraging.

Radical politics and food growing go together. The word "radical" itself is, after all, derived from the plant world. *Radix* is the Latin for root, and while radical has come to mean far-reaching social or political change, the word has retained the sense of addressing root causes. Lack of affordable fresh food in the town was an issue, but growing food was not so much intended as the solution, rather as a medium through which to effect change. The hope was that when produce was picked, cooked, and shared, conversations would be stimulated that prompted people to think differently about what we eat and how we live. Warhurst and Clear talk of "propaganda gardening," which is apposite because the word "propaganda" also originates from the plant world. The Incredible Edible experiment has proved that propagating plants can be a highly effective form of communication.

It was not long before changes became evident in the local community. The first to emerge was that levels of antisocial behavior and vandalism in the town went down. As Clear says, "People respect food, they don't attack it." Gradually, the boarded-up shops on the main street began to disappear and cafés and restaurants started to open up. There is now a thriving market where people can buy locally grown produce. School gardening has taken off, and the secondary school has acquired an orchard with vegetable plots and bees. A new training for young people who want to gain a qualification in horticulture has been set up. The local authority got behind the project and decided to review its vacant land to see what could be released for growing food. This was significant in a place where back-to-back housing meant limited garden space and that, in 2008, had only fifteen community garden plots. A measure of the changes is that a recent survey showed that three-quarters of residents are now growing some of their own food.

According to Clear, most of the key people behind the project are "women of a certain age, all driven by social justice," and, she added, "we are working harder than we ever have before." Indeed, when I met them, she and her friend Estelle Brown had just finished sowing five thousand vegetable, flower, and herb seeds that were lined up in trays on Clear's kitchen windowsill. The movement is not reliant on any external funding. Instead, they want to see how far they can go with the power of cooperation and the currency of kindness. "Once you get into grants," Clear says, "there are outcomes to meet." Although Incredible Edible has developed strong links with the town council, the police, and local schools, for the most part they have never sought permission for what they do. They know it will entail layers of bureaucracy. "It's not," as Clear puts it, "that people actually want to say no; they just don't know how to say yes." If objections do arise, which happens rarely, they simply ask for forgiveness.

When collective gardening takes place in Todmorden, on alternate Sundays, about thirty people usually turn up. The volunteers range in age from three to seventy-three and span the social spectrum. People work in small groups on various sites around the town; some pick up litter, others garden. Then they come together for a simple communal lunch in a disused church. For some of the volunteers, particularly the ones who live in assisted living, this fortnightly event is the mainstay of their social life. The ethos, as Clear describes it, is "to let people do things in their own time and in their own way." A sign of change, she explained, may be someone "speaking when they weren't speaking before or something even more simple like taking their coat off." She calls it "people growing."

Clear is talking about combating the plague of loneliness that increasingly defines our times. With one in four people suffering from feelings of isolation, loneliness has never been more prevalent than it is now. Until recently, the adverse effects were thought to be mainly psychological, but now it is known to be a physical health issue, as well. A lack of social connections is associated with a 30 percent greater risk of early death from all causes, an increase that is equivalent to being obese or smoking fifteen cigarettes a day. Loneliness has become a major public health problem.

Across the ages, human beings have found ways to inhabit the most inhospitable climates and terrains, but whether in the arctic, at altitude, in the jungle or the desert, people have always lived in small, cohesive groups. This is the first time in the history of our species that large parts of the world's population are living in a state of disconnection, not only from nature but from one another. Community gardening addresses both kinds of disconnection. People are able to connect to a place and attach to a group. Both involve a sense of belonging, and the crisis of modern life is at root a crisis of belonging.

The Incredible Edible model has spread far beyond Todmorden. There are now 120 similar not-for-profit societies in the UK, all bearing the same name. Around the world, Incredible Edible is represented on every continent, with a thousand groups now in existence. In France, where the concept has proved popular, they are called the *Incroyables Comestibles*, and the slogan is translated to "*nourriture à partager*" (food to share). The Incredible Edible network is a loose affiliation: different groups operate in different ways, but they all have the same aim of creating kinder, greener, better connected communities.

It is perhaps no accident that a horticultural movement should have sprung up from this region of England with such vigor. This, after all, is where the Industrial Revolution began. It seems fitting that the part of the world where industrialization was pioneered should be at the forefront of addressing the predicament of post-industrial decline. Urban horticulture then and urban horticulture now share much in common, but one difference stands out. Back then socializing focused on the enormously popular local shows and competitions. These days, competing has seeped into almost every corner of life. Community gardening fulfills a different set of needs. Many people want a break from competing and seek its opposite, which modern life lacks—cooperation.

Looking back through history, it seems that the value we place on cultivating the earth is unduly caught up with our man-made economic cycles—people turn back to the land in times of recession and rapid social change. It is symptomatic of the age we live in that gardening has become a global social movement. The problems associated with urbanization and the consequences of technology supplanting industry are occurring all around the world. As community gardener Mark Harding put it, when industry spits you out, there is "always a place for you in nature."

Harding has helped run the urban farm at Oranjezicht in Cape Town, South Africa, since 2014. Prior to this he had been made redundant after twenty years of working as a welder. Three years of unemployment and depression followed, until he started working on the farm. As a young man, he had been attracted to the "illusion of the city." The problem, he explained, "is that it leaves you nothing to fall back on." These days he feels more grounded: "Now I have something I can call reality." Working with the earth has given him a sense of resilience and a feeling of security that his skills will always be useful: "I'm capable of growing food and I can take that talent anywhere."

The Oranjezicht urban farm is in one of the suburbs of Cape Town, on the site of a small park that had fallen into disuse and become a dumping ground. The project primarily has an educational mission, and a thousand children visit each year to learn about planting seeds, making compost, and nutrition. Cape Town has been undergoing rapid urbanization, and there are high levels of unemployment. Multinational outlets have proliferated selling cheap fast food, high in fats and sugar. As a result, urban poverty is increasingly linked to obesity, diabetes, and heart disease. The urban farm, which produces affordable organic produce, has played a major role in awakening people to the politics of food, both its availability and how it's grown. In a region that has suffered a series of terrible droughts, Oranjezicht has helped drive forward the idea that produce needs to be grown according to the season.

The biggest success of all has been the Oranjezicht food market. What started as a few stands on the farm has become a hugely popular weekly event that now takes place on the waterfront in the city. The market helps to support more than forty organic gardens and farms in the locality, as well as small food producers selling bread and other artisan foods.

The cofounder of the farm, Sheryl Ozinsky, describes how the Oranjezicht vision has grown: "urban agriculture is more than growing veggies. We want to educate people, build communities, re-think how food markets operate. We want to tear down the high walls of our suburbs and create spaces where neighbors can meet and mingle, where people use public parks and green spaces, where communities walk, cycle, and bus together." The project is about making connections and breaking down racial and social barriers. Growing food for Harding is, as he describes it, a "healthy way of fighting back." He speaks of how "the big corporations pick varieties for long shelf life, but they're less nutritious," and of his regret that he has only woken up to these issues rather late in life. Through his work on the farm he has assumed a new sense of identity as a "green rebel."

• • •

The politics of food has become an inescapable aspect of contemporary community gardening around the world. Ron Finley, an African-American artist and garden activist based in South Central LA, is another "green rebel," and he's taken the identity to another level. This part of LA is one of the largest "food deserts" in the US, with plentiful fast-food outlets and liquor stores but no accessibility to fresh produce. The area also suffers from gang violence and drive-by shootings. Finley argues that while the "drive-bys" get more publicity, the fast-food outlets, or "drive-thrus," are actually killing far more people. The toll is all too apparent. Levels of obesity run at more than 30 percent, and dialysis centers and motorized wheelchairs are becoming more and more common.

Finley became so fed up having to make a forty-five-minute trip in his car to buy fresh food that he started sowing vegetables and planting fruit trees on the narrow strip of land outside his home. Within months, the strip of land, which had previously been used a dumping ground, had become productive. Finley shared the harvest of kale, sweetcorn, peppers, pumpkins, and melons with others living on the street. But the following year he was served with a warrant for gardening on city land without a permit. Although he was forced to remove the plants, he immediately started a petition to allow him to reinstate them.

This was in 2010, only a year or so after First Lady Michelle Obama had dug up part of the South Lawn of the White House and involved elementary school children in planting and harvesting vegetables there. Obama's "Let's Move" campaign was aimed at addressing the alarming rise of obesity and diabetes in children. The zeitgeist was changing. The *Los Angeles Times* publicized Finley's campaign; his action was successful, and the city subsequently revised its regulations on urban cultivation. Finley now runs a project that supports people growing food on vacant lots. Styling himself as the "gangsta gardener"—with the slogan "Let the shovel be your weapon of choice" —he strives to make gardening cool and relevant to a generation of schoolkids whose parents, and in many cases grandparents, have never gardened.

One of Finley's main missions is to combat the stigma attached to working on the land. The history of farming in the US is one of racial exploitation through slavery and sharecropping. The legacy manifests itself today in an assumption, as Finley describes it, "that something terrible must have happened to you that you need to grow your own food—yet you are being self-sustaining." He thinks that people have lost a basic instinct to feed themselves and that "no one is really asking why the fast-food chains dominate to the extent they do." To be able to grow your own food may not be a human right, but it is a fundamental freedom. As Finley puts it: "If you don't have a hand in your own food, you are enslaved." The food deserts, he argues, should really be called "food prisons" because "if you want to find healthy food, you have to escape from them." Finley wants to create a momentum for change.

Gardening as a form of political resistance has a long history that can be traced back to the Diggers in seventeenth-century England, who, in the context of social unrest and high food prices, asserted the right to grow food on common land. Modern guerrilla gardening acquired its name in the early 1970s when the nearly bankrupt city of New York was spiraling into decline. The Green Guerrillas, as they called themselves, reclaimed derelict city plots and set up community gardens, invoking America's food-producing "victory gardens" of the First and Second World Wars. Some guerrilla gardeners have specialized in flowers more than food, such as Richard Reynolds, who started a movement in London at the turn of the millennium by planting flowers secretly at night outside his tower block in South London. Following this, groups of volunteers came together in an attempt to bring the beauty of nature to the most run-down parts of the city.

The Green Guerrillas remains an active organization in New

York today. There are eight hundred gardens associated with it, which is an impressive legacy. Like Incredible Edible, the movement quickly gained the approval of the city authorities, although later there would be further battles. One of the pitfalls of community gardening is the gentrification that often follows the creation of an attractive green space. At its worst, the very people that a project was intended to help can end up being priced out. During the 1990s, the Green Guerrillas fought to avoid just that situation when the city started selling land for development, putting six hundred community gardens at threat. Only after a lengthy battle were they rescued and preserved.

Terry Keller, one of the original Green Guerrillas, went on to work with the New York Botanical Garden (NYBG) on a highly successful outreach project restoring vacant lots in the deprived area of the South Bronx. The New Roots Community Farm, which runs alongside the Grand Concourse—the major thoroughfare through the Bronx—has recently been developed here. Converting the derelict site, devoid of any plant life, into a half-acre thriving farm entailed a great deal of hard work. The ground slopes steeply, and during the summer of 2012 large numbers of volunteers were involved in helping to dig the trenches that were needed to channel storm-water runoff and prevent soil erosion. The New York City Department of Sanitation supplied a large amount of free compost, and NYBG provided composting expertise. Fruit trees, including cherries, figs, persimmons, and pomegranates, were planted and beehives installed. All the work of soil preparation paid off, and the newly established raised beds were soon growing an array of produce including tomatoes, kale, watermelons, and peppers. Wildlife quickly started making itself at home: along with dragonflies, numerous butterflies, including painted ladies, black swallowtails, and red admirals began to appear.

Bronx Green-Up coordinates the farm in collaboration with refugee organization the International Rescue Committee. The project brings together people from diverse places and different cultures. New arrivals, fleeing from countries such as The Gambia or Afghanistan, work alongside residents who have been settled for longer, from places like Central America or the Caribbean. The challenges that face someone new to a strange city are massive, even more so when they are suffering from trauma or depression, as many of the refugees at New Roots are. Gardening can help them on many different levels, but above all the farm gives them a place where they begin to feel they belong.

Studies have shown that urban gardens like this are highly effective at promoting social integration. They lend themselves to becoming cultural and social neighborhood centers, and by providing a safe "third space" outside home or work, they can help reduce community tensions. Their role in fostering community cohesiveness is particularly valuable in ethnically diverse neighborhoods, where this can otherwise be hard to achieve. According to the Baltimore-based Johns Hopkins Center for a Livable Future, food is central to this effect: "The strong sociocultural values surrounding food growing, cooking, and sharing, help facilitate the role of gardens as a social bridge." Urban farms create a culture of collaboration, if not through shared produce, then shared pleasure. The power of gardening to shift relationships between people and bring about social change like this arises to a large extent from an effect of mutual benefit.

All organisms have a basic biological need to shape their environment, but in the city most of the shaping effect is the other way around, because people are not empowered to shape their surroundings. When the urban environment breaks down, things go wild. Urban wilderness consists of abandoned houses, broken glass, rusting metal, and weeds that have grown as tall as people. Above all, it means dangerous territory. The more an area deteriorates, the less time most of the residents spend outside in it. This makes it possible for gangs to control the streets. A vicious circle of increasing violence then sets in as conditions deteriorate further.

The first remedy for tackling this is to improve the surroundings. Reducing gun crime is a major priority for many large cities in the US, and the demographics clearly show that this crime is concentrated in the poorest, most derelict districts. In Chicago, for example, the violence is mainly concentrated in the south and west sides of the city, where levels of unemployment are high and the largely African-American communities have suffered decades of disinvestment. In 2014, there were more than twenty thousand vacant lots in Chicago, of which thirteen thousand were owned by the city. The "Large Lots" program, which was piloted in 2014 and launched in 2016, has targeted the worst-affected neighborhoods and enabled residents to buy a vacant lot near their home for only $1, provided they agree not to sell it for at least five years and undertake to tend it in the meantime. Altogether, four thousand lots across Chicago have been distributed in this way, with the aim that turning derelict land into gardens will strengthen the fragmented communities around them.

Urban "cleaning and greening" projects such as this are inspired by a series of groundbreaking studies that have taken place in Philadelphia over the last two decades. The research is led by Charles Branas, professor of epidemiology at Columbia University, and may be the only randomized controlled trial of environmental manipulation that's been carried out in a city. Philadelphia's LandCare Program was established in 1999 in collaboration with the Pennsylvania Horticultural Society, and is considered a model. Since then, volunteers have cleared hundreds of blighted spaces and abandoned lots in the city, removing rubbish and debris, sowing grass, planting trees, and erecting low wooden fences. The neighborhoods that benefited from these interventions were decided through a process of random allocation.

This long-running research project has compared the rates of violence in areas with similar demographics: the contrast between streets where lots have been transformed and those where they have not is striking. The latest study, published in 2018, found that the beneficial effects were greatest in neighborhoods below the poverty line. In these, the crime rate dropped by more than 13 percent, and gun violence by nearly 30 percent. By monitoring the city as a whole, the researchers were able to establish that these reductions were genuine, and the problems had not simply shifted to the next or nearby area.

In the course of the study certain approaches were found to be more effective: researchers discovered that when chain-link fencing was used to protect the plots, people felt kept out and started using the lots as a place to chuck their trash. In contrast, when wooden split-rail fencing was used, a clear sociability effect emerged. This lower-level fencing is easy to climb over, and it's possible to sit on the rail. As a result, people used the spaces for relaxation and socializing. Neighbors who would not otherwise have set eyes on one another started having conversations, and local children had somewhere safe to play out of doors. Keeping the gardens to a basic layout, with just lawn and a few trees, meant there were reassuringly good sight lines—important in potentially hostile areas. The simplicity also gave people scope to modify the gardens, so they began to invest in them.

The researchers found that people living near the newly greened lots reported feeling 60 percent less fearful about going outside. This large response is in keeping with other research by the same team who discovered that walking past derelict lots in the immediate surrounding of their homes caused a spike in people's heart rates of nine beats a minute. The finding shows that people do not habituate to urban decay; rather, it poses a constant source of background threat. Derelict surroundings also function as a mirror that lowers self-worth and gives rise to a feeling that nobody cares. Persistent feelings of being abandoned and forgotten are likely to make people feel depressed. Indeed, the follow-up study confirmed this, when it identified that feelings of depression and poor mental health for people living near the newly planted lots had almost halved. These are large effects, by any standards. Urban planning has, however, repeatedly neglected people's need for neighborhood green space. The Philadelphia research shows that a relatively low-cost landscape intervention can have profound effects on health and crime.

When it comes to breaking the cycles of violence and drug addiction that feed on inner-city deprivation, proximity of safe green space is particularly important for young people. Urban farm youth projects can be a highly effective way of providing this. The Chicago Botanic Garden, for example, has a longstanding commitment to community outreach projects. During the last fifteen years they have opened eleven farms in impoverished parts of Chicago, aimed at addressing health and educational inequalities. Some of these offer trainings for school leavers who want to learn to grow food and start businesses. Others are for younger people. Each year between May and October, the organization employs a hundred schoolchildren between the ages of fifteen and eighteen to work and train on their Windy City Harvest Youth Farm Program.

The youth program director, Eliza Fournier, explains that when the kids start attending, most of them are in a state of "plant blindness." Very few have a yard at home, and they have no idea whether they're going to like working with plants or not. So much of what plants provide is hidden from us. One of the first questions Fournier asks the group is whether they like pizza. Of course they all do. "If you like pizza, you like plants," she tells them and then explains how all of our food is ultimately derived from plant life. Putting their hands in the soil is a new experience for most of the participants, and it can take some getting used to the idea, as one girl put it, "that food that comes out of the dirt is good for you."

Washington Park is in one of the city's South Side food deserts. The youth farm here is enclosed within cast iron railings. Surrounded by tall trees, with raised beds among the grass, it feels more like a garden than an urban farm. Within weeks of starting, Fournier observes the kids becoming fitter and beginning to eat more healthily. She thinks it's important that "they get to be a kid as well as to work," and at the start of each session, they play simple team-building games, so there is a chance to have fun.

Safety is a basic unmet need for many of these young people. Along the perimeter of the garden there are fruit trees planted to commemorate peers who have died from gun violence. Many of the students are living not only in unsafe neighborhoods, but in homes that are not safe either, while some are effectively homeless, getting by through couch surfing. The farm becomes their "safe place," and they know if they need help, the staff will listen to their problems. Working in a haven of green like this gives rise to a range of "enriched environment" effects: reducing stress, promoting learning, and increasing sociability. Through gardening in small teams, the participants learn how to work collaboratively and resolve conflict when it arises, and when the weekly market starts up in summer, they also learn about relating to the public. At the end of each season, each young person receives "straight talking" feedback from staff about their work; the kind of thoughtful attention that most have never received before. Gradually, they gain in confidence and become less defensive.

The broader aims of the project are to promote social and emotional learning through gardening. Lives can be changed by projects such as this, and there is reason to think that levels of violence, addiction, and teenage pregnancy can be reduced. Outcomes like this are difficult to assess accurately, but what is striking is the basic statistic that 91 percent of the young people who attend the Windy City Youth Farm projects stay in education afterward or go on to do a vocational training. These are much higher figures than would be expected in this demographic group.

The University of Illinois recently carried out an assessment of a range of different types of youth programs. The study concluded that the Windy City Harvest Youth farms excelled at teaching life skills and providing career opportunities, and also helped strengthen family dynamics. This last gives an indication of how far-reaching the effects can be. As Fournier says, "Caring for plants provides a meaningful way to talk about caring for people." The garden functions as a model that helps the kids believe in the possibility of building a different kind of life for themselves.

No other species shares food in the way we do. In terms of our evolution, it is central to what it means to be human, yet modern life has eroded this powerful source of connection between people. The rise of convenience meals combined with busy, stressful lifestyles means that families eat together far less than they used to. Fournier emphasizes the extent to which food is a "great connector" and therefore plays a central role in the program. Once a week, the participants cook a meal in the garden and enjoy it together. For many, it's a chance to try new foods, but something much more important is also taking place.

As a species, we are adapted to living in relatively small groups of people. If we scale up too much, we lose the vital connections that sustain us. This is relevant not only to our emotional well-being, but according to the theory of "natural pedagogy," it's important for our cognitive development too. The cognitive scientists who founded the theory, György Gergely and Gergely Csibra, argue that the sharing of knowledge between close members of a group or tribe was so important to survival that a special channel evolved in the brain that functioned like a fast track for the transfer of cultural information. That special channel is opened when we feel trust. Gergely and Csibra call the phenomenon "epistemic trust" and believe it is what enabled our remote ancestors to develop an increasingly sophisticated range of skills, including tool making and the preparing and cooking of food.

Social learning is a powerful tool, but children who grow up in danger and fear learn not to be curious. Living in a state of mistrust leads people to turn away, and they stop learning from others. By contrast, if trust can be established, the brain is better able to create new neural networks. Land-based projects that involve growing, harvesting, and sharing food, such as the Windy City Youth farms, derive much of their power from replicating many of the basic life skill activities through which social learning evolved.

The standard approach to education today hugely underestimates the crucial role that social bonds play in facilitating learning. A failure like this to appreciate the importance of our biological roots has arisen alongside the modern idea that we can reinvent ourselves. As Jung pointed out: "We would laugh at the idea of a plant or an animal inventing itself, yet there are many people who believe that the psyche or the mind invented itself and thus brought itself into being." Yet the brain is the product of millennia of adaptation. As Jung put it: "The mind has grown to its present state of consciousness as an acorn grows into an oak."

For our hunter-gatherer ancestors, the identification of plants within a locality and an understanding of which ones were good to eat, medically useful, or toxic formed the first complex knowledge base. Cultural information like this is passed down through the generations, enabling people to accumulate and refine their pool of knowledge. But if the link is broken, human societies become equally vulnerable to losing knowledge and skills. It is only a matter of a generation or two. Look how fast the culture of care and the culture of work has changed; how quickly a relationship with the land has been lost.

The study of botany, which was so popular in the nineteenth century, suffered a decline in the course of the twentieth century. For many people being brought up in cities today, plants have almost entirely lost a sense of relevance or value. The term "plant blindness" that Fournier used was coined at the turn of the millennium by two American botanists, James Wandersee and Elisabeth Schussler. They were concerned that a progressive disconnection from nature meant that the fundamental role plants play in sustaining life has dropped from our collective consciousness.

The situation, they believe, has not been helped by the fact that the brain is prone to filtering out plants from our awareness. Our perceptual system is acutely sensitive to certain patterns, particularly any cues that resemble the human face. Most plants lack this kind of salience, although flowers can grab our attention in this way. Furthermore, the visual cortex prioritizes stimuli that are moving or potentially threatening. Since plants are relatively static and slow-changing, they slip into the background. This means that unless people are helped to open their eyes, there is a risk that the plant kingdom will remain closed to them.

Wandersee and Schussler observe that a love of plants often arises through the influence of a "plant mentor": most of us need to be introduced to the world of plants by someone who already values and understands them. A young man called Daniel, whom I interviewed on a community garden project, described such an experience. He had spent most of his teens in online gaming and had been feeling lost for some time. When he first came to the community garden a few streets away from where he lived, he felt even more lost. Plants seemed to him like a "beautiful but alien world," and he had no idea how to relate to them. One of the garden coordinators, a man who was only a few years older than Daniel, engaged him in getting his hands in the earth and showed him the basics of plant care. That process had, as Daniel put it, "opened me up." After that, he really took to plants. He distinctly recalled coming to the garden one day and feeling "now I understand how you work." He spent more and more time in the garden. A big driver for him was that, in contrast to gaming, gardening gave him something "real" he could do. Working with plants had a transformative effect on Daniel. He volunteered for a time abroad and ended up teaching gardening in a makeshift school within a Greek refugee camp, so he became a plant mentor himself. Through gardening, he realized he could do something that made a difference.

For Daniel, who was so at home in the world of technology, the natural world was an "alien" world. In growing up, he had found a niche for himself through gaming but it had left him chronically disenchanted with life. The choice today that many boys face is between spending time online in various forms of combat or hanging out on streets, where gangs and violence are a fact of life. Urban environments do not offer many alternatives, particularly for children from low-income families. When I asked the kids on the Windy City Harvest Youth farm what they would be doing if they weren't attending the project, the three main answers they gave were: in bed, online, or in trouble.

Boys are sometimes put off gardening because they see it as nurturing rather than manly. Some youth projects call themselves farms rather than gardens specifically to try to overcome this issue, but whatever name it goes by, cultivating the earth is about potency as well as nurture. So we find in ancient Greece that Priapus, the male god of fertility, presided over the growing of fruits, vegetables, and vineyards, and he is sometimes depicted with a huge phallus and a display of his garden produce.

There is vegetable empowerment to be found too in the story of "Jack and the Beanstalk"—an old English fairy tale whose origins lie in an ancient myth dating back five thousand years. The supposedly "magic" seed that Jack wastes his impoverished mother's last few coins on makes him look like a foolish, gullible boy, but then it sprouts a huge bean plant. He climbs up it, confronts a tyrannical giant, and reclaims all that has been stolen from his family. The story is about a boy's journey to manhood through realizing his potency, as well as a parable of social justice. In terms of radical solutions, there are all manner of "tyrannical giants" that gardening can help overcome—from individual problems like stress and demotivation to social and economic issues such as fragmented communities, lack of access to fresh food, and urban decay. Wherever they are in the world today, these are the issues that inner-city cultivation projects are trying to address. They demonstrate that growing food can be a way of growing a better society.

Cultivating the earth is empowering, and sharing its fruits promotes trust and cooperation more effectively than anything else. We all need to feel a sense of potency and to give and receive nurture. These dual aspects of human nature are brought together through the alchemy of gardening. The simple truth is that if every city or town was conceived of as a garden, and if people were allowed and encouraged to tend a part of their neighborhood, then people as well as plants would have a better chance to flourish.

CHAPTER 9

War and Gardening

Soldier of the Gordon Highlanders
(51st Division) tending his trench garden.
Heninel, October 23, 1917.

Yet shall the garden with the state of war
Aptly contrast, a miniature endeavour
To hold the graces and the courtesies
Against a horrid wilderness.

Vita Sackville-West (1892–1962)

More than once in the course of writing this book I have felt rueful about sitting at my desk while Tom was outside in the sunlight getting on with things in the garden. One autumn this feeling was particularly strong.

All summer long, I had been researching the origins of therapeutic horticulture in relation to the First World War. Industrialized warfare had been deployed on a scale that had never been seen before, and the devastating consequences strengthened the idea that people needed to get back to working the land. I had also been investigating the life of my grandfather, Ted May. What I eventually discovered about the degradations and cruelties that the prisoners of war in Turkey were subjected to shook me to the core. By the time autumn arrived, devoting so much time to thinking about war was beginning to have a negative effect on me. I realized I needed to put my research to one side and spend some time in the garden.

Several large boxes of bulbs were stacked up in our shed, so I loaded myself up with some bags of scillas and joined Tom, who was working in one of our large flower beds. What a relief to get my hands back in the earth! Working with a dibber and relishing the smell of fresh, clean soil, it was not long before I found a rhythm and felt at one with the task. The weather was mild for the time of year, and the warmth of the sun helped dispel a creeping inner chill that I had begun to feel. As I continued, it occurred to me that planting a bulb is like setting a little time bomb of hope in motion. All winter long the scillas I was distributing would lie in the dark earth, then silently detonate in spring, covering the ground in shards of brilliant blue.

The way that seeds, bulbs, and corms rise up out of the ground, transforming themselves from something dry and seemingly lifeless, is something we can ordinarily take for granted. The experience of war, however, is one in which nothing can be taken for granted. All the structures and assumptions that seem to hold life together are called into question. At the same time, the effects of simple things like natural beauty and human kindness are intensified. Extreme situations such as those encountered in the trenches and those endured by prisoners of war strip life right back and expose the value of experiences that might otherwise be obscured.

Warfare and gardening are in many ways the opposite of each other. Both are about territory, attacking or defending it on the one hand and cultivating it on the other. The idea that one activity might counterbalance the other has ancient roots. In the great civilizations of Mesopotamia the skills involved in combat and cultivation were given equal weight. Writing in 329 BC, Xenophon (424–401 BC), for example, not only designed his own garden but grew and planted many of the trees in it himself.

The warrior and the cultivator represent the twin poles of human nature: aggression and destructiveness versus peacefulness and creativity. In 1918, during the First World War, Winston Churchill drew on this ancient dichotomy in an interview reported by the poet Siegfried Sassoon. Sassoon had been decorated for bravery in combat, but he was also well known as an antiwar spokesman. Churchill, then minister of munitions, summoned him to a meeting during the closing months of the war. As the interview progressed, Sassoon realized that Churchill wanted to "have it out with him." Their exchange, which lasted an hour, culminated in Churchill pacing the room with a large cigar in the corner of his mouth while proclaiming "an emphatic vindication of militarism." Reflecting on the encounter afterward, Sassoon wrote: "Had he been entirely serious, I wondered, when he said that 'war is the normal occupation of man'? He had indeed qualified the statement by adding 'war—and gardening.'"

Churchill was serious about both war and gardening. Garden making was important to him throughout his life. Three years earlier he had been demoted from his post as first lord of the admiralty following the appalling failure of the Dardanelles naval campaign and the Gallipoli landings. During that summer, the "carnage & ruin," as he described it, preyed on his mind, and his garden at Hoe Farm in Surrey proved to be a lifeline.

• • •

It is one thing for gardens to provide respite from war but quite another to create them in the very midst of it. Yet this is what happened during the long, drawn-out fighting on the Western Front. Pretty flowers may seem trivial when shells are dropping all around, but in that landscape of utmost devastation, the beauty of nature, especially that of flowers, provided a psychological lifeline in a way that nothing else could. Gardens were created by soldiers, chaplains, doctors, and nurses. Some were small, some substantial, some were more decorative, others more productive. It helped that the conditions in France and Flanders lent themselves to it. The climate, the rich soil, the long stalemates and periods of inaction all combined to make gardening possible. Trench warfare revealed the power of the garden to answer to some of humankind's deepest existential needs.

One of the many gardens on the Western Front was created by John Stanhope Walker, a hospital chaplain at a casualty clearing station near the river Somme. Walker arrived in December 1915 and the following spring started making a garden as a place of refuge. At the beginning of July, the Battle of the Somme commenced, and the clearing station was swamped with casualties. A thousand badly wounded men were brought in almost every single day, and Walker buried nine hundred of them in three months. Lasting 141 days, the Somme offensive became one of the bloodiest battles in history. Of the 3 million men who fought there, more than a million were killed and maimed.

In his letters home, Walker described how the clearing station could barely cope. The wounded were "literally piled up—beds gone, lucky to get space on floor of tent, hut or ward." He worked as long as he could keep going through the day and night: "Chaps with fearful wounds lying in agony, many so patient, some make a noise, one goes to a stretcher, lays one's hand on the forehead, it is cold, strike a match, he is dead—here a Communion, there an absolution, there a drink, there a madman, there a hot water bottle and so on." In the face of all this, the flowers he had planted came into their own: "The garden is really gorgeous and the sides of the tent are down so the patients just gaze out at it."

Working with so much "broken humanity" left Walker at times feeling horribly incompetent, and he was disappointed that only a small proportion of the convalescent men made the effort to attend his services: "Tommy does not want religion. I don't persuade him." But if his sermons didn't attract their interest, his garden did. In mid July he wrote: "The garden is very bright with flowers now, the first row of peas is ready, the huge pods are much admired by the blood-stained warriors. Green tomatoes have formed and small marrows, we have had some very nice carrots." Praise for his garden came from other quarters too. He was particularly pleased that the surgeon general, Sir Anthony Bowlby, appreciated the garden: "He is very much struck with my flowers and he says he will have me mentioned in despatches for the size of my beans and peas."

In August, after the British had advanced, Walker and a colleague took a day off to visit the battlefield for the first time: "Oh what sights, the multitudes scattered over miles and miles, the immensity of war as it now was revealed . . . an absolute scene of destruction, miles and miles of country battered beyond all possible recognition." They walked on and entered the newly captured territory: "German trenches pounded to a mass of earth and barbed wire. Huge mine craters made a miniature lake and mountain district. Here where bricks and mortar are freely mixed with mud is Fricourt, there where gaunt boughless trees stand splintered is Mametz."

Some of the German dugouts had survived the onslaught. The two men clambered down and entered one. It was lined with wood like "a Swiss chalet" and had been made surprisingly homey with a carpet and a little bed. The outside of the dugout had been cared for too. They discovered a garden complete with "auriculas, shrubs and roses in tubs, window boxes and flower pots." The garden that Walker had created at the casualty clearing station was behind the lines, but this carefully tended patch was right in the middle of the fighting.

Astonishing as it may seem, dugout gardens were not that unusual and they were created by soldiers on both sides. The American journalist Carita Spencer documented some of the British soldiers' gardening activities when she visited the war zone at La Panne near Ypres. Along the rear side of the trenches there, some of the men had installed a line of small gardens: "First they had a little vegetable garden, and next to it for beauty's sake a little flower garden, and next to that a little graveyard, and then the succession repeated." Living "week in week out in the range of shell fire," she observed, meant that "life and death take on a new relationship. Death may come at any moment, and yet meantime life must be lived."

Alexander Douglas Gillespie, a young officer serving with the Argyll and Sutherland Highlanders, arrived in France in February 1915, shortly after his brother had been killed in action. In March Gillespie created a garden by transplanting sweet violets he found growing on the bank of an old flooded trench, and he retrieved a spent German shell casing which he used as a flower pot. He and his men had been wretched in the previous month's incessant rain, and the planted shell casing boosted their morale: "Now I have got the violets planted in it and set outside the dug out, and this pleases the Jocks very much."

Gillespie and his platoon were moved around between different trenches, but throughout that spring and early summer garden making took place in most of them. He asked his parents to send out nasturtium seeds and sowed them under cover of darkness one night in late March, and in early summer he wrote of sowing marigolds, poppies, and stocks, seeds that had been sent out to another junior officer.

The networks of trenches were dug arbitrarily through fields, orchards, and domestic gardens, wherever the lines happened to be. Sometimes flowers that had been disturbed sprouted anew from the trench walls and grew down, bringing color into the trenches. The dugout gardens themselves were partly created by sourcing plants from abandoned gardens nearby. At the start of May, Gillespie spent an afternoon in a village where he was billeted "getting plants from a ruined village for our trench gardens—wallflowers, peonies, pansies and many others; rather cruel to transplant them perhaps, but there are plenty left." Some of the plants didn't thrive in their new homes, but it was the doing of it that mattered more than anything else.

A few days later, on returning to the trenches, Gillespie wrote of "wearing respirators round our necks, and watching the wind, in case the gas should come drifting down." He then continued: "The gardens are all flourishing—lily of the valley, pansies, forget-me-nots, and all the old favourites. We are kept busy watering them."

In mid June, Gillespie's platoon was moved to a trench in close proximity to the German front line, where the levels of bombardment meant that gardening was not possible, but three weeks later, he was back in one of his old trenches. Here, the German lines were in some places only 350 yards away, and both sides looked out onto "a wide field of blood-red poppies." The garden he had previously made was also flourishing: "We have a wonderful trench of Madonna lilies in the garden. I don't know what it is that makes them glow in the half-light of morning or evening, but they are at their best then, and shining as I write." Then, just before he signed off, having requested some flypaper against the swarming flies, he conveyed a piece of bad news: "Today, in the middle of a peaceful sunny afternoon a big shell suddenly swooped down from nowhere into the trench, killed five and wounded four."

There is something inescapably baffling about this juxtaposition of life and death—the beauty of the lilies amid the deadly shell attack—but perhaps it is only baffling when viewed from outside? For it is said that soldiers in the trenches dreamed of their mothers and their gardens—dreams that expressed their longing for the safety and sanity of home. Flowers brought associations of familiarity and sanity into the madness and horror of war, and in the context of such extreme trauma and estrangement, they provided a psychological lifeline.

In September, when Gillespie was billeted in a local village, he went in search of the garden in which his brother Tom had spent time shortly before he was killed. Having walked several miles, he found the château and discovered that it was still occupied. The view of the garden from the veranda matched the image on his brother's last postcard home. He thanked the woman who owned the house for being "so kind" to Tom when he had been billeted with her the previous year. It was, Gillespie wrote, a "very charming spot. . . . There were ducks and water-fowl swimming in the pond, and some beds of flowers." This, as things turned out, was also Gillespie's last break from the trenches, for he was killed soon afterward, aged twenty-six, leading an attack on the first day of the Battle of Loos.

In a letter he wrote to his former headmaster shortly before he died, Gillespie proposed an act of reclamation that is currently coming to fruition through a centenary project called the Western Front Walk. When peace finally came, Gillespie wanted no-man's-land to be planted with shade trees and fruit trees, creating a pilgrimage walk from Switzerland to the English Channel. He envisaged that it "might make the most beautiful road in all the world" and that walking along it people might "think and learn about what war means."

As the war progressed into its third year, the military began to harness the gardening activity that had been spontaneously set in motion. Vegetable plots behind the lines were established on such a large scale that by 1918, the Western Front was self-sufficient in fresh produce. The dugout gardens that were created in the first spring of the war were motivated by much more than a need for food; they were an attempt, as Vita Sackville-West described it in her epic poem *The Garden*, "to hold the graces and the courtesies." They expressed a wish to feel human and a will to be civilized, to be more than an animal in a mud-filled burrow or a cog in the giant war machine.

The trench gardens were, in their way, a version of swords to plowshares. Gas cans were converted to watering cans, and bayonets were put to alternate use in cultivating the ground. All the values that gardens represent are in opposition to war, and in them the historian Kenneth Helphand identifies a potential antiwar message: In his book *Defiant Gardens* he writes: "Peace is not just the absence of war but a positive assertive state. . . . The garden is not just a retreat and a respite, but an assertion of a proposed condition, a model to be emulated." The role of gardening in wartime can, Helphand believes, renew our appreciation of the garden's "transformative power to beautify, comfort, and convey meaning."

What feels homey, what gives hope, what strikes the eye as beautiful are all dependant on the surroundings in which we find ourselves. Cultivating the earth in the context of a battlefield throws the power of the garden into sharp relief, and when so much is beyond repair, to be able to change something for the better is extremely important.

In *Greening the Red Zone*, the socio-ecologist Keith Tidball describes how within conflict zones and following natural disasters people instinctively turn to nature. "It seems counter-intuitive," he writes, that people in these situations "would engage in the simple act of gardening, tree-planting, or other greening activities." Yet there are plenty of accounts that observe people "benefiting from the therapeutic qualities of nature contact to ease trauma and to aid the process of recovery." Tidball regards this behavior as an expression of what he calls "urgent biophilia."

The urgency of the need to keep a love of nature alive, and by extension a love of life, was an important survival strategy for many of the soldiers confronted by the horrors of the trenches. Much as in Freud's Eros pitted against Thanatos, flowers provided these men with a form of ammunition against fear and despair. Whether this helped reduce the longer-term impact of trauma or not is impossible to judge, for it was an utterly uneven battle, and the exposure to so much death and destruction pushed many men beyond the limits of human endurance.

The great war poet Wilfred Owen wrote to his mother a few months before he suffered a breakdown, that while he could endure the freezing weather and a great deal of other hardship and discomfort, having to live with the "universal pervasion" of ugliness in a landscape that was "unnatural, broken, blasted" was much harder to bear. Worst of all, he continued, was the "distortion of the dead, whose unburiable bodies sit outside the dug-outs all day. . . . THAT is what saps the soldierly spirit."

Owen's poem "Mental Cases" is based on his own experience when, in May 1917, he was sent to the casualty clearing center for nervous cases at Gailly. He was confused, experiencing tremors, and had developed a stammer. For the afflicted men in the poem, there is no consolation to be found in nature, and even "dawn breaks open like a wound that bleeds afresh." Plagued by terrifying nightmares, at times Owen believed himself to be alienated from the natural order.

The following month, Owen was transferred to Craiglockhart Hospital, outside Edinburgh, having been given a diagnosis of neurasthenia. This was the disorder invented by George Beard a few decades earlier to describe enervated city-dwelling intellectuals. Now, as a result of the war, it acquired a new application. The term "shell shock" was emotive; it had caught the popular imagination, and as the war dragged on, medical officers were increasingly discouraged from using it. Neurasthenia became the catch-all diagnosis for traumatized servicemen, but its connotation of nerve weakness did not do justice to their condition. These were men who had been sapped of their vital forces by prolonged exposure to stress and fear and whose peace of mind had, in many cases, been irreversibly shattered.

Owen was fortunate that he ended up at Craiglockhart and was not subjected to electric shock treatments or to the bed-rest-and-milk-diet cure, both of which were used in other military hospitals. In contrast, the regime at Craiglockhart was based on a belief in the therapeutic power of connecting with nature. Owen's physician, Arthur Brock, thought it was important to "give Nature a chance." He believed that war trauma caused a violent detachment from the environment and that a physical engagement with the environment was necessary to reverse it. The mainstay of his approach was the plots of land he had set up within the hospital grounds where his patients grew vegetables and kept chickens as part of the therapy. Before the war Craiglockhart had been a hydropathic spa, and the gardening activities also involved caring for its grounds, including the tennis courts, croquet lawn, and bowling green that were for the men's recreational use. Brock encouraged his patients to engage with their surroundings in other ways too, through walks in the nearby Pentland Hills and field studies of the local botany and geology.

Brock's ideas were based on those of his friend and mentor the Scottish social reformer Patrick Geddes. Geddes was a pioneer in both environmental education and town planning, and gardening was at the center of his approach. Before the war he had reinvigorated the slum areas of Edinburgh by making community gardens on vacant lots. He believed that people needed to live by Voltaire's maxim *"Il faut cultiver notre jardin"* ("We must cultivate our garden"). The cultivation of people and place was encapsulated in his concept of "Place-Work-Folk," a triadic relationship that he regarded as the basic building block of society. The combined effects of industrialization and city living had, he observed, weakened the connections between people and place, resulting in negative effects on social and individual health. In Geddes's formulation, the work of gardening re-created those connections.

There was another influence at Craiglockhart in the form of Sigmund Freud. Brock and his colleague William Rivers believed that the advice that was often given to banish traumatic memories from the mind would only delay the men's recovery; instead they encouraged their patients to face their disturbing memories in a way that made them tolerable. In a letter to Freud, Brock wrote, "The most characteristic feature of Neurasthenia . . . was just this lack of solidarity, this segregation of parts," and described how his patients could not function within a community because they had become "like the fragments of their minds, isolated units, unrelated in space and time."

By contributing to the community, Brock thought, the men could regain self-worth and experience a sense of integration. He drew up individual treatment plans of various activities based on his patient's interests and skills. Unusually for his time, he believed that the prime task of the physician was to help the patient to help himself (although there are accounts of him dragooning men out of bed to go on early morning walks). Rivers, said to be the more charismatic man, focused on individual psychotherapy, while Brock created a therapeutic community. Regardless of the different methods, the aim of treatment at Craiglockhart was to help the men confront reality. This meant forms of escape like movies were frowned on. The "picture house" unhelpfully offered, Brock thought, "brighter prospects by far than the real world."

The battle for the mind has to be fought for a long time, well after the physical battles are over. In spite of all the activities and intellectual stimulation on offer during the day, for many of the men at Craiglockhart the nights remained a terrible ordeal, when their traumas and fears would revisit them in the dark. Brock, who was a classicist, used the myth of Antaeus to dignify these struggles. The giant Antaeus was possessed of formidable strength, but he was only unbeatable as long as his feet were in contact with the ground. Hercules discovered Antaeus's secret and defeated him in a wrestling match by lifting him up in the air. As Brock explained, "Every officer who comes to Craiglockhart recognises that, in a way, he is himself Antaeus who has been taken from his Mother Earth and well-nigh crushed to death by the war giant or military machine.... Antaeus typifies the occupation cure at Craiglockhart. His story is the justification of our activities."

Engaging in outdoor physical work and making an impact on their environment in various ways were all part of empowering the men to face what Brock referred to as their "phantoms of the mind." The detachment from the environment that Brock described is what these days we would call dissociation. The therapeutic value of grounding in the aftermath of trauma is now recognized. Physical activity and bodily awareness can help reverse the sense of detachment and unreality to which dissociation gives rise. Bessel van der Kolk, professor of psychiatry and director of the Trauma Center in Boston, argues that traumatic experiences are essentially disempowering and therefore people need to reestablish a sense of physical efficacy as a biological organism in order to recover from trauma.

In his biography of Owen, Dominic Hibberd suggests that Owen's experience of being blasted into the air by a mortar bomb as he slept meant that Brock's theories about the need to re-ground made sense to him. Owen's mother was a keen gardener and he had gardened with his grandfather as a boy. He was knowledgeable enough to deliver a lecture entitled "Do plants think?" to the Field

Club, from memory, arguing that in their responsiveness to sunlight, water, and temperature, plants are possessed of something akin to our sensory system. He also gave a paper on "The classification of soils, soil air, soil water, root absorption and fertility."

Owen spent four months at Craiglockhart, and from the beginning Brock recognized his artistic spirit, suggesting he take the subject of Antaeus for a poem. Published later as "The Wrestlers," it depicts Antaeus's feet like a plant's roots sucking "secret virtue of the earth." As Owen's writing developed, Brock encouraged him to ground his poems in his own experience of war, thereby putting his traumas and nightmares to creative use. Owen's great friend Siegfried Sassoon later recalled that "Dr. Brock, who was in charge of his case, had been completely successful in restoring the balance of his nerves." The problem with "getting dangerously well," as Owen himself described it, was the inevitable return to the front, and although for him this was delayed, he would be killed in action just one week before the war finally ended.

The fighting in the trenches is a defining feature, if not *the* defining feature, of the First World War. I had grown up understanding much more about the kind of war that Wilfred Owen fought in and much less about what my grandfather's war experiences involved. As a child I knew he had been prisoner of war, but I knew it simply as a statement of fact. I had little idea of what might be hidden behind the term. I also had no understanding of what being a submariner might have involved.

Ted was only fifteen when, in 1910, he joined the Royal Navy. He must have been keen to sign up, because he persuaded his father to add a year to his age. The following year, he trained as a Marconi wireless operator. Those crystal sets and spark transmitters communicating in Morse code were the start of a new telecommunications era. Not for a moment do I think that Ted was anything like a would-be gardener at that stage in his life. In fact, I suspect he was getting away from everything that working on the land entailed; the new technologies of the day and a life at sea would have been far more attractive options.

Like wireless telegraphy, submarines were a new invention. Their use in war had never been tested, and within the naval establishment they were a source of controversy. Admiral Sir Arthur Wilson, the controller of the Royal Navy, objected to their deployment because in his view they were "underhand, unfair, and damned un-English." He and Churchill were said to regard the submariners as pirates. The submariners in turn cultivated a swashbuckling kind of image and were notorious for being unconventional. You had to have a do-or-die mentality to be a submariner. If you got into trouble against the enemy deep out at sea, you could not expect to survive, and over the course of the war, one in three submariners did not return. Rudyard Kipling admired them and wrote about their exploits in his poem "The Trade," describing their officers looking like "unwashed chauffeurs" in their dirty white wool sweaters.

The early submarines were extremely rudimentary, and the engines were horribly noisy. When they were submerged, the air inside quickly became hot and stale, smelling of oil, sweat, and diesel. There was no sanitation, only an oil-filled bucket, and the interior was gloomily lit by the boat's batteries. The men did not clean their teeth while out to sea, and constipation and headaches from lack of oxygen were the norm. In heavy conditions, the crew of thirty men had to contend with the submarine constantly rolling and "pumping," that is vertically falling up to twenty feet. Working in these cramped, airless conditions, however, gave rise to a strong camaraderie and may have helped the men survive the very different kind of confinement they had to endure later on.

Ted's tiny, faded diary, with its neatly formed pencil entries, starts at the beginning of the war when he was the wireless operator on the E9 submarine, in the North Sea. In 1914 the E9 saw action in the Battle of Heligoland Bight and the Cuxhaven air raids and was the first British submarine to sink a German warship. Early in 1915, Ted was transferred to another submarine, the E15, which patrolled the seas near Malta and the Greek islands while the Anglo-French fleet was trying to gain control of the Dardanelles. This narrow, thirty-five-mile, winding channel, which connects the Aegean with the Black Sea via the Sea of Marmara and the Bosporus Strait, was of key strategic significance in the First World War.

The shores of the Dardanelles had been heavily fortified, and the straits themselves were full of mines. On March 18, 1915, the Allied bombardment of the straits culminated in a huge naval battle in which the Anglo-French fleet suffered terrible losses. Three warships were sunk, three put out of service, and a thousand Allied lives lost. The question then arose as to whether one of the British E-class submarines could make it through the straits and disrupt the Turkish lines of communication in the run-up to the proposed land invasion at Gallipoli. A French submarine had already been sunk after hitting one of the mines a few months earlier, and avoiding that fate would mean navigating under ten minefields at depths of up to ninety feet.

The captain of the E15, Theodore Brodie, volunteered to try. Just hours before the mission was due to start, Brodie's twin brother, Lieutenant Commander Charles Brodie, came to bid him farewell. The E15 was "cluttered up with gear and food for three weeks patrol," and the sight struck Charles Brodie "as a nightmare of chaotic discomfort." The men, he observed, "had been working all night, and were tired and unkempt but eager, and to my eyes very young"—and Ted was the youngest of them all. Undertaking the passage through the straits would entail what Charles Brodie described as six hours of "blind death." Submerged much of the time too deep for the periscope, they would have to steer by feel and sound, changing direction if they heard the chains of the mines rattling along the hull. But the mines were by no means the only hazard. The straits are known for being fast and turbulent; with a fresh water layer on top and salt water below, the currents run at different speeds simultaneously.

As morning broke on April 17, the E15 was only a third of the way through the straits when it was caught in a fierce eddy current by Kephez Point, right under the guns of Fort Dardanus. Ted's diary entry records that they were "soon high and dry." A torpedo boat immediately trained on them, and "the Turkish batteries then opened fire on us, one large shell entering our conning tower and killing the captain as he was going onto the bridge. Several shells came through the boat, one entering the engines and bursting several oil pipes and thick smoke began to come from aft but we could not see what had happened there." Chlorine gas had in fact been released as the acid in the batteries hit the water, suffocating six of the crew.

The surviving submariners were not only under fire but were faced with a three-quarter-mile-long swim to the shore. Ted wrote: "Several men would not attempt it, and I think it was because of this that so many were injured." Once on the beach, they were rounded up: "All our clothes were taken away and we were given old soldiers suits, filthy and alive with vermin. We were then told to march having no boots, no caps and no underclothing. The wounded were removed to hospital in carts." Having been paraded around Constantinople, they were taken to Stamboul prison, which is where they were on April 25, when the ill-fated Allied landings and slaughter took place on the beaches of Gallipoli.

The following week, the captured submariners were transported to Afyon-Kara-Hissar, the Opium Black Fort, a three-day train journey away in the highlands of Anatolia. "Kara," as Ted referred to it, was a clearing and distribution center for the prison camps. "Here we were put in a room that beggars description," he wrote. "I have seen stables and pigsties at home, but never have I seen human beings put into such a place." They were kept in confinement twenty-three hours of the day, all the men cramped into a tiny room with no furniture and no bedding, and apart from being filthy, the place was swarming with lice, fleas, and vermin. After a month of being locked up in these conditions, they were put to work, eleven to twelve hours a day, breaking stones on the roads.

The camp was ruled by a Turkish naval officer who was known for the cowhide whip with which he flogged the POWs for the most trivial of offenses. The captives had to buy their food and clothing, everything except a tiny ration of dry black bread. Ted notes in his diary that after a month of hard labor "on no pay with many promises," the American ambassador sent them a Turkish pound per man and "never I think were men more grateful for a bit of money." The last event that Ted records took place in the middle of that first summer. The men were ordered to set off on foot for the country and marched across rough terrain until dark. They spent the night in an open field. "Between the crowd of us I do not think we could have mustered a decent suit of clothes or a pair of boots." The war still had more than three years to run, and that long, cold night that Ted records out in the open, foreshadowed the terrible lack of protection they were to experience in the months and years to come.

The POW experience in Turkey is not well documented, even though more than sixteen thousand British and Indian servicemen were taken captive. There are, however, a small number of diaries kept by captured men from which I was able to glean some information. During January 1916, the captured crew of the E15 and Australian AE2 submarines were subjected to a four-day-long forced march. They had to cover twenty miles a day through sparse and hostile terrain. It was bitterly cold, and most were barefoot; some had old boots or Turkish slippers, and others found rags with which to bind their feet. They were starving, nearly frozen, and constantly slipping into pools of water and mud. Some men simply fell by the wayside. Eventually, the prisoners reached Angora, which at three thousand feet has a harsh climate at the best of times, but that year the snow was thick. From there many of them were transported to the village of Belemedik, to start work on building railway tunnels through the Taurus Mountains of southern Turkey for the new train line from Berlin to Baghdad. As the months wore on at Belemedik, malaria and typhus broke out and dysentery became rife. By the end of the war nearly 70 percent of the Allied POWs held in Turkey had died.

Keeping any kind of written material, as some men did, was extremely risky. Diaries had to be ingeniously hidden. Even though Ted had ceased maintaining a record, he hung on to his pocket diary. As a talisman of his former days, it must have felt crucial to keep it safe, a means of holding on to an identity that was being ruthlessly stripped away. It contained a record of happier times, the success of the E9 in the North Sea, which he was proud to have been part of, the glorious spring weather they had enjoyed in the Greek islands, and whatever escapade he encoded in the entry he made in Malta: "I went ashore and enjoyed myself immensely."

Planning escape attempts helped maintain morale among the men and kept their hopes alive. The difficulty lay not so much in slipping past the Turkish guards; the real problem lay in traversing the vast and mountainous terrain that surrounded them. There were no maps to be had, water was scarce, and food often unobtainable. Men sometimes escaped only to hand themselves in a few weeks later. The mystery of Ted being reported dead twice during the war may well have been on account of his having disappeared during failed escape attempts.

In the last year of the war, Ted was in a camp at Gebze on the shores of the Sea of Marmara, laboring in a cement factory not far from where he was captured. It was from here that he and a small party of fellow POWs finally escaped by boat, surviving for twenty-three days on water alone. We know that at some stage Ted was picked up by the hospital ship *St. Margaret of Scotland*, which was anchored in the eastern Mediterranean.

Soon after Ted had reached safety on the *St. Margaret*, he was lying in bed when an American orderly appeared with a large can of soup. Ted watched as the orderly opened the can and then disappeared to collect a saucepan. A starving man does not miss an opportunity. He sprang up, grabbed the can, and gulped the soup down in one go. It was far too much and far too soon. The violent spasms he was seized by as his body ejected the soup were, he would say later, like nothing else he had ever felt. In recollecting this experience, he conveyed to my mother how horribly ill he felt that day, but of the suffering he had endured during his years of forced labor, and the horrors he had witnessed, he did not speak.

In time, Ted gained just enough strength on board the hospital ship to make his way back across Europe to England, to be reunited with his fiancée, Fanny. What must she have felt when he turned up so emaciated and aged, in his battered old raincoat with a Turkish fez on his head? Years of hard labor and malnourishment, followed by the four-thousand-mile-long journey, had weakened him almost to the point of extinction. It can be hard enough to bring the body back to life after such extreme experiences, but coaxing the mind back takes even longer. With Fanny's patient nursing Ted began to put on weight, but in September 1919, he was discharged from the navy with a diagnosis of neurasthenia.

So much gets written about the horrors and glories of war, so much less about the long, slow process of recovery and rebuilding afterward. It is necessarily slow, for what has to be avoided is too much too soon. Just as Ted's starving body convulsed in pain from the soup, so the traumatized mind cannot cope with too much stimulation. Anything sudden or unexpected floods it, and the slightest ambiguity is prone to being misread, provoking flashbacks or mental shutdown. A feeling of shelter and safety is crucial. New experiences need to be in a form that is unthreatening and digestible; only then can they be sustaining.

During the war, a Swiss physician, Adolf Vischer, visited POW camps in England and Germany. He described a condition he named "barbed-wire syndrome," which arose through prolonged incarceration and was characterized by symptoms such as confusion, memory loss, poor motivation, and debilitating anxiety. The powerlessness of the predicament along with feelings of shame and survivor guilt easily preyed on the prisoners' minds. Barbed-wire syndrome, like shell shock, was regarded as a form of neurasthenia.

Once back home, it could be hard for released POWs to feel that their own suffering was warranted when so many of their comrades were maimed or dead. The long-term outcome for former First World War POWs was particularly poor, and their mortality rates during the 1920s and '30s were five times higher than that of other veterans. Malnourishment and infections had left many of them with poor physical health, and they were prone to depression, mood swings, anxiety, and suicide.

When it came to helping these men regain something of their former vitality, Vischer thought that apart from being reunited with their families at the earliest opportunity, they needed to return to some form of work. He discouraged manufacturing on account of its joyless monotony but thought that cultivating the land was of "infinite value." It could provide, he wrote, "an ideal occupation for the released prisoner" because "it binds man to his native soil. No herded existence with chance acquaintances is involved, no agitation; it is independent of human influence." Like Brock, Vischer recognized that a process of reattachment needed to take place.

For POWs and men returning from the front lines, there were many adjustments to be made. Memories of home that sustained them during their absence had become fixed and idealized, and the reality they returned to was inevitably different. To make it even harder, the war had set in motion a great deal of social and cultural change, so that home really was a different place. It created a set of conditions in which an unhelpful nostalgia arose, either for home before the war or for the lost camaraderie of service life. Unless attachments could be forged anew, such men were at risk of withdrawing from life, becoming unemployable and socially adrift. Indeed, by the 1920s there was national concern about the plight of demobilized men and their high levels of sickness and unemployment. British newspapers regularly reported on rehabilitation programs set up to train them for new roles.

The Ministry of Labour and charitable organizations like the Salvation Army and the British County Homestead Association set up trainings, many of which were in horticulture and agriculture, with the aim of improving the veterans' "health and their prospects." When Sir Arthur Griffith Boscawen MP, parliamentary secretary to the Board of Agriculture, opened a training center in Kent, he expressed the mood of the time when he spoke of "fitting our gallant soldiers to occupy a position on the land" and invoked the health-giving properties of "life in the beautiful country, in the fresh air." These men, he proclaimed, "were anxious to cultivate a smallholding, a bit of the land for which they fought. Therefore proper training was of great importance."

In the early summer of 1920 Ted embarked on one such training. The main clue I had about Ted's rehabilitation was a much folded handwritten letter dated May 24, 1921, penned by his instructor, Mr. W. H. Cole from the Horticulture Section at Sarisbury Court, near Southampton. It certifies that during his twelve months training in "all branches of horticulture," he had acquired a good practical knowledge of "the cultivation of hardy fruit and vegetables also vines, peaches, tomato, melons and cucumbers under glass" as well as "herbaceous plants and roses."

The mansion at Sarisbury Court (also known as Holly Hill House) had been owned by the US government during the war and run as a military hospital, taking wounded men off ships straight from nearby Southampton docks. After the war was over, the British government bought it back and the Ministry of Labour set up a range of residential courses for ex-servicemen there. The house had extensive gardens, thought to have been laid out in the mid-nineteenth century by Joseph Paxton, famous for designing the Crystal Palace in London for the Great Exhibition of 1851. The grounds, which ran down to the shores of the River Hamble, included a series of terraced lakes as well as cascades, a grotto, and a large walled garden.

The sales catalogue of 1927 gives a good idea of what the gardens would have been like when Ted was there. It lists ten large greenhouses, some as much as forty feet long, which were heated and home to various exotics. There were two Peach Houses, two Vineries, one stocked with "Black Hambro" vines, a Palm House, a Tomato House, a Cucumber House, and a Carnation House. There was also a Mushroom House and a Fruit Store. Altogether there were four-and-a-half acres of garden, of which two-and-a-quarter acres were walled and are described as well stocked with bush fruit and trees.

These days there is a public park on the site, called Holly Hill. The walled garden has been built on and the greenhouses long since demolished, but wandering around the lake gardens, with their luxuriant growth, waterfalls, and islands covered in tree ferns, had a deeply calming effect on me. Just before I left, I stumbled on an area called the sunken garden, standing in the middle of which were two magnificent camellias, both in full flower. They were tall enough for me to stand under and gaze up into their dark pink flowers. Then I took in the fan palms that were growing around them and realized that this was the site of one of the heated greenhouses.

How welcome must have been the warmth and light in those greenhouses? How restorative to work in this garden surrounded by the fruits of the earth, learning to have a hand in their making? I see Ted as someone with an instinct for getting hold of life. In saying that, I am thinking of the young man who didn't hesitate to jump into the treacherous waters of the Dardanelles, or who seized the can of soup, or who set off on the longest of journeys, heading home overland. I think he grabbed at this experience too.

In the long term, Ted's year at Sarisbury Court didn't lead to employment in horticulture, but in the short term it did. Soon afterward, he traveled to Canada, taking with him Mr. Cole's letter, which, after describing his experience, contained the following recommendation: "I am pleased to state he is an intelligent, hard working, trustworthy and sober man and I therefore have much pleasure in recommending him to anyone requiring the services of a good man." Ted arrived in Winnipeg in the summer of 1923 and worked on the harvest before finding a position as a gardener on a ranch in Vermilion, Alberta. His two years of outdoor work there helped him recover his strength and resilience.

Clinicians such as Brock and Vischer certainly thought that working the land was particularly helpful for men like Ted, but there was little in the way of follow-up after the war to ascertain the effectiveness of such treatments. To complicate matters, the dream of returning to the land was vulnerable to unfortunate economic realities. In Britain, the wartime effort to boost food production in the colonies created a glut of cheap imported food and led to a collapse of food prices in the 1920s. As a result, many small farmers struggled to make a living. Working on the land can be harsh and cruel, and for some men in those postwar years it was a case of dashed hopes along with grind and toil.

The best evidence of beneficial effects comes from an American physician, Norman Fenton, who worked in one of the base hospitals in France in 1917 and carried out a follow-up study afterward.

Between 1924 and 1925, he surveyed 750 men he had treated who had been given a diagnosis of neurasthenia. Fenton's study revealed that seven years after the war, many of the afflicted men were still unhealthy and suffering from nervous problems. The amount of help they were offered afterward made a huge difference to their recovery, and the ones who received emotional support and found a source of motivation fared much better. Fenton was particularly interested to find out what line of work the men were best able to cope with afterward. The answer was "agriculture far above all others." The information he collected showed that "many who had difficulty working at manufacturing trades in towns or cities have been able to make a fairly successful readaptation in agricultural work. Some have even improved as to be self-supporting and gradually losing all their symptoms."

When Ted returned from Canada after his two years there, it was the end of his outdoor working life. Horticultural jobs were in all likelihood in short supply, but his training in telegraphy meant he found employment in the postal service. Then a few years later he and Fanny were able to buy their own small plot of land. On family visits when we were children, it was not Ted's flowers and vegetables that interested my brother and me. What we loved best were the times he let us go with him into the aviary he had built in his garden and help feed his birds or peep at newly hatched chicks. As I look back now, Ted's care of these little captives stands out in stark contrast to his own experience of being held in captivity.

Trauma changes the inner landscape in a way that is fundamentally displacing, and the physicality of gardening in this context is important—it is about getting dirt under your fingernails, planting yourself in the soil, rebuilding a sense of connection to place and to life in the process. Ted's year at Sarisbury Court, with its "Peach Houses, Vineries, Palm House, Tomato and Cucumber Houses and Fruit Store," was life-changing and set in motion a love of growing plants and tending a patch of earth.

Making a garden often involves a re-creation, an attempt to bring into life another place that has imprinted itself onto us and inspired us. The extensive greenhouses at Sarisbury Court where Ted worked and convalesced does much to explain his later expertise and his devotion to his greenhouse and orchids, as well as his pride in the Macpenny Mist Propagator which gave him such good results.

CHAPTER 10

The Last Season of Life

Winter in the Barn Garden.

*May I walk every day on the banks of the water,
may my soul rest on the branches of the trees which I
planted, may I refresh myself under the shadow of my
sycomore.*

Egyptian tomb inscription, ca. 1400 BCE

In the dark days of winter, the garden is three-quarters asleep. It is
a season of letting go and a time of forgetting. The tug of life that
needs attending to has relaxed its hold, but not for long; soon there
will be new growth to nurture and bring on. Even in December, it

is pressing up already. Amid the dead, discarded leaves, fresh green shoots are rising from the earth.

In the course of a year, a plant goes through all the stages of life, from seed to procreation and death, yet it is not the kind of death we undergo because the plant world is so adept at resurrecting itself. Our own mortality breaks the continuity of time. We foresee a future lost and everything we love being wrenched away. No wonder we try to banish death from life. But this, as the great essayist and philosopher Montaigne argued, is a mistake and only intensifies our fear of death. Instead of regarding death as a kind of adversary, to be fought on the battlefield, Montaigne thought we need to experience death as something more ordinary: "We must rid it of its strangeness, come to know it, get used to it." It is not that Montaigne found this easy himself, quite the contrary; when he was a young man, his enjoyment of life was diminished by his fears of dying.

When it came to contemplating how his own life might end, Montaigne hoped that it would happen in his garden: "I want death to find me planting my cabbages, but careless of death, and still more of my unfinished garden." Montaigne understood that living is always a process, that nothing is fixed, however much we long for it to be, and that however long or short our life span, none of us can complete everything we have planned or hoped for. But as much as his cabbage patch symbolizes the unfinished life, it also evokes the continuity of life, for it is as if in breaking off midsentence, our words and thoughts can live on through the real or metaphorical cabbages we have planted.

The year after I qualified as a doctor, something happened that I associate with Montaigne and his wish to die in his cabbage patch. I was working on a cardiology unit at the time, and my daily ward tasks were often interrupted by emergency admissions. That particular morning was no exception, and when the alert went out that a man in his late seventies was on his way to emergency having suffered a cardiac arrest, I went straight down to the resuscitation room. The rest of the crash team were already assembling, and we waited while the clock on the wall ticked precious minutes away.

Then the room was propelled into action as the ambulance crew burst in through the doors. The stretcher they carried bore a man in the winter of life with white hair and a long gray beard. To my eyes, at least, he looked like Old Father Time, a figure straight out of a picture book. Evidence of his recent activities added to my impression, for death had found him mowing his lawn. He must have lain on the newly cut grass, because his jacket, trousers, and wellington boots were all covered in fine lawn clippings. When he was transferred from the stretcher onto a gurney, some of the greenery fell to the floor and then spread itself further as his clothes were cut off his body. The smell of mown grass filled the air while we focused on the strict and briskly timed routine with which resuscitation attempts are conducted.

Afterward, when one of my senior colleagues went to speak to the man's wife, I caught a glimpse of her looking small and frail with someone younger, possibly a daughter, by her side. Perhaps, while he was in the garden, she had been inside preparing their lunch? It must have seemed like an ordinary day with no foreboding of the swift, cruel severance to come.

When those lawn clippings scattered themselves in the white, sterile room that day, it seemed to me that two versions of death were juxtaposed in front of our eyes. With its high-tech screens and beeping machines, this was a space equipped to conquer the forces that extinguish life, and we were treating the body as a failing machine, but it is to earth that we ultimately return, and the green blades of grass asserted the inescapable naturalness of the fact.

We have separated ourselves from nature to such an extent that we forget we are part of a vast and living continuum, that the atoms in our bodies are derived from the products of the earth and that in time they will slip back into the chain of life. This continuity between us and the natural world is not only in death; even as we go about our day-to-day lives, our skin is turning to dust and the carbon dioxide we expire is contributing to the growth of plants.

Although we live in a technological age and hide behind our machines, our difficulty with assimilating this kind of understanding is not a modern phenomenon. The naturalness of death does not come intuitively to us and probably never has. It is simply that we have found stronger and more sophisticated ways of distancing ourselves from it.

That we are part of nature in this way seemed profoundly shocking to Sigmund Freud when he first encountered the idea. He was only six years old, and his mother had just explained to him that we are all made of earth and therefore must return to the earth. He resolutely refused to believe her. In an effort to convince him, she rubbed the palms of her hands together, which is what she did when making dumplings, except on this occasion she was rubbing skin on skin. Freud described how his mother then showed him "the blackish scales of epidermis produced by the friction as proof that we were made of earth." Her actions had the desired effect: "My astonishment at this demonstration knew no bounds and I acquiesced in the belief which I was later to hear expressed in the words: 'Du bist der Natur einen Tod schuldig,'" or "Thou owest Nature a Death."

Four years before, when he was two years old, Freud's baby brother Julius had died. Periodically, throughout his life, Freud suffered from attacks of what he called "*Todesangst*," or the fear of death, and he came to understand how much this feeling of terror is related to the instinct to "kill or be killed." He noted that among hunter-gatherer tribes, death is not necessarily recognized as a natural process; it is attributed to the action of an enemy or a malevolent spirit.

He also thought that deep down we all believe we are immortal because our own death cannot be represented in the unconscious. The logical statement "all men must die," he argued, is meaningless when applied to ourselves, for even when we imagine ourselves dead, we are still present as a spectator. Recent research at Bar Ilan University in Israel has shown this effect in action. In a series of studies, the researchers observed that the brain's prediction system showed a tendency to categorize death as something that happens to other people rather than ourselves. While resisting the idea that death is directly related to us might confer protection from overwhelming anxiety, it means that much of the time we live in denial of our own mortality. We can either ignore death or live in fear—it is the bit in between that is harder. If we think about dying too much it interferes with living, but if we never think about death, we remain perilously unprepared.

People have always tried to naturalize human origins and endings. Take the numerous ancient myths that tell of how the first people on earth were formed from soil or clay. In ancient Greek mythology Prometheus shaped man out of mud, and Athena breathed life into the figure, while the Bible tells of God's creation of Adam from the dust of the earth. These narratives are more than accounts of how the world first came to be peopled; they also carry the message that Freud's mother conveyed. They are a reminder that, however distinct from soil and plant life flesh and blood may be, we are made of earth and must return from whence we came.

This way of understanding death can be traced back to the beginning of cultivation in prehistory. The archaeologist Timothy Taylor argues that horticulture brought with it not only a different way of life, but a new set of symbols: "This was when the earth first began to be widely seen as Mother Earth providing a womb into which the dead could be placed like seeds awaiting a new spring." In his book *The Buried Soul*, Taylor links the emergence of beliefs about the afterlife to observations of seed germination in particular: "The dry seed, placed in the ground, would not be reborn with-out the powers, or 'gods' of sun and rain exerting themselves in correct measure. Similarly, the gods' approval was needed for the dead to be reborn." In other words, the regeneration of seeds may have provided a model for the development of ideas regarding the possibility of resurrection and rebirth.

The metaphor of seed germination in relation to the afterlife can be found in the Bible, but the idea is largely implicit. In the much older ancient Egyptian religion, however, it was explicit. The Tomb of the Vines on the West Bank of Luxor in Egypt, for example, bears this inscription: "May he grant that his dead body may germinate like a seed in the Netherworld." This exqui-sitely decorated tomb belongs to Sennefer, a nobleman who was entrusted with overseeing the gardens in the city, which is why it is also known as the Gardener's Tomb. The inscription is addressed to Osiris, the god who was believed to guide the dead on their passage to the underworld. This god was also associated with the growth of new vegetation, and rituals that involved the germina-tion of seeds symbolized his resurrection in spring.

Entering the tomb down a long, steep narrow stairway, you see that the entire ceiling of this intimate, underground space is cov-ered with painted vines and bunches of grapes that are so well pre-served and hang so low, it feels as if you could almost pick them. The decorated pillars contain scenes from Sennefer's life, and in one he is portrayed in the afterlife, where he sits in the shade of a sacred fig tree (*Ficus sycomorus*), inhaling the scent of a lotus flower.

The ancient Egyptian practice of mummification was not only a way of protecting the body from decay, but also placed the body like a seed in a husk. The symbolism was further reinforced by the sowing of real seeds inside some tombs. Known as Osiris beds, these receptacles of earth were formed into the shape of the god Osiris. They varied in size; some were even life-sized, like the one that had been shut in a large box discovered in Tutankhamen's tomb. When it was finally opened in the 1920s, withered shoots of barley were found to have grown three inches high.

Paintings of gardens also appear on ancient Egyptian tomb walls. They symbolize a resting place and a source of sustenance for the deceased on their journey to the world beyond. These images are not overly elaborate or idealized; they are of rectangular plots irrigated with water channels and resemble the deceased's real gardens. Typically centered on a pond replete with fish, they have shaded walkways of date palms, figs, and pomegranates, along with vines and flowers.

The fear of death is a primal fear generated by the instinct for survival. The ancient Egyptians dealt with that fear by focusing on the journey beyond, but there is also a psychological journey we have to make in this life in order to reconcile ourselves to death. The symbolism of the garden can console and sustain us as we undertake it.

Gardening is about a balance of different forces, human and natural, life and death. When it comes to contemplating the inevitability of death, decay, and decomposition, however, much of the garden's power derives from a direct and earthy engagement with it. If you are not a gardener, it may seem strange to think that scrabbling about in the soil can be a source of existential meaning, but gardening gives rise to its own philosophy, and it is one that gets worked out in the flower beds.

The death of someone we love is a traumatic wrench—the finality, the irreversibility, and the inhumanness—it is beyond our grasp. Death fractures our sense of the continuity of time, of a future with this person alongside us. Everything has to be reconfigured. There is a great deal of work in this, not work we have done before, because each loss is different. I think it is how it comes about that death, the most natural, inevitable biological happening, can come to feel so unnatural. Our innermost nature rises up in the urge to revolt against it, as if death should not be.

The American poet Stanley Kunitz published a remarkable book in 2005 shortly before his hundredth birthday, a year after his wife's death and, as it turned out, a year before his own. *The Wild Braid* contains interviews and writings in which he reflects on a lifetime spent writing, teaching, and gardening. He describes how a shadow was cast over his childhood by his father's suicide before he was born. Later, when he was in his teens, the same terrible shadow fell again when his stepfather died suddenly from a heart attack. In the face of this shocking loss, Kunitz was beset by primal fear. He became afraid to fall asleep because in his mind, unconsciousness was associated with death. His structures were profoundly shaken and he realized how vulnerable life is: "There was so much death around me in my family that I had to become reconciled to it or else suffer the consequences psychologically. It was impossible to live with that fear every day, every night."

A few years after his stepfather died, Kunitz started working on a neighboring farm. Tilling the earth, as Kunitz writes, creates a connection between the self and "the rest of the natural universe." In witnessing the cycles of growth and decay, for the first time, he understood, as he put it, "that death is absolutely essential for the survival of life itself on the planet."

As Montaigne described, the task of living is made much harder when we see death as an adversary, to be battled with at all costs. When we take the strangeness out of death and make it more ordinary, the prospect of dying can seem less terrifying. As Kunitz reached an understanding that death is a necessary part of life, his anxiety lifted and he experienced a new energy: "When I came to that realization, I felt as if I'd been reborn. And it was purely internal."

In his late fifties, Kunitz started creating a garden on a steeply sloping sand dune area in front of his house in Provincetown. Like recovering peace of mind from the fears of death that had assailed him earlier in life, his garden's construction, so near the sea, was an act of reclamation. He was carving out more of a hold on life for himself. First, he built three brick terraces and then laid down pathways made from crushed clamshells. Next, he set about enriching the sand with soil and compost, as well as seaweed that he collected from the shore. It took years, but over time, the garden came to support a diversity of plants—some sixty-nine species—as well as creating a haven for wildlife. Such was the tangle of brightly colored flowers within it that it was likened to a jewelry box

There is no escaping the fact that things die in the garden, and our mortality is, as Kunitz put it, "the hard reality, perhaps the hardest reality that we have to reckon with." The lifespan of a flowering plant can be "so short," he writes, "so abbreviated by the changing seasons, it seems to be a compressed parable of the human experience." For him, even the compost heap serves as a reminder that "we are all candidates for composting." Creativity is one of the ways we work out our relationship to the nature of our existence. Kunitz likens the process of gardening to writing a poem; in fact, he sees his garden as a "living poem." Both can give us an imaginative way of living in the world, but the garden and the work we do in it are inescapably physical.

Gardening involves an interplay of forces, human and natural, which is why for Kunitz, his garden is a "co-creation." Much as he responded to the garden, it responded to him. In old age, when he felt the life force within him waning, he experienced caring for plants as a kind of procreative intercourse: "As one grows older and older there is a need to renew that energy associated with the erotic impulse." The garden took on a form in his mind as what he calls "an abiding companion," a kind of muse: "I never am absent from the garden even when I'm away from it." In 2003, when he was seriously unwell and nearly died in the hospital, he believed that it was his longing to get back to his garden that helped him recover.

The garden is an imagined place as much as it is a real one. People dream about their gardens and make plans for them. For many people, the amount of time they spend thinking about the garden far outweighs the time they actually spend relaxing or working in it. Even tending a window box can open a door onto another world.

The writer Diana Athill started gardening in her sixties, a phase of her life that also saw the start of a second career as an author. Until she was unexpectedly entrusted with the care of her cousin's garden, she had "never so much as pulled up a piece of groundsel." Left to get on with the responsibility that had been imposed on her, her gardening life started with a bang: "When I planted something for the first time in my life and it actually grew, I became hooked, and hooked I remained." During her seventies and eighties she continued to be an active gardener. She loved the way it absorbed her and "quite took one out of oneself, always a most refreshing and beneficial experience." The two main pleasures of gardening for her were the joy of making something happen and spending time in the company of plants "full of the mystery of life, just as we are ourselves."

I first met Athill when she was ninety-seven and came to visit our garden with her nephew Phil and his wife Annabel in high summer. The full circuit of our plot is rather demanding, so Phil pushed her in a wheelchair while Annabel held up a parasol to protect her from the sun. Athill was quick to notice all sorts of details, so we made regular stops to look at individual plants and trees. She was stylishly dressed, and the directness of her opinions was at times disarming. It struck me that she had found a way to accept the limitations of old age, while at the same time remaining resolutely undiminished by them.

In her nineties, Athill moved into a retirement home in a leafy part of North London. Fortunately it had a large garden and there was a beautiful magnolia tree growing right outside her window. Her room came with a balcony on which she installed two large pots and three window boxes. In what she referred to as "advanced old age," her enjoyment of the garden inevitably became more hands-off, but she still took care of her potted plants. She was, as she put it, "mad" about flowers and about color. Her exuberant display included agapanthus, sweet peas, and morning glory, and although she disapproved of them in earlier life, she grew begonias. Her favorite was "a gorgeous Mae West of a flower" with the reddest and pinkest of blooms that are "champion lasters," and all through the summer months, she would sit in their company and enjoy "an unexpected moment of sunshine."

In autumn, she planted out violas: "dear valiant violas, which look so delicate but flower steadily from October through to May, shrinking a little from a really severe frost, but always recovering so gallantly." Just like her, it seemed, for Athill was clear that being very old is far from easy; but flowers and trees provided her with a form of pleasure that did not, like so many other things in old age, have to be relinquished.

Both Athill and Kunitz embarked on their garden projects after midlife, and it's not far-fetched to attribute some of their health and longevity to gardening. When the fact of our mortality presses in on us, as it generally starts to do in middle age, we can experience a surge of creative energy, as they both did. Erik Erikson, the developmental psychologist and psychoanalyst, called this phenomenon *generativity*. He believed that being able to be generative in various ways during the second half of life was important for our emotional well-being. By generativity, Erikson meant taking a perspective that stretches beyond our own life. There is an overlap with creativity, but it is also about the skills and knowledge we pass on to the next generation and the things that will live on after us, that give us a way to keep looking forward. In contrast, if the passing of time makes us feel "what is the point?" we are likely to enter a state of "stagnation," so that life loses meaning and purpose.

The largest psychological study of aging and quality of life that has ever been carried out, the Harvard Grant Study, involved more than a thousand people and ran for many decades. One of the most striking findings was that men and women who developed ways of being generative in their fifties were three times more likely to be thriving at eighty. This finding surprised the researchers, who had expected to find economic factors playing a significant role in the quality of life of the elderly, but the correlation was not that strong. Just as surprising was the finding that physical health itself was not particularly linked to how people coped with the changes and losses involved in aging. The crucial factors turned out to be people's emotional lives and the kind of the activities they engaged in. Loneliness, unhappy relationships, and a lack of purpose were shown to be the biggest contributors to a poor quality of life in older age.

In *Aging Well*, the psychiatrist George Vaillant, who was lead researcher on the project for thirty years, wrote that it is not so much about what kinds of adversity life might throw at us as it is about how we deal with them. The most important thing, which he thinks can't be emphasized strongly enough, is the need to cultivate our closest relationships, as these are what sustain us more than anything else. The next most important thing is how we spend our time, not so much in productivity but in generativity and various forms of "creative play." Of course, there are many ways of doing this, but gardening is undoubtedly one of them.

Donald Winnicott was known for adopting a playful and creative approach both in his psychoanalytic theories and his own life. Not surprisingly, he also loved tending plants. He took pride in the garden on the roof of his London house and cared for his cottage garden in Devon. His wife Clare Winnicott has described how he retained his talent for play well into old age, even continuing to ride his bicycle downhill with his feet on the handlebars.

Soon after he turned seventy, Winnicott suffered a series of major heart attacks which prompted him to start working on an autobiography. In the margin of his notes, he entered the following plea: "Oh God! May I be alive when I die." How many of us feel the same? Winnicott's cry from the heart expresses the wish to inhabit the world fully and be spared the depression that so often accompanies terminal decline.

Clare Winnicott relates how, having suffered "about six coronaries and recovered from them," Donald still didn't stop himself from doing anything. Age seventy-four, a few months before he died, she found him in the garden of his home in Devon up in a tree. When she exclaimed, "What the *hell* are you doing up there?," Winnicott replied: "I've always wanted to top this tree off. It spoils the view from our window." A job, perhaps, that he had not got around to, but finally with time running out, he did. The symbolism is striking—he was not ready to die, he wanted a longer view of life ahead—and, of course, there is nothing like unleashing a bit of aggression to help us feel alive.

That same autumn, thoughts of death increasingly preoccupied Winnicott. At the start of one of the final lectures he gave, he spoke of his predicament in the following way: "A great deal of growing is growing downwards. If I live long enough I hope I may dwindle and become small enough to get through the little hole called dying." The task of dying for Winnicott involved a central dilemma: how to grow downward and feel fully alive at the same time. In framing old age and decline with an illusion of choice and presenting our final exit as a reversal of the way we enter the world, he employed his trademark humor to lend a little bit of mastery to his otherwise helpless situation.

The growing downward that Winnicott described afflicts us all, and brings with it an unavoidable sense of loss. As we decline, there is no escaping the way that the canvas of life shrinks. Many things are taken away from us or are no longer accessible. Our plans and our dreams have to shrink too. In the face of this, gardening can help maintain a sense of purpose. It can be a way of grappling with our place in the world and help us feel we have some grip on life, that at least there is *something* that's under our control and not everything is running through our fingers. Concerns about mortality may be the least conscious part of it, but there is nothing that compensates us for growing downward better than something that is growing upward.

For gardening to be affirmative like this, it needs to be on a manageable scale. Looking out of a window at a neglected and overgrown patch that has previously been a source of pride can be worse than having no garden at all—a painful reminder of not being able to cope. Garden sharing schemes can offer a solution to this predicament. The Edinburgh Garden Partners program in Scotland, for example, matches people who are keen to grow food but lack access to a plot of land with people who need help with a garden that they can no longer manage. There are clear benefits on both sides. The shared sense of interest can lead to a renewed sense of pleasure and the formation of friendships can help to combat the isolation of old age. Research on a similar program that ran for a number of years in Wandsworth, South London, found that the quality of life of the elderly garden owners was significantly improved—their levels of physical activity increased, and symptoms such as anxiety and depression were reduced.

To tackle the problems of old age in contemporary society, we need to come up with creative solutions like this, but for the most part we lack a viable model. As the years of advanced old age grow longer, it is more important than ever that we attend to them. What is the point of living another decade or two if the quality of life is abysmal? So often, the elderly are sidelined and "parked" out of sight, and there is a lack of respect for their needs and a lack of interest in what they have to offer in the way of life wisdom and memories. Diana Athill was fully aware of how fortunate she was to have access to such a beautiful garden and grow plants on her balcony. Many retirement homes are not like this; in fact, most are not. Life in residential care is all too often a restricted indoor life. It consists of set routines that roll themselves out in a relatively unattractive and unchanging environment. Existence is reduced to waiting—waiting for the next dose of medication and waiting for the next meal. It is essentially a matter of waiting to die.

In *Being Mortal*, Atul Gawande explains how important it is to have a source of meaning as the end of life approaches. Sadly, most care homes do nothing to help provide this: "As people become aware of the finitude of their life," he writes, "they do not ask for much. They do not seek more riches. They do not seek more power. They ask only to be permitted, insofar as possible, to keep shaping the story of their life in the world." Institutions don't normally allow for much individual life-shaping but it doesn't have to be this way.

Gawande goes on to describe what happened at the Chase Memorial Nursing Home in New York when pets and plants were introduced. The changes involved establishing a vegetable patch and flower garden and installing hundreds of potted plants. Rabbits, hens, parakeets, cats, and dogs also injected life into the place. The results were dramatic: people who had barely spoken started interacting, others who had been inactive were drawn into new activities, and those who had been anxious and agitated were calmer and happier.

Over a two-year period, the changes were measured and the findings were compared to an ordinary nursing home nearby. Not only were the residents at Chase Memorial less depressed and more alert, the death rate fell 15 percent and the number of prescriptions for medication halved. These are strong outcomes from simple changes. As Gawande writes, feelings of effacement and exclusion were reversed: "The terror of sickness and old age is not merely the terror of the losses one is forced to endure but also the terror of isolation."

Loneliness can be one of the most painful aspects of growing old. A low-grade state of separation distress can set in with detrimental effects on health. The last paper that the psychoanalyst

Melanie Klein wrote, a year before she died, was on the subject of loneliness. The extent to which we feel lonely when we are isolated depends to a large extent on what we make of our earlier life experiences. Feelings of resentment and grievance about the fact that many pleasures are no longer available can act as confirmation of life's emptiness and serve only to reinforce the lonely state. By contrast, memories of happier times, Klein observed, can be an emotional resource, particularly if we cultivate gratitude for the past.

The enjoyment of beauty can provide a kind of companionship that helps to alleviate feelings of isolation. The philosopher Roger Scruton described how our pleasure in beauty is "like a gift offered to the object which is in turn a gift offered to me," and he argued, "in this respect it resembles the pleasure that people experience in the company of their friends." To feel that something is beautiful is also linked to gratitude, and the experience helps us feel at home in the world. The love of flowers certainly did this for Freud. In a letter he sent to the American poet H.D. in his eightieth year, thanking her for a datura plant that she had sent him as a Christmas present, Freud wrote: "In front of my window ... stands a proud sweet-smelling plant. Only twice have I seen it bloom in a garden, at the Lago di Garda and in the Val Lugano. It reminds me of those bygone days when I was still able to move around and visit the sunshine of southern nature myself."

Freud's travels would have given him plenty of other memories to draw on. On his first visit to Italy, for instance, he encountered an unforgettable garden. Near the end of his trip, feeling footsore and weary, he and his brother Alexander arrived at the Torre del Gallo in the hills outside Florence. They stayed for four days. As he described in a letter to Martha, this place offered no ordinary respite: "One gets round to nothing in this heavenly beauty, it's paralysing. . . . The Paradise Garden plays its part, luring us into hours of slumber under the fig trees." The sensuality of the place extended to its produce: "The whole meal comes from the garden except the excellent beef. Fresh figs, peaches, almonds from the trees that we have already gotten to know personally." The grounds, which had panoramic views over Florence, were large enough to wander about in freely and take in "the whole dizziness of southern beauty."

What could be more luxurious than ripe peaches, fresh from the tree, imparting the sun's heat so fragrantly to the mouth? What could be more restful than lying under a fig tree, drifting in and out of consciousness with half-hidden thoughts bobbing about? How easy it would be on a hot summer day in a place like this to slip into daydreams with only the gentle humming of the insects and the slightest breeze as disturbance—no shouting in the streets, or sudden intrusions to jolt you from your reverie. Paradise offers a supremely safe and gratifying experience that takes us back to the earliest phase of our lives. We witness it in the blissful state of a well-fed baby lying soothed and sleepy, for whom the comfort of familiar voices fading in the background means there is nothing whatsoever to fear.

Freud never lost his appetite for beauty and spent increasing amounts of time in the garden as he aged. When he was in his late sixties, a cancerous growth was removed from his mouth, following which his doctors forbade him to travel. He found it hard to reconcile himself to the physical restrictions imposed on him and the prospect, as he put it, of living "life under a sentence." He started a pattern of renting a villa in the suburbs of Vienna for the spring and summer months each year, and his patients would drive out to see him. The main requirement for Freud was to have access to a lovely garden. In the villa at Pötzleinsdorf he found "unbelievable beauty, peace and closeness to nature," and he enjoyed the "idyllically quiet and beautiful" villa at Berchtesgaden, but it was the villa at Grinzing that had the loveliest setting of all. He once described it as "beautiful like a fairy tale," and having found this place, he did not want to stay anywhere else, returning to it in subsequent years.

His son Martin recalled that the grounds of the villa at Grinzing were "large enough to be called a park in which one could get lost" and that it had a "fine orchard which offered delicious early apricots." Ten acres were enclosed within its walls, and it had views over the vineyards to the landscape beyond. Freud had an outdoor swing bed, shaded by a canopy, that was made especially for him, and when he was at Grinzing, he would read, slumber, and receive visitors in it. The garden here was a fitting place, he declared, in which to "die in beauty." By this stage, although he continued to work, Freud had more or less withdrawn from public life. In the course of his illness, he would undergo a total of thirty-three surgical interventions on his jaw and mouth. These prolonged his life but often left him in pain, and he experienced numerous complications and infections.

During an interview with the American journalist George Viereck that took place shortly after his seventieth birthday, Freud repeatedly spoke of his love of flowers. The interview took place in the garden, and as they set off on their walk Freud said: "I enjoyed many things—the comradeship of my wife, my children, the sunsets. I watched the plants grow in the springtime." Experience had taught him, he added, "to accept life with cheerful humility." Viereck could not help but notice an impediment in Freud's speech. As a result of surgery to remove the tumor in his mouth, Freud had a mechanical device replacing part of his jaw. The mechanism, he told Viereck, consumed his precious energy, but he was still able to enjoy his work, his family, and his garden: "I am grateful," he said to Viereck, "for the absence of pain, and for life's little pleasures, for my children and for my flowers!"

Freud was unwilling to be drawn into speaking on the subject of his legacy, and when Viereck pressed him, he came to a halt and "tenderly caressed a blossoming bush with his sensitive hands whilst saying 'I am far more interested in this blossom, than in anything that may happen to me after I am dead.'" Having covered other subjects as they walked and talked, Freud returned to this one at the end of the interview. His parting words to Viereck were: "Flowers fortunately have neither character nor complexities. I love my flowers. And I am not unhappy—at least not more unhappy than others."

The restrictions of old age and illness limit the potential for experiences of novelty, but a garden offers a setting in which the closer we look, the more we see. When a tree comes into blossom overnight or the first peony opens, we cannot help but look on the world with fresh eyes. Hanns Sachs, an old friend of Freud's, noted how Freud observed "every particle of his garden with the same zest and told as many interesting things about what happened there as about the art and civilisation of foreign countries and their faraway past, the relics of which he had studied on the spot in more vigorous times."

As he approached his eighties and his condition deteriorated further, Freud was sometimes gripped by a "dread of renewed suffering." Nazism was on the rise, and the world outside the garden was rapidly becoming frightening and bewildering. His works had been among those destroyed in the book burnings of Berlin in May 1933, and the Gestapo continued to confiscate them from bookstores. "Everything around me is getting darker, more threatening," Freud wrote, but he did not want to go into exile, as some colleagues and friends had begun to do. "Where would I turn in my dependency and physical helplessness?" he asked his friend Arnold Zweig. Even if a place were to be found for him and his family, he was unsure if his health could withstand such an uprooting, so he decided, for the time being at least, to "sit it out resignedly."

When Sachs visited him at Grinzing shortly after his eightieth birthday, he found him much changed. Recent surgery for a recurrence of the cancer had left Freud "bowed-down, icy-grey, shrivelled." Nevertheless, he was determined not to miss his daily excursions around the garden: "When he had a good day he, who had been such an indefatigable walker, was able to climb step by step the ascending garden path, at other times he moved in a wheel chair while I walked at his side. He spoke little of his work but pointed out the interesting things in his garden." Even in his frail state, Freud stuck to the habit of consciously directing his mind toward sources of interest and beauty outside himself.

When life forecloses on us, the lack of a sense of a future is the hardest thing to deal with. It requires us to make the most of a little and find small things to look forward to. This strategy had also been employed by Montaigne, who found that an effective way of managing the losses of old age was to "run through the bad and settle on the good." If his mind wandered onto negative thoughts when he was taking his daily walk in his orchard, Montaigne would consciously shift his attention back to his surroundings to make sure he cherished them. The small pleasures of life are not so small really; it is just that we get into the habit of taking them for granted.

In the spring of 1938, Freud was unable to return to his Grinzing refuge. Under the Nazi regime, he was a virtual prisoner in his Berggasse Street apartment. Representations from abroad were made on his behalf, including one from President Roosevelt. He endured months of uncertainty about his status, until finally, in early June, he and his immediate family were allowed to travel to England. In spite of his efforts to bring three of his sisters with him, they were not allowed to accompany him; forced to remain in Vienna, they later died in Auschwitz.

Freud was overwhelmed by the generosity that greeted him when he arrived in London. Antiquities were sent to him by strangers who had heard about the loss of his precious collection which, along with his savings, had been confiscated by the Nazis. Word had also spread of his passion for flowers. Florist vans arrived bearing plants and bouquets in such numbers, that with characteristic black humor, Freud quipped, "We are buried in flowers."

It was high summer, and the garden of the family's first and temporary home on Elsworthy Road in Swiss Cottage was ablaze with color. It bordered on the park at Primrose Hill and was a source of great joy. Freud wrote of how from his window he could see nothing but greenery: "My room looks out onto a veranda which overlooks our own garden framed with flower beds and gives onto a large tree-studded park." A brief home movie taken by his great friend the Princess Marie Bonaparte shows the family taking tea on the veranda. The shot then moves to Freud standing with two of his grandsons, Lucian and Stephen, gazing at the fish in a lily pond. It is said that this garden helped re-animate Freud, and the camera certainly catches a spring in his step as he spots something in the water and crosses to the other side of the pond.

As a refugee in a strange country, the familiar plants and trees at Elsworthy Road provided Freud with a feeling of reassurance. "It is as though we were living in Grinzing, " he wrote. There was also a potted plant that provided a link with home. I learned of its existence when a friend gave me a cutting that originated from it. It is a zimmerlinde, or *Sparrmannia Africana*, otherwise known as a house lime, and it is believed that the Freuds brought it with them as a small cutting from a larger plant growing in the conservatory at Berggasse Street. With its large, fresh green leaves and pretty white flowers, the zimmerlinde is a vigorous grower, and judging by the rate at which ours has grown, by the following spring, Freud's plant would have been a few feet tall.

The Freud family moved into their new London home on Maresfield Gardens in September 1938. Ernest Jones observed "how much he enjoyed the pretty garden" there. Compared to the Viennese gardens that Freud had loved, this house had a relatively small yard, but it was the first garden that the family had owned, and Freud wanted to see it through all the four seasons, something he had never been able to do in the gardens of the villas he had rented. He shared his love of nature most strongly with his daughter Anna Freud, now a pioneering child psychoanalyst, and it was she who tended the plants.

Freud's son Ernst, the architect, had installed wide French doors at the back of the house, which opened from his father's study into the garden, so that Freud's desk was bathed in sunlight and had a lovely view. The sheltered garden proved the perfect place in which to re-erect Freud's Grinzing garden swing bed, which had traveled with him to London. A home movie taken in October that year shows Freud being tucked into it and covered with blankets to keep him warm. Sachs recalls how the old trees in the neighboring gardens "greeted one over the walls" and gave the garden a feeling of seclusion. Many of the plants, such as the clematis, roses, and hydrangeas that were there in Freud's time, are still growing today in the garden of the Freud Museum, at the same address.

A few months after his arrival in England, the Nazi administration decided to release his precious collection of antiquities. After it was delivered, Freud wrote to his friend and colleague Jeanne Lampl-de Groot: "All the Egyptians, Chinese and Greeks have arrived, have stood up to the journey with very little damage, and look more impressive here than in Berggasse." This event was a cause of great excitement throughout the house and a huge relief to Freud, but for him the feeling was tempered by a kind of flatness: "There is just one thing," he wrote, "a collection to which there are no new additions is really dead."

His antiquities would be an important part of his legacy, but that phase of his life was now over; he could no longer make the collection grow because he lacked both funds and energy to seek out new acquisitions. Besides, possessions have a static quality, and they tend to loosen their hold on people as they approach the

230

deathbed. We have to breathe life into them through investing them with significance, whereas the beauty of the natural world breathes life into us. Unlike Freud's collection of antiquities, his garden was still growing and was something that he and Anna could make plans for.

In his work on the psychology of dying, the psychiatrist Robert Lifton showed the importance of finding ways to symbolize immortality. In doing this, he was building on Freud's idea that the unconscious mind has no way of representing our own death. Lifton argued that we need to deny death, at least in part, and that this paradoxically helps us to accept its reality. The prospect of annihilation is too terrifying; the mind cannot assimilate it, and we have to find ways to make dying less absolute. We can achieve this through various forms of what Lifton called "symbolical survival," which according to him includes our genes living on in the next generation, as well as beliefs about the afterlife, our own creativity, and the continuity of nature.

Our deep existential need for symbolic survival is one of the reasons why when people are confronted with death, their relationship with nature often takes on a whole new significance. This aspect of nature is consoling not only to the dying but to the bereaved too. Planting a tree in remembrance of someone who has died provides a potent source of symbolic survival. We know that time will fade our memories, but the tree will bring new growth. It puts down deep roots like a guarantee against oblivion.

The love of flowers is a love that can be shared and throughout life Freud took great pleasure in giving flowers to women he admired. When Virginia Woolf paid him a visit at Maresfield Gardens, he didn't miss the opportunity. Leonard documented how he was "extraordinarily courteous in a formal old-fashioned way" and "almost ceremoniously presented Virginia with a flower." Progressive

231

illness and decline can be so brutal and cruel. Quite how disabled and frail Freud became over that winter is documented in Virginia Woolf's diary entry for January 29, 1939. She records his "paralysed spasmodic movements, inarticulate: but alert." His speech may have been impaired, but flowers have a language of their own, and the flower Freud gave her was one of his favorites: a narcissus.

The arrival of spring that year was enormously important to the dying Freud. It was too early to erect the swing bed, but he could sit out in the loggia that Ernst had built onto the back of the house. Open to the elements on one side, it provided a sheltered space from which the garden could be enjoyed when the weather was too cold for his outdoor bed. Known as threshold spaces, constructions like loggias, conservatories, verandas, and balconies provide an experience of being half-inside, half-outside; the best of both worlds.

Structures like this are increasingly recognized for the role they can play in the care of the elderly and the dying. When life is on the threshold itself, a physical threshold is helpful. To be able to watch the wind scudding the clouds across the sky means that life is not completely closing in. When the feet can't travel, the eyes can still roam, and when the birds sing, the mind can sometimes soar and inhabit the trees alongside them.

By the early summer, in common with most people in the closing stages of life, Freud was sleeping a lot. As often as he could, he did this outdoors. His family would sometimes sit around him as he lay on his garden bed, but he was never alone, for his dog, Lun, whom he was devoted to, was a constant companion. Freud would lie in the garden, as Sachs describes, "sometimes in light slumber, sometimes caressing his chow who did not leave his side for a moment." As the summer progressed, the open wound on Freud's jaw developed a deep-rooted infection that showed no signs of shifting. For many years, eating had been difficult, but now it became even harder, and he grew weaker as a result. His bed was brought down from his room upstairs, and his study was converted into a sickroom so that he could lie and look out at the garden.

In early September, the skin over his cheekbone showed signs of gangrene and started to give off an appalling stench. This development proved to be the end of his relationship with Lun. The dog's instincts came to the fore, and she reacted in accordance with a state of primal fear. When Lun was brought into Freud's study, she crouched in the farthest corner and could not be prodded into coming near him. There was at least still the garden to turn to for solace. The French doors were kept open as much as possible, and Freud's bed was positioned so he could gaze out at the flowers he loved. Flowers can be guaranteed not to reject us.

In the last few weeks of his life, Anna as his main nurse was assisted by Ernst's wife, Lucie. In a letter written the following month, Lucie records how in spite of Freud being in so much pain, "a peaceful, cheerful, almost homely mood prevailed in the sick room." In his waking moments he was "indescribably friendly and loving with all of us, touchingly patient in putting up with everything."

Freud once wrote that dying is an achievement, that when we hear news of someone's death, we can feel something like admiration for the task completed. It is, after all, an existential accomplishment to detach yourself from your loved ones and let go of life. Freud died in the early hours of September 23, 1939, a year and a week since the family had taken up residence in the house. When Freud had first arrived, he wanted to see the garden through all four seasons. That wish was fulfilled. The garden accompanied him through the last year of his life.

In the refuge of a garden, we are surrounded by Mother Nature at her most benign and beautiful. We are protected from all things capricious and hostile. In such moments of peace, all is well with the world. When faced with the need to prepare for death, the psyche needs to find a resting place, and Freud found one in the garden.

This resting place concerns more than nature's calming and

soothing effects; a garden stimulates the imagination and triggers recollections as well. For Freud there were so many beautiful places enshrined in memory: the Grinzing garden, "like a fairy tale" that he loved to walk in, and the Torre del Gallo, "the paradise garden" that captivated him when he was footsore and weary. Then there were his trips to the mountains, where he sought out orchids and wild strawberries, and the shady groves in the woods in which he felt so at home, and his boyhood wanderings in the wildflower meadows near where he was born, and last of all, the arms of his youthful mother, she who first taught him about death.

Our mother's arms are, after all, the very first place we come to know. Freud noted the significance of this earlier in his life when he wrote of how "the Mother Earth" receives us again. But, he added, "it is in vain that the old man yearns after the love of woman as once he had it from his mother; the third of the Fates alone, the silent goddess of Death, will take him into her arms."

The idea of death as a return is powerfully expressed in Helen Dunmore's last book of poetry, *Inside the Wave*. In it, she charts her journey toward death and her need to find a resting place. The last poem, written only ten days before she died, is called "Hold Out Your Arms." It starts with her asking for death's "motherly caress," and she focuses on the irises in her garden: "the bearded iris that bakes its rhizomes / Beside the wall," whose scent "flashes with loveliness." She wonders how death will take her and then realizes:

> there's no need to ask:
> A mother will always lift a child
> As a rhizome
> Must lift up a flower.

Then she takes the personification further:

As you push back my hair
—Which could do with a comb
But never mind—
You murmur
"We're nearly there."

Death is faceless, and anything that is faceless is terrifying, as is the prospect of falling into a void. We feel safer when we can reach out to something familiar, as if in grasping hold of one hand, we can let go of another. Dunmore places her trust in the iris and its rhizome, and it gives her a sense that a natural process is unfolding.

The different ways in which we symbolize death determine how frightening or not it is, and how natural or unnatural it feels. Since the beginning of culture, plants and flowers have influenced people's understanding of living and dying. They lend structure to our thinking in a way that helps ward off fear and despair. The return of spring each year can be endlessly relied on, and in not dying when we die, we have a sense of goodness going forward. This is the garden's most enduring consolation.

CHAPTER 11

Garden Time

A secluded part of Alnarp Rehabilitation
Garden, Sweden.

*Gardening imparts an organic perspective on the passage
of time.*

William Cowper (1731–1800)

When life comes adrift, garden time can get you going again. One
spring, a few years back, when I was recovering from a period of
illness and intense work stress, I had my own experience of this.

For the previous thirteen years, I had been working as a consult-
ant psychiatrist running a National Health Service psychotherapy

department. Given the severity and complexity of the patients that we looked after, I was used to carrying a high level of responsibility and managing a certain amount of stress, but then the service I worked for was required to find major savings, as much as 20 percent, over the next four years. Mental health care had always been underfunded, and it seemed so very wrong that it was being cut further.

There followed a period of organizational restructuring that led to the closure of specialist teams, including the one that I ran. A number of my colleagues were laid off, and in the months that followed some others decided to leave. The loss of the psychotherapy team combined with an increase in my workload had left me feeling powerless and isolated. Nevertheless, I resolved to carry on. The following year, I was stopped in my tracks by a sudden attack of inflammatory arthritis. I had always had a strong commitment to my job, but I was off work and immobilized for long enough to realize that I could no longer ignore its effect on my health. The extent of this became clearer after I left the following summer, because no sooner had I done so, than I was laid low by an attack of shingles.

As that autumn progressed, I hoped for a resurgence of energy, but it didn't come. The lethargy dragged on into winter, and the wintery feeling dragged on into March. Usually when spring arrives, I can't wait to get out to the greenhouse, but that year was different. Even though I had long ago ordered a selection of seeds, they were all still sitting in their packets.

One weekend morning, Tom suggested we get started in the greenhouse together. It was certainly in need of a clean. We set to work, clearing out dead leaves, old broken pots, and all the rest of the previous year's debris. Then we rearranged the plants on the shelving and filled up the repotting buckets with fresh compost. Just as we were finishing off, I began rifling through my box of seed packets, and for the first time, I started planning what to sow.

The following day, right after breakfast, I went outside, intending to pop into the greenhouse and make a start on a few seed trays, but I hadn't been out there long before I was gripped by an urgent need to get things into the ground. I worked through my feelings of tiredness as if nothing else mattered. By the end of that day, there were lettuces, carrots, spinach, beetroot, kale, coriander, parsley, basil, and more—all sown in seed trays or lined out in the vegetable patch. I sowed flowers too—calendula, larkspur, sweet peas, and cosmos—all these things no longer nascent in my mind, but actually in the soil, soon to grow. Throughout the previous months, I had been marooned, a hapless surfer watching the waves rolling by. But that day was different, I caught a ride on the wave of time—garden time that is—which with its seasonal pull and energy of new growth can carry you along.

Seeds have tomorrow ready-built into them. They set off the pleasure of planning and new possibilities. They give you a toehold in the future, and it's a future you can easily imagine. You have the knowledge that whatever else happens, at least the lettuce and calendula will grow. There may be pests and bad weather to contend with, but you can hedge your bets, and if some things fail, others will likely thrive.

All the time, in all sorts of ways, we are investing in an unknown future, but when events conspire and life feels out of control, it is hard to dare to dream. The garden is a safe place to begin, and it gives you structure and discipline too—it is not about unboundaried possibilities. There is no negotiating with the march of the seasons or the pace of the natural growth force. You cannot slow them down or speed them up. You have to submit to the rhythm of garden time and you have to work within that frame.

The pace is at its most exhilarating in spring and early summer. However much this motivates me, there are times when the rolling sequence of tasks becomes too much and just looking at the garden can make me feel weary. I want to say, "Can't you just slow down a little! Can we have an extra week in the month, please?" But then I realize it is me who needs to slow down.

We talk of a sense of time, but there is no dedicated center for perceiving it in the brain, no sensory organ that detects its passing. The neuroscientist David Eagleman, who researches the perception of time, refers to it as a distributed property of the brain. It is, he says, "metasensory; it rides on top of all the others." In effect, we experience the passage of time through a complex weaving together of emotion, sensation, and memory, and this means our experience of time is closely linked to our sense of self—in fact some people regard it as a product of the self because of the degree to which our feelings radically alter our perception of time's passing.

We can live in the present, dwell in the past, and project into the future. Time is a construct, and our experience of life is heavily influenced by how we think about the passing of time, and the habits we form around it. Time can be understood as a series of recurring cycles, or we can think of it, as we mostly do these days, in its more modern, linear form.

Cyclical time was the first way of understanding time and made sense for people who lived close to the earth, but the circularity of time was not only about the recurrence of the seasons; the earliest narratives took a circular form too. In myths, legends, and folktales, we find the figure of a hero who sets off on a quest and then returns to recount his adventures. The Arthurian knights are a classic example: a narrative loop brings the hero back to the place where he started, and it is only on his homecoming that his story is woven together. This circular narrative structure lies deep in our psychological ancestry; it goes back to the hunter-gatherer way of life and tales of excursions told in the evening by the campfire.

The mind does not employ a linear approach to time because the brain is a predictive organ. We make endless returns to the past in order to make sense of the present and anticipate the future. If we have a period of being consumed by activity or have been overtaken by fast-paced events, we need eventually to bring ourselves back to a calmer state, for it is only then that we can reflect on and assimilate the things that have happened to us. The parasympathetic rest-and-digest state is about both physical and psychological digestion because it is not only the food in our gut but our feelings that need to be metabolized. This process is how we construct our own narrative. If we lack time and mental space for this, experience feels more like one disparate or unconnected event after another. Life starts to lack meaning.

The garden is a place that brings us back to the basic biological rhythms of life. The pace of life is the pace of plants; we are forced to slow down, and the feeling of safe enclosure and familiarity helps shift us to a more reflective state of mind. The garden gives us a cyclical narrative too. The seasons come around again, and we have a sense of return; some things are altered, some things are the same. The structure of seasonal time has consolations. Kinder to the psyche, it lets you learn, because you get second chances. If something fails this year, you know you can try again at the same time next year.

Linear time is more uncompromising, and its finite quality is harder to live by. It's like an arrow on a fixed trajectory that doesn't recognize our bodies' need for cycles of rest and recovery, or that the land needs this too. When everything is about utilizing time for maximum output, we become preoccupied with not wasting time and feel we don't have enough time. We end up trying to live by a clock that we are always trying to beat.

Living life as a series of buzzes and adrenaline rushes can easily become addictive, and an underlying exhaustion, paradoxically, makes the pattern harder to take a break from. This can turn into a way of escaping from problems rather than sorting them out, making it easier to keep up the pace rather than slow down and set aside time to take stock.

In this age of fast food, speed dating, 1-click ordering, same day delivery—the quicker all manner of needs are satisfied the better.

The endless stream of posts, notifications, alerts, emails, and tweets requires us to absorb so much new information that it is hard to assess what might be relevant. There is a lack of time to digest experience, understand it, or even remember it, because our individual and collective memories are increasingly outsourced to the cloud.

Our sense of time passing is, in fact, closely linked to the amount of memory we lay down. Time spent in new places or in situations that require us to notice a lot of detail always seems to last longer, because we are laying down more memories. In contrast, time spent on the internet flies by almost faster than anything else, for it does not require the same kind of attention and we are not laying down much in the way of memory.

Our autobiographical timeline is composed of memories, but our sense of time elapsed is often hazy. This is because memory has a much stronger relationship to place than it does to the chronology of the clock. It is why we are often unsure about how long ago something happened but invariably know where it happened. Our remote ancestors living in the wild needed to map terrain and recall the whereabouts of resources, so there are evolutionary reasons why location might function as something like an index card to the memory system. In consequence, over the course of our lives, places become intimately woven into our autobiographical narrative and our sense of self.

The relationship to both time and place has been disrupted. If we want, we can do almost anything at any time of the clock and have access to it wherever we are. The digital world makes it hard to fully inhabit the place we are in; it keeps us semi-distracted and partially elsewhere. Furthermore, the differentiation between work time and rest time, daytime and nighttime has been eroded. Sleep is when the microglia cells in the brain carry out their restorative pruning and weeding activities, but many people run short on this most basic form of rest and recovery time.

• • •

Rising job insecurity and competitive cultures of overwork have led to a dramatic increase in workplace-based stress over the last couple of decades. Cities are full of offices in which people continue the working day well into the evening, and there are plenty of organizations in which it is considered a badge of honor not to take all your paid holiday leave. Many teachers, doctors, and nurses are struggling with increased demand to meet targets in services that are under-resourced. Whatever the line of work, it has become the norm for people to be at risk of burnout. Stress has recently become the most common single reason for people to take sick leave from work.

Burnout is what happens when there is not enough recovery time and the ability to regulate stress is lost. It increases the risk of depression and is linked to higher rates of a number of physical disorders, including heart disease and diabetes. Physical or mental collapse caused by overwork or stress was given the name "burn-out" in 1974 by the psychologist Herbert Freudenberger. One of the most important centers for treating burnout and stress disorders through horticulture is in Sweden. Over the last fifteen years or more, Professor Patrik Grahn and his colleagues at the University of Agricultural Sciences in Alnarp have developed an intensive twelve-week program of garden therapy. They have published numerous studies demonstrating the benefit of what has become known as "the Alnarp model."

The ethos is multidisciplinary. Grahn, who has a background in landscape architecture, designed the garden, and a team consisting of an occupational therapist, a physiotherapist, a psychodynamic psychotherapist, and a horticulturalist deliver the program. The majority of their patients are women, from professions like teaching, nursing, medicine, and law, who are on long-term sick leave and have not responded to other treatments. Typically, they are high-achieving, conscientious people whose health has collapsed through a combination of work overload and family commitments. They suffer from anxiety, and their lack of mental and physical energy means they find it hard to concentrate or make decisions. Because their self-esteem is strongly invested in performing well at work, they struggle with feelings of guilt and shame about not being able to work.

The Alnarp therapy garden is enclosed within a russet-red picket fence on the edge of the university campus. The program is run from a traditional wooden building in the center of the five-acre site. The main room has a simple, homey feel and opens onto a wooden deck overlooking the vegetable beds. Beyond these, there is an attractive open view over a meadow and woodland. Standing on the deck, you don't feel that this setup is part of a university or that there is a busy campus close by; only the distant noise of traffic on the highway breaks the feeling of total seclusion.

The garden encompasses both wild and cultivated nature because people have different needs at different stages of their treatment. The cultivation areas include two greenhouses and a mixture of raised and low-level beds for vegetables, fruits, and herbs. In contrast, the wilder parts of the garden offer an experience of nature free from a compulsion to do anything. There are also a number of secluded "garden rooms" where people can seek refuge.

The participants, most of whom have not gardened before, attend four mornings a week for twelve weeks. After a few days of settling in, the therapist tells them to choose a restful place where they can spend time alone. Some carry mattresses out to the wilder parts of the garden; others use the hammock, the swing seat, or one of the benches in the garden rooms. Through their illness they have become disconnected from their bodies and from the world. They need to find a way to reestablish contact at the most basic level through their senses and feelings.

One of the garden rooms has a particularly inviting small wood-land corner with a hammock strung up between the trees. In May, when I visited, this part of the garden was looking fresh and green, with white tulips in flower. The hammock had been put up that week. Each year, the miscanthus grass grows up in front of it, creating a private enclosure for rest and repose, as the smell of cinnamon wafts in the air from the nearby katsura tree. This woodland corner also contains a pond that is surrounded by mossy stones with a large boulder at one end.

The presence of trees, stones, and water is important in the thinking behind the garden design, which partly draws on the work of the American psychiatrist and psychoanalyst Harold Searles. He was writing in the 1960s, and even then was troubled by the extent to which technology was interfering with people's ability to relate to nature. "Over recent decades," he wrote, "we have come from dwelling in another world in which the living works of nature either predominated or were near at hand, to dwelling in an environment dominated by a technology which is wondrously powerful and yet nevertheless dead." He believed that our capacity to experience profound meaning through the natural world is often only revealed when we are in crisis. For someone who has become disconnected from life, a relationship to a much simpler form of life offers a crucial sense of reconnection. Searles identified a hierarchy of complexity, with relationships to people being the most complex, followed by animals, then plants, then stones.

Johan Ottosson, who works with Grahn, experienced this first-hand nearly twenty years ago when he was knocked off his bicycle and suffered a devastating head injury that left him with a permanent disability. He later wrote about his experience in *The Importance of Nature in Coping with a Crisis*, a paper that has informed the work at Alnarp. Ottosson describes how his trauma threw him into a state of deep psychological disconnection. As he began to recover from his injuries, he took to walking in the park that surrounded the hospital where he was receiving treatment. Here he encountered a large "untouched stone" that seemed, in some way, "to speak" to him. With its "blanket of lichen and moss," it gave him his first experience of "calm and harmony" since the accident.

Through returning to the stone, he developed a relationship with it that allowed him to begin opening himself up to the world again. Everything in his life had been changed in a split second. In the context of this, the timeless quality of the stone had a reassuring effect on him: "The stone had been there long before the first human being had walked past. Countless generations, each with lives and fates of their own, had passed." His contact with the stone was profoundly stabilizing.

The staff at Alnarp regularly observe the need to revert to simpler relations with trees, water, or stones. Their participants are free to choose what they want to commune with, and occasionally someone will clamber up to sit on the flat top of the large boulder by the pond. Finding a safe way of beginning to relate to the world like this helps them emerge from their closed-in state. After a week or two, their feelings of curiosity begin to return, and they start exploring the rest of the garden. As they do so, there are plenty of opportunities for foraging, and the wild strawberries, in particular, are popular.

After about six weeks, most of the participants are experiencing a better quality of sleep, and their physical and mental energy is improving. Their scores on rating scales for feelings of empowerment and emotional coherence are monitored, and by now these are showing improvement. They are able to get stuck into longer spells of garden work, which helps relieve the muscular tension that many of them suffer from. Part of the state of disconnection is that they have long since stopped listening to warning signals from their bodies. Now they are encouraged to tune in and take breaks when they feel tired.

Many garden tasks are of the repetitive type that allow participants to find a sense of rhythm. When this happens, mind, body, and environment can come together and function in harmony. Entering into what is known as a *flow* state is profoundly restorative on several levels. It strengthens parasympathetic functioning and promotes brain health through increasing levels of a whole range of antidepressant neurotransmitters, like endorphins, serotonin, and dopamine, as well as raising levels of BDNF. The combined effect is one of pleasurable and relaxed focus.

Flow states were first described by the psychologist Mihaly Csikszentmihalyi in the 1980s when he was conducting research into the characteristics of emotionally satisfying work. He identified how athletes, artists, musicians, gardeners, and craftsmen, to name a few, are all engaged in activities where they can get into "the zone" and feel at one with what they are doing. The result, as Csikszentmihalyi describes, is that "the ego falls away. Time flies. Every action, movement, and thought follows inevitably from the previous one." Flow doesn't occur in all activities that are rhythmical, because if they are not absorbing enough, the mind can still ruminate on things. Csikszentmihalyi established that flow states are more likely to occur when there is a matching of skills and challenge, so that the task is neither too easy nor too difficult.

People often describe a pleasurable feeling of "losing themselves" when they become fully immersed in doing something, and this is what Csikszentmihalyi is referring to when he says, "the ego falls away." This unconstrained state of losing yourself arises because flow temporarily slows down activity in the prefrontal cortex, a state that is called hypo-frontality, so for the duration, we are less self-scrutinizing and can more freely experience creative thoughts. We all need periods of time in which we feel free from self-criticism and judgment, but it brings particular relief to someone suffering from depression and anxiety, because the self-monitoring circuits that link the frontal cortex to the more primitive parts of the brain, including the amygdala, are overactive in these conditions.

As the Alnarp garden participants become more in touch with their bodies and feelings, they start to connect with deep, raw emotions relating to aspects of their past that they have previously been unable to acknowledge. Some are able to express these feelings in the group sessions or one-to-one sessions with their therapist, while others take themselves off to a far-flung part of the garden, where, unobserved and unheard, they can let their feelings go.

After this stage of emotional catharsis, a new phase starts in which the symbolic meaning that can be derived from gardening becomes more important. The way that it emerges is different for each person and depends on an individual's life history and particular problems. Caring for a seedling can help someone realize how little they have been caring for themselves. Pulling up weeds can encourage an inner process of letting toxic feelings go, and working with the compost heap can strengthen a belief that something good can follow bad. The therapists understand that much of this goes on unconsciously and try to help people put their experiences into words.

In the last few weeks of the Alnarp program, time is devoted to group activities. The focus of the program becomes more sociable, and the participants are generally ready to cope with this development. A follow-up study has shown that one year later, more than 60 percent of participants had returned to some kind of work or training, and their visits to the family doctor have dropped on average from thirty a year to five. Because it helps people on long-term sick leave return to work, the Alnarp program is regarded as a cost-effective intervention by the county council, who support it as a result.

Anna María Pálsdóttir, one of the lead researchers on the Alnarp garden, has produced a study called *The Journey of Recovery*, which is based on in-depth interviews with participants both during and three months after treatment. These revealed that the "unconditional" acceptance of nature was therapeutically important to them. When fears of rejection and feelings of guilt and shame are strong, it can be hard in human interactions to allow yourself to be vulnerable like this. Finding a safe container for feelings in nature can be the start of a process that eventually helps people move on to more in-depth talking therapy.

Through spending time close to nature the participants learn, as Pálsdóttir puts it, "that there is a time for everything." They come to understand that when life becomes overly pressured, it starts to lack meaning and that a pause does not mean losing time if it brings with it a deeper connection to life. One woman spoke of how simply observing "a mini world that moves along at its own pace" gave rise to feelings of "happiness that you don't find at the hospital." Seedlings, trees, and stones have life cycles both much shorter and much longer than our own. The spectrum of time that can be experienced in a garden is an important part of the therapeutic effect.

Donald Winnicott once wrote of how a breakdown can be a breakthrough. The reason the breakdown occurs is that the coping strategies and psychological defenses that have served someone so far stop working and start causing problems of their own. A new attitude to life needs to emerge, and in this respect, tending plants can teach us how to live.

Caring for plants can help someone uncover a sense of self-compassion so that the sense of failure and harsh self-criticism that accompany depression can begin to soften. Pálsdóttir found that, three months after completing the treatment, the participants had all changed their lifestyles. They had acquired an understanding of their own rhythms of rest and revitalization and were finding ways to spend time in nature each week. Some were going on long walks, others had started gardening at home, and a number had taken on work in a community garden.

Gardening can be understood as a form of space-time medicine. Working outdoors helps expand our sense of mental space, and the growth cycles of plants can alter the relationship we have with time. There is an old riff that Susan Sontag once quoted that goes like this: "Time exists in order that everything doesn't happen all at once . . . and space exists so that it doesn't all happen to you." When we are ill, the reverse of both these things is true. Depression, trauma, and anxiety all shrink our temporal horizons and contract our sense of mental space. Feelings of hopelessness and fear foreshorten the future. The past and the present become more or less merged through dwelling on old hurts and the inward turn of the mind means it feels as if "everything" is happening to you.

The experience of slow time has an important role to play in counteracting this. Slow time does not mean doing things more slowly. People suffering from burnout and depression have slowed down considerably and not been restored. Slow time is entering into a living relationship with the present. Carl Jung cultivated this experience himself through spending time at his tower on the lakeshore at Bollingen. Here, lacking electricity, he entered into the natural rhythms of life. He would write in the morning, and then after a siesta, he would work outdoors, tending his potato patch and his maize field as well as chopping wood. During the war, he cultivated more land, and apart from corn and potatoes, he grew beans, wheat, and poppies for oil. These activities always restored and refreshed him. "For it is the body, the feeling, the instincts, which connect us with the soil," he wrote. Through grounding himself in nature, he experienced the immense interconnectedness of life: "At times I feel as if I am spread out over the landscape and inside things, and am myself living in every tree, in the splashing of the waves, in the clouds and the animals that come and go, in the procession of the seasons." For Jung, such experiences were a way of accessing the "two-million-year-old man that is in all of us."

The green exercise guru Jules Pretty, professor of environment and society at Essex University, thinks immersive experiences like this are a crucial part of nature's benefits for our mental health. Slow looking and slow listening nourishes and revitalizes us. Modern lifestyles, however, leave us short of opportunities for this kind of immersion—although many people seek it out in their spare time, through activities such as hiking, fishing, bird-watching, and gardening.

Pretty's team have carried out research that shows spending time in nature not only helps recovery from stress but helps people manage subsequent stress; in other words, it can act like a buffer that increases resilience. Another of their studies on community gardeners found they had higher levels of well-being than similar non-gardeners. Tending their plot helped reduce their levels of tension, anger, and confusion. Just one session a week of thirty minutes was enough to bring about significant improvements in mood and self-esteem.

Caring for a plot in a community garden is about putting down roots. In the UK, allotment plots are still measured in the ancient Anglo-Saxon pole system and are typically sized around five poles, which is 150 square yards. Many plot holders spend six to eight hours a week gardening in summer and about two hours in winter. Figures show that once people get past the first two years, they tend to stick with it.

On the outskirts of a town near where I live there are some allotment gardens tucked away in a field close to a railway line. Their patchwork of green and brown is a medley of conformity and individuality. The collection of small sheds, plastic compost bins, fruit cages, and bean poles give rise to a feeling of gentle industry. In summer, the plots are brimming with vegetables, but some of the allotment holders grow color too—clouds of pink and purple sweet peas and stands of bright yellow sunflowers.

Dorothy is one of the allotment holders here. She is in her early thirties and is a slight, rather elfin figure with long blond hair. As she told me, she sees herself as part of a generation who are turning back, as she put it, "to low-tech stuff." She refers to a wider social awakening in which "people are starting to realize that they're not happy when everything is done for them." Waiting lists for allotments are notoriously long, and Dorothy had been waiting for a number of years before her name came up. When it finally did, she was pregnant with her first child, a boy called Robin. The allotment was always going to be her project, not her husband's, and they both wondered if it was too much for her to take on at that point, but after all the waiting, she couldn't bear to let the opportunity go.

The plot Dorothy was allocated had fallen into neglect and was full of couch grass. Her heart sank at first, but she enlisted help from a friend who plowed it up for her with his tractor. Since then she has been working on improving the soil, composting everything and returning it to the ground. One of the first things she planted was an apple tree, and then lots of strawberry runners, so that now about a fifth of the plot is devoted to strawberries.

A hedgerow full of overgrown oak and hawthorn surrounds the site and it feels quiet and secluded. It is a perfect setting for Dorothy and her two children because she feels they will be safe even if they try to stray. But they rarely wander: Robin's younger sister, Poppy, likes to crawl about eating strawberries, while Dorothy gets on with weeding and Robin plays with his bulldozer in an area she has marked out for him with canes.

Regardless of what age we are, gardening can be a form of play. Winnicott described the psychological significance of the ability to play in the following way: "It is in playing and only in playing that an individual child . . . is able to be creative and . . . it is only in being creative that the individual finds the self." In this sense, play is not the distraction or diversion it might seem to be; it is a restorative activity that is highly invested with meaning. This has certainly been true for Dorothy, who has found that "if really big things are going on in your life, then you can make sense of them through the garden."

Part of that sustaining effect for Dorothy is about revisiting her childhood. She related memories of being with her father on his allotment. There were times when he pushed her along in a wheel-barrow, and she recalled "using rhubarb as an umbrella." In summer, she and her sister would make beds under the rhubarb plants. On one occasion, they fell asleep and their father found them lying curled up together in the shade of the giant leaves.

At home Dorothy and her husband only have a tiny outdoor space, and she finds looking after Robin, who is a "very physical" little boy, much easier on the allotment. Everyone there is friendly and the children have a ready-made supply of grandparents. She has made some friends there herself and likes the way there is a lack of competitiveness about gardening, so it feels easy to ask for advice and swap ideas. But while it can be sociable, it is important to Dorothy that it is not too sociable. Generally, people get on with doing their own thing, so that it is easy to spend time in solitude.

Having a baby is one of the most life-affirming and creative experiences, but it is also one of the most draining and demanding. Dorothy chose to give up work to be a full-time mother after Poppy arrived. About six months later, she found herself crying every day. She went into "a low spiral" and was prescribed antidepressants, which she took for a short time. Most of all, she was struggling with a loss of self-esteem: "You are a mum and you're not earning any money and you feel a bit demoted."

The allotment helped lift her out of that downward spiral. In particular, she found that nature's time frame, with its "window of opportunity," was a good antidote to procrastination. As she explained: "The garden gives you a purpose and a schedule. It regulates you, keeps you on your toes." This was not the case with other activities. "If I'm doing a patchwork quilt, it can sit in the drawer for years—there is no momentum."

The pull of the earthly calendar meant that Dorothy ended up getting her garlic in the ground with just an hour to go before she needed to collect Robin from preschool. "It was pelting down with rain, but I did it anyway—it was so good to be in the elements. It was such bad weather, I was almost laughing, but there was a real a sense of satisfaction that I got them all in the ground."

The garden has also given her a place of her own: "somewhere not at home that is my own space." This feeling of "being away" is important for her and is "more positive than just retreating, because I get stuff done." At home, she measures how well she is managing by the state of the house, which means she is constantly tidying up and dealing with the children's mess. Inevitably, almost as soon as something is done, it is undone, but dirt is not dirt in the garden, it is productive soil. As Dorothy put it: "You can't impose too much order on it. That's why it's good for you. You can't clean mud, you cultivate it."

In contrast to vacuuming and picking up toys around the house, Dorothy finds the tangible rewards in the garden deeply fulfilling. Last year she grew "huge leeks" as well lots of other produce, like chard, beetroot, and pumpkin. As she put it: "To be able to plant something, grow it, harvest it, and feed you and your children with it is very satisfying." The neuroscientist Kelly Lambert thinks that a belief in our ability to shape our lives originates through shaping our physical surroundings. When actions produce a result we can see, feel, and touch, we begin to feel more connected to the world around us and have an increased sense of control. "In our drive to do less physical work to acquire what we want and need, we've lost something vital to our mental well-being," she writes.

According to Lambert, the brain is tuned into manipulating the environment. When opportunities to do this are lacking, our sense of mastery over the world is diminished and we become more vulnerable to depression and anxiety. Her experiments on rats have demonstrated that when they have to make an effort to acquire their food rather than being passively fed, they show more determination when faced with obstacles. She calls this phenomenon "learned persistence." A similar effect in humans, she believes, leads us to acquire a sense of optimism about our ability to influence our own life situations. This is in contrast to "learned helplessness," which involves feeling at the mercy of external events. She thinks we need constant boosters or reminders of the control we have and that these change the physiology and chemical makeup of what she calls "the effort-driven rewards circuit," activating it in an energized way.

Lambert has come to believe that working with our hands is vitally important to health and points out that a large portion of the human brain is dedicated specifically to the movement of the hands. There are many different ways of working with our hands, including DIY and handicrafts, but the advantage of gardening is, as Dorothy finds, that you can't procrastinate. Lambert thinks the unpredictability is important too. We need to plan for different outcomes in a process she calls "a contingency workout."

While developing the ability to be in the present moment gets a lot of emphasis in the treatment of stress these days, we also need to cultivate a future orientation. During the course of our prehistory, people first started to plan for the future and trust in the outcomes of their efforts through cultivation. In the garden, there is always something to be planning for or looking forward to, and as one season ends, the work of the next season takes over. Positive feelings of anticipation like this contribute to a sense of the continuity of life that can be stabilizing. Last autumn, Dorothy let Robin grow a pumpkin on her plot. "It was huge," she told me, and "I can't tell you how much satisfaction and fun we got from it. He was so proud carrying it in from the car, and his father said, 'That's a big one!'" They saved some of the seeds, so that Robin can grow some more next year.

The sense of pride that Dorothy feels in the produce she grows, and that she so enjoyed seeing in her son, is what she calls "more pure." Gardening, she thinks, is less linked to vanity because "it's not just you, it's you and the planet." No sooner had she said this, than she exclaimed, "No—it is the universe, because it's about the sun and the earth." Dorothy was talking about something that lies far beyond human time: "I'm not religious," she said, "but I do get something spiritual from it."

Jung wrote: "Man feels himself isolated in the cosmos. He is no longer involved in nature and has lost his emotional participation in natural events, which hitherto had a symbolic meaning for him." A sense of spiritual connection like the one Dorothy described is something that many gardeners know and recognize. Feelings of connectedness like this are, in their very nature, difficult to verbalize, and this has led to these kinds of experiences being neglected in most of the research studies into the beneficial effects of gardening. The horticultural researcher Joe Sempik argues that they need to be taken into account because they bring such an important sense of meaning and purpose into people's lives.

Dorothy related an experience like this that happened when she was in the middle of her "low spiral." She had not managed to get to the allotment for a while, but just before Poppy's christening when she was getting ready for the celebration, she went to check on things. To her amazement she saw that her plot was almost entirely covered in opium poppies, which were in full bloom. There had been no sign of them the year before, but as she told me, "they must have been in the ground all the time." A host of purple flowers, poppies for Poppy—it could not have been more fortuitous. "They were *so* beautiful," she said, and tears sprang to her eyes. This unexpected gift came in her time of need, and she picked large bunches of them to bring home.

Dorothy used to be painfully aware of the fleeting nature of everything in life. She told me that for many years the feeling was at its worst in summer, when she would constantly feel time was slipping by. If we experience time as a series of moments lost, then all we can do is regret their passing, but there is less need to feel regret when they are part of a larger story. The allotment has given Dorothy that larger story.

CHAPTER 12

View from the Hospital

Tulips in the Barn vegetable garden.

In many cases, gardens and nature are more powerful than any medication.

Oliver Sacks (1933–2015)

Tulips are simply made to be in a vase. They put on a performance like no other flower, and they die so elegantly too. We grow them in our raised beds in the vegetable garden at home, set out in straight lines: reds, yellows, purples, and oranges—like a parade of glory that greets us as we stagger, sun-starved, out of winter.

We try out new types each year, but nothing displaces our old favorites from their place in the pageant: the statuesque tangerine Ballerina, the raspberry ripple Carnaval de Nice, the exotic dark Abu Hassan, and best of all, the irresistibly cheerful red-and-yellow striped Mickey Mouse.

Back in the days when you were allowed to bring flowers into the hospital in the UK, I went to visit a cherished friend clutching a bunch of the most vibrant tulips I could find in our garden. Her world had been turned upside down by the recent diagnosis of a rare condition for which she needed major surgery, and the outcome, at that point, was worryingly uncertain. I found her marooned in bed looking anxious and pale, but as I brandished the tulips, a broad smile cascaded over her face. A wave of positive feeling flowed between us, and with her eyes fixed on their tutti-frutti colors, she let out a celebratory "Wow!"

Those tulips were an instance of flower power in action. Beautiful flowers are known to trigger a true smile, an involuntary smile, known as a Duchenne smile, which, unlike a polite smile, lights up the whole face indicating genuine pleasure. Such phenomena are rarely researched, but in 2005 a study carried out at Rutgers University in New Jersey made an attempt to do this. Jeannette Haviland-Jones and colleagues tested the effects of receiving flowers against other comparable gifts. The results showed that being given a bouquet won hands-down. Everyone who was given flowers smiled a "true smile" and experienced a longer lasting sense of good mood.

Not long ago, I fell and fractured my hip. Unable to move and in pain, I lay awaiting surgery. Overnight, I had become a refugee in the land of the sick and immobile, while everyone in the land of the healthy, or so it seemed, was carrying on with his or her busy life. Surrounded by white walls, I felt trapped in a place that was cold and clinical. My sense of confinement would have been much worse if not for the daylight from the window by my bed. I was lucky in this respect, although the view itself did not offer much comfort, as I was looking out onto a grubby white-tiled wall.

Behind this, I could see a higher red brick wall with plants growing in the crevices of the mortar. My eyes repeatedly returned to these tiny tufts of green, as if striving for a sign of life or hope. I was frightened—it was a bad break—and for all the wonders of modern medicine, there were still many uncertainties.

The day before I was due to undergo hip replacement surgery, a friend brought me a postcard of a painting, which I propped up on my bedside table. This picture, *The Dessert: Harmony in Red* by Matisse, is a great painting—one of his greatest. Surrounded as I was by blank walls, I craved color, and this image became my anchor. The soft, deep red of the room in the painting was food for my eyes and gave me a separate world that I could enter into. The decorations of blue flowers, baskets, and flowing branches spoke to me of beauty and elegance, and at the same time, the scene of a female figure poised in her task of arranging fruit on a platter felt reassuringly domestic. One other ingredient in the painting helped to sustain me—a window looking out onto a garden. Like a picture within a picture, this glimpse of green grass, blossom-covered trees, and yellow flowers compensated for the dismal wall outside my real window.

The majority of hospitals designed in the second part of the twentieth century prioritized functionalism, infection control, and technology, resulting in a clinical idiom that makes many people feel unduly anxious. Most hospitals in the UK now exclude gifts of flowers as a precaution against bacterial contamination, as do an increasing number of US hospitals. The buildings themselves typically lack daylight, greenery, and fresh air—basic deprivations that are a cause of stress for patients and their families, as well as staff. The emotional needs of people admitted to the hospital have come to be neglected, and nature is often regarded as either an irrelevance or a threat. Unlike prisoners, who have the right to spend time outdoors in the open air each day, hospital patients, even long-stay ones, do not. This is in spite of the fact that fresh air and daylight are good for mental health and, according to recent research, are also "forgotten antibiotics," because light and airy hospital rooms have been found to be associated with shorter stays and lower infection rates.

Florence Nightingale recognized these health-giving factors in the nineteenth century. She believed that hospital wards needed plenty of natural light and a good circulation of fresh air. She also observed that patients recovered more quickly if they were wheeled outdoors. After her experience of nursing in the Crimean War, Nightingale wrote: "I shall never forget the rapture of fever patients over a bunch of bright-coloured flowers. I remember (in my own case) a nosegay of wild flowers being sent me, and from that moment recovery becoming more rapid." This is from her *Notes on Nursing*, published in 1859, the contents of which make it clear that she understood the power of patients' surroundings to influence physical healing. "People say the effect is only on the mind," she declared. "It is no such thing. The effect is on the body, too. Little as we know about the way in which we are affected by form, by colour, and light, we do know this, that they have an actual physical effect."

Nightingale witnessed the suffering of patients being nursed in huts with only the knots in the wooden walls as a view. Flowers and bedside windows could, she believed, offer an important source of aesthetic nourishment. But she saw nurses denying patients "a glass of cut-flowers, or a growing plant" on grounds of "unhealth-iness," and observed how the cravings of the sick for color and variety were dismissed by nurses as their "fancies." Far from being fanciful, she believed these longings were an indication of what would aid recovery.

This aspect of Nightingale's thinking is currently experiencing a comeback. Increasingly, it is recognized that the environment should not be regarded as something separate from treatment but as a fundamental part of it, and as such, needs attending to. The British Medical Association, for example, issued a new set of guidelines in 2011 calling for increased psychological awareness in hospital design and recommending that all new hospitals should include a garden.

A number of research studies have contributed to an evidence base for views of nature in a range of different clinical settings. These include a cardiac intensive care unit, a bronchoscopy clinic, and a burns unit. Roger Ulrich, the pioneering environmental psychologist, carried out the first study of this kind, *View Through a Window May Influence Recovery from Surgery*, in 1984, and the experience of having a tree outside his window during a period of childhood illness inspired his investigations. The study took place in a suburban Pennsylvania hospital and involved two groups of patients recovering from gall-bladder surgery. One group had windows looking toward some deciduous trees, while the other group looked out at a brown brick wall. The patients with a view of trees fared better; they had lower levels of stress, more positive mood, required fewer doses of pain medication, and were discharged on average a day sooner. The research also showed that the patients with the view of trees had far fewer negative comments in the nurses' notes, suggesting that their lowered stress levels resulted in them making fewer demands.

A skeptic might wonder whether other forms of distraction like watching TV while in the hospital might have the same effect. From the findings of recent research carried out by a team from the University of Kansas, it appears that this is not the case. All the patients in this study had a TV, while half of them also had a flowering plant near their bed. In total ninety patients having their appendix removed were randomly allocated to either type of room. In the period in which they were recovering from surgery, the patients with flowers reported better moods, less anxiety, and had lower blood pressure and heart rate readings. Their intake of pain medication was also significantly reduced. This led the researchers to conclude that flowering plants are an "inexpensive, and effective medicine for patients recovering from surgery." They also reported that participants interpreted the presence of the plants as a sign that the hospital was a caring place; in other words, the presence of greenery and flowers promoted feelings such as trust and reassurance.

All the benefits of nature for health discussed in previous chapters are of course relevant here, but particularly important in the hospital context is the way that basic emotions like hope and fear can dramatically influence the experience of illness and sometimes its outcome. The presence of gardens and flowering plants are a sign of a cared for place, thereby giving rise to a form of "placebo effect." The term "placebo" means "to please" and is used for the control pills in drug trials as well as the positive expectations that arise through empathetic interactions with health staff. While a placebo is entirely based on feeling and belief, the effect in the brain is real and comes about through release of endorphins, which are mood boosting, calming, and pain relieving. Uplifting qualities of a building are thought to have a similar effect, which is why the architectural writer Charles Jencks, founder of the charity that builds the Maggie's Cancer Caring Centres in the UK, refers to the role of hospital surroundings as "the design placebo effect." The Maggie's Centres, which are run by welcoming volunteer staff, are intended as an antidote to what Jencks refers to as "the factory" of the hospital. They are designed by different leading architects, so the aesthetics of each one varies, but they all maximize the design placebo effect through use of light, beauty, homeyness, and gardens.

When we are sick, the artifice of life is stripped away. We are thrown back to the basics, and in that process thrown back to a black-and-white experience of the world in which things are quickly labeled good or bad, safe or dangerous. This is particularly true with ambiguous imagery, because if we are anxious, given the slightest of cues we will project fearful things onto the environment around us. Ulrich's research on the effects of art in hospitals confirms the extent to which art needs to be carefully chosen. He found that over a fifteen-year period in a Swedish psychiatric hospital, it was only the abstract paintings that were attacked, never the ones depicting natural scenery. A further study on patients recovering from heart surgery revealed that abstract art was less calming than pictures of the natural world, and one image in particular that contained straight lines was found to be positively stressful, perhaps through contributing to feelings of being confined or closed in.

Ulrich also cites the example of a semi-abstract sculpture installation of large, angular, birdlike shapes cast in metal, that was commissioned for a cancer treatment center. No one involved at the planning stages for *The Bird Garden*, as it was called, had spotted the menacing potential in the sculpture's form, but it soon became apparent after the birds were installed. More than 20 percent of the patients reported negative reactions to them; not simply disliking them—some people perceived them as hostile and menacing. The sculptures preyed on patients' fears of cancer, and it was not long before they had to be removed.

The *Bird Garden* sculpture is an example of how our experience of life is influenced by a process of imaginative projection. This phenomenon was given the name "*einfühlung*" in the nineteenth century by German philosopher Robert Vischer. The word means "in-feeling," and he coined it to capture the way we feel our way into the world around us through what he believed was a form of kinesthetic or internal simulation of it. Vischer was way ahead of his time. The prevailing model then was of a brain that passively registers what we see—much as a camera does. We now know this is not the case. The brain simulates actions and movements as we watch them. This complex process originates in the activity of specialized cells called mirror neurons. These neurons are found in the motor parts of the cortex, and as we observe movement, they fire up as if we are making the movements ourselves; all that is lacking is the instruction to the muscle pathways to perform them. Vischer thought of *einfühlung* as a process of "inner imitation," which is more or less what it is.

Mirror neurons come in a range of different types, and they play an important role in the mirroring of facial expression that accompanies mother-infant bonding; they also contribute to our capacity for empathy. Most of the research interest in them so far has focused on these areas, but recent studies have shown that mirror neuron cells are involved much more generally in how we experience our physical surroundings. This is perhaps not surprising because hunter-gatherer survival depended on being able to detect subtle movements in the landscape. The Italian neuroscientist Vittorio Gallese, who heads one of the main research teams specializing in the mirror neuron system, has described how it might be "a pinecone falling on a garden bench in the park, or drips splashing on the leaves of a plant during a downpour" that set our mirror neurons to work.

A process of inner simulation means that we read the environment in the same way that we read body language. The phenomenon accounts for how we can take vicarious pleasure in things around us and feel a sense of empathy toward all sorts of aspects of the natural world. The fascination of watching a bird on the wing as it glides in the thermals is that we, in part, glide along with it. Because the experience is being actively simulated within us, we can project ourselves into the bird as if we are accompanying it on its flight.

The effect of watching movements in nature when we are sick and frail may not be so different from the effect we can perceive in babies, who are endlessly fascinated by moving objects like mobiles or swaying branches. It also means that when the body is weak and physical movements are restricted, the motor parts of the brain can still be stimulated in a pleasurable way.

When he worked at the Beth Abraham Hospital in Manhattan, the great neurologist Oliver Sacks regularly took his patients across the road for walks in the New York Botanical Garden. For Sacks, two types of non-pharmaceutical therapy were particularly important in chronic neurological diseases: music and gardens, because, he wrote, they both have "calming and organizing effects on our brains." He observed that patients with neurological disorders like Parkinson's and Tourette's could sometimes get temporary relief from their symptoms in a natural setting. There are other conditions in which an effect of calming and focusing the mind is seen, particularly Alzheimer's and attention deficit disorder (ADD), and it may be that an innate neurological response to nature that we can all benefit from is simply more apparent when the nervous system is disordered. Either way, Sacks believed the brain was directly altered: "The effects of nature's qualities on health," he wrote, "are not only spiritual and emotional but physical and neurological. I have no doubt that they reflect deep changes in the brain's physiology, and perhaps even its structure."

Sacks's opinion is backed up by some recent research findings. Flowering plants and garden settings have, for example, been found to alter the brain's electrical activity through increasing levels of alpha waves. Alpha rhythm is a form of neurological nourishment; it lifts mood through release of serotonin, and we can benefit from these effects for a while afterward.

Indoor settings tend to be static and unvarying, but the nervous system is geared to perceive difference and change. We need sensory stimulation; it is one of the things that help us feel alive, and there is an optimal state between over- and understimulation. The sound of wind in the trees or gently flowing water is restful because, within a predictable range, it is endlessly variable. This effect has been called difference-within-sameness, and it means our senses are both responsive and relaxed. The visual patterns that we find in nature also provide a gentle form of stimulation. Natural forms exhibit a type of geometry known as "self-similarity," in which patterns are repeated on different scales, like variations on a theme. Fractal patterning, as it is known, is perhaps most clearly illustrated in the structure of a tree. All the different parts of the tree, from the veins in a leaf to the stems and roots, have a similar pattern of branching, and yet each instance of it is subtly different. The brain is essentially a pattern-seeking organ and needs to make rapid predictions from a vast array of incoming sensory information. Fractal patterning makes the brain's task easier because there is a strong element of predictability, so that at a glance, the visual cortex can fill in gaps and assemble a larger picture.

These kinds of patterns make natural scenery conducive to what is called "fluent visual processing." This means that we can, with a relaxed gaze, sweep over the environment and take it in through making a minimum number of visual stops along the way. The Dutch environmental psychologist Agnes van den Berg, from Wageningen University, studies these patterns and thinks they make a significant contribution to the restfulness we experience in nature. She explains that built environments are full of irregular, angular patterns, and research has shown that when we scan them, our eyes need to make many more stops in order to collate the visual information. We are not conscious of our eyes doing this, but all the same it means using more energy to process what we are seeing. In contrast, nature is less taxing to interpret—or as van den Berg puts it, "nature is easy on the mind." When the body is sick and our energy is low, sensory stimulation needs to be at just the right level, neither too much nor too little, and the gentle forms of nature provide it best.

· · ·

Nature has a way of awakening our emotional lives. However much we may come to understand about the neurological effects of natural stimuli on us, this aspect may remain more of a mystery, depending as it does on our state of mind. There are times when we look but do not see and listen but do not hear. The visionary artist and poet William Blake understood that our experience of the world is strongly influenced by the receptiveness of the mind. He wrote of how "the tree which moves some to tears of joy is in the eyes of others only a green thing which stands in the way."

The writer Eve Ensler has chronicled an extraordinary encounter she had with a tree when she was admitted to the hospital. At the outset, however, much as Blake described, the tree outside her window was no more than a "green thing" that stood in her way. Ensler had recently been diagnosed with a large, cancerous tumor in her uterus and was seriously unwell. In *The Body of the World*, she recounts arriving at the hospital in a state of utter exhaustion. Her room was reassuringly pretty and clean, but the view from her window was not so welcome, obscured as it was by a tree. Too weak to watch a movie or call a friend, all she could do was lie on her bed and stare at that tree. She thought she would go mad from boredom, and the tree annoyed her. She explains: "I was raised in America. All value lies in the future, in the dream, in production. There is no present tense. There is no value in what is, only in what might be made or exploited from what already exists." In this mindset a tree only has value if it is chopped up and used for wood. In other words, if it is a dead tree.

The first few days passed in a similar fashion, with Ensler's eyes unresponsive to nature. Then something shifted—she began to see the tree no longer as an obstructive object—but alive in all its detail: "On Tuesday I meditated on bark; on Friday, the green leaves shimmering in late afternoon light. For hours I lost myself, my body, my being dissolving into tree." Such intense intimacy, with a tree of all things, is entirely new to her: "To actually lie in my hospital bed and see tree, enter the tree, to find the green life inherent in the tree, this was the awakening. Each morning I could not wait to focus on tree. I would let the tree take me. Each day it was different, based on the light or wind or rain. The tree was a tonic and a cure, a guru and a teaching." Like an ever-present companion she can learn from, the tree cures her of her unresponsive eyes. By the time Ensler starts her chemotherapy treatment, she is filled by nature and reveling in an "insane delight over the gentle white May blossoms that were beginning to flower everywhere."

All her life Ensler had felt estranged from her body and from the earth. She had experienced abuse as a child and as an adult. She had grown up not realizing her body needed care. For years, she longed for a connection with her mother but was unable to find a "way in." As a result, in her passage through life, she feels she has been a "visitor" rather than an "inhabitant"; but the tree changed that by simply being there and asking nothing of her. In a way that is hard to fully explain, through discovering how to inhabit the tree, she feels she has re-found her mother.

Not many people would choose to spend hours on end gazing at a tree. Ensler certainly didn't, but being sick forces us to stop and slow down. Serious illness involves a major adjustment. A watershed has been crossed, and life will never return to what it was before. The healing that needs to take place is not only about physical survival. We need to reassess what matters, adjust our priorities, and go forward in a different way.

Ensler's awakening and her newfound sense of connectedness, powerful as these experiences were, are far from unique. A recent review of the evidence for people diagnosed with cancer found that through being ill, many of them had formed an entirely new relationship with the natural world. Furthermore, time spent in nature helped give rise to a fresh perspective on life. When we are faced with illness, receiving support from others in making the transitions involved is important, but ultimately, we have to make these changes on our own. In a natural setting, we are always surrounded by life. This makes it possible to feel alone but not isolated and provides a uniquely consoling form of solitude.

When I interviewed Olivia Chapple, cofounder of a UK charity called Horatio's Garden, she emphasized the therapeutic importance of being alone but not isolated. Horatio's Garden creates and maintains gardens in spinal injury centers in the UK. Over the last eight years Olivia has witnessed the enormous sense of consolation that a beautiful garden can bring to people facing a life-changing disability. In spite of the fact that spinal injury patients need to be in the hospital for six to twelve months, the only outdoor spaces they could previously access were the tarmac-covered parking lots.

The designer Cleve West created the first of these gardens at the Duke of Cornwall Spinal Treatment Centre in Salisbury Hospital. On his initial visit to the site, he asked to be pushed around in a bed and a wheelchair. He was shocked at how much every little bump in the ground was transmitted and how vulnerable and out of control he felt. This experience gave him a new perspective on the design process.

A preliminary consultation with the patients had revealed that what they most wanted was a place to escape from the clinical environment. Just two words dominated their list of priorities: "beautiful" and "accessible." Their rehabilitation programs were largely focused on physical needs rather than emotional or social ones, and in keeping with this the staff initially conceptualized the garden as an opportunity to maximize physical therapy. In contrast, the patients were emphasizing their need for emotional sustenance and their longing for a place where they didn't have to "do therapy," but could temporarily return to something like "normal" life.

The patients' priorities of beauty and accessibility became the central focus for West's design. He created a garden filled with perennial plants that provide structure as well as lots of seasonal

variation and color. Along one side of the garden there is a trel-
lis walkway with trained apples growing over it. Here, in summer
patients can lie protected by the dappled shade, with the soothing
sound of water trickling through the long stone rill that runs close
by. Although there is a greenhouse in the garden, and there is some
scope for physical therapy, it doesn't feel like a place where you are
expected to do things. It is a place that simply asks to be inhabited.
As I sat on one of the long, curving, dry stone walls that transect
the garden and gazed toward the green hill that lies beyond, I was
struck by how easy it was to forget you were on hospital territory.

The charity was founded by Olivia, a retired GP, and her husband, David Chapple, a neurosurgeon, but would not have come
into existence without their eldest son, Horatio. At the age of sixteen, Horatio worked as a volunteer at the spinal injuries unit in
Salisbury. He became increasingly concerned by the lack of outdoor space for patients and could not understand why no one
seemed to recognize the basic human need for contact with nature.
He then started a campaign to raise money to create a garden on
the vacant lot next to the unit. That same summer Horatio was
killed in a tragic accident on a school expedition. Following this,
his parents decided to take his vision forward, and two years later
the garden he had envisaged came into being.

There are eleven spinal injury centers in the UK. Until 2012
none of them had gardens, but now six of them do. Each of these
specialist units covers a large area of the country, and for many
patients this means being far from friends and family. A spinal
injury is one of the most devastating conditions anyone can face.
It means the future ahead is totally altered. Relationships, work,
hobbies—nothing is unaffected, and with so many restrictions on
life, it can be hard to see a way forward. A huge physical adjustment is required, but the mental adjustment is just as profound,
and the sense of isolation, with everything that has to be come to
terms with, can be terrible.

Olivia describes wheeling patients out to the garden for the very first time after a lengthy initial phase of total bed rest on the ward. After everything people have been through, to see the sky and feel the sun's warmth is a momentous experience, and many shed tears. Greg was in his early twenties when he suffered a terrible injury in a car accident. He described how in the fresh air among the plants and trees he experienced his first feelings of freedom from confinement: "You are not the property of the hospital anymore," he told me. Having the garden to turn to helped Greg recover his sense of identity; as he put it: "I got back my self." Such simple words, and yet they convey the profoundest of effects—to feel you have lost your self and then to recover it. The truth is that in connecting with nature we connect with ourselves, sometimes to the very core of our being.

In his book *A Leg to Stand On*, Oliver Sacks describes his own experience of recovering his sense of identity through nature. He charts his confinement and sensory deprivation in the hospital following a traumatic accident to his left leg. Cut off from the outside world, in a windowless room for three weeks, he shrinks within himself, and the shocking thing is that it all happens so fast: "We speak, glibly, of 'institutionalisation,'" he writes, "without the smallest personal sense of what is involved—how insidious, and universal, is the contraction in all realms . . . and how swiftly it can happen to anyone, to oneself."

On his last day in the hospital before going to a convalescent home, by which time he has not been outdoors for a month, Sacks was taken outside to the garden in a wheelchair. The sense of reversal was as swift as it was powerful: "A pure and intense joy, a blessing, the sun on my face and the wind in my hair, to hear birds, to see, touch and fondle the living plants. Some essential connection and communion with nature was re-established after the horrible isolation and alienation I had known. Some part of me came alive, when I was taken to the garden, which had been starved, and died,

271

perhaps without my knowing it." To be sick or badly injured, Sacks writes, means you need an "in-between" place, a "quiet place, a haven, a shelter." You can't be "thrown back into the world straight-away."

An important aspect of the garden as an "in-between" place for Greg was that it helped him keep in touch with his friends during the length of his stay. Spending time outside together in the sun-shine made everything feel more "normal," as he put it. "It's some-where you'd both like to be." The patients' relatives are in need of this kind of feeling too because a trauma like this affects the whole family. Each of the Horatio's gardens is different, but they all have secluded places and nooks where patients and their visitors can be together in relative privacy. The garden as a place that he wanted to be was also important to Greg in getting through the endlessly repetitive rehabilitation exercises he had to do, like picking up a clothespin and putting it back in a box. Greg is far from alone in feeling these beneficial effects. Many people testify to the invalu-able support they have derived from the gardens and the extent to which the beauty of nature has supported them through the long, slow process of rehabilitation.

For patients who are currently receiving treatment on one of the spinal injury units, the gap between the ward and the world beyond can feel like an unbridgeable gulf, but the garden brings the outside world in and in doing so acts like a bridge. A signifi-cant contribution to this effect arises through the volunteers who tend the garden. As they are all regulars, the patients get to know them. This provides an opportunity to have "normal" conversations such as sharing enjoyment of the flowers. The patients can also practice talking about their injuries; an invaluable preparation for when they eventually leave the hospital. Sometimes patients them-selves return as volunteers, and for people who have been recently admitted it can be helpful to see someone in a wheelchair working in the garden: someone whose life has moved on. Gardens have a way of gathering life unto themselves, especially in summer when people can congregate in them. Horatio's has hosted concerts as well as food and plant fairs, and some patients have chosen to return and get married or hold christenings in one of the gardens, such is the significance of this place in their lives.

A therapeutic garden is a health intervention and, as a form of treatment, needs to be carefully tailored to the people who will be using it. For spinal injury patients, the requirement for smooth surfaces and thresholds is paramount because the smallest of jolts can trigger painful muscle spasms. Otherwise, the more beauty and variety there is, the better, as long as the patients have access to shade.

The Pamela Barnett Centre at Ravenswood Village in Berkshire provides a different kind of garden that has also been carefully designed to meet the residents' needs. The center is a home for adults with severe learning disabilities. They lack language and also have impaired nonverbal communication skills. This condition makes them difficult to reach on any level. Most also suffer from hypostimulation, which means they need a lot of sensory input. When this is lacking, they create their own stimulation by banging or tapping noisily.

Nature, however, is able to reach them. The movements, sounds, and textures of plants, birds, and insects are a source of endless fascination. Gayle Souter-Brown and Katy Bott from Greenstone Design UK, a practice that specializes in health-care settings, designed the garden for maximum variation, with lots of different leaves, flowers, and edible fruits. The structural design is curvilinear and invites exploration with interconnecting paths. Within the garden, different zones have different characters: there is a little bog area, a Zen gravel garden, a fish pond, and a small corner of meadow. The residents revel in the sensory immersion and sense of

273

freedom they can experience outside. The garden is also used for a form of therapy called *intensive interaction*, in which the therapist sits with the patient and tries to tune in to his or her emotional state through the patient's breathing, vocalizations, eye movements, and other body signs. This becomes the basis for reciprocal communication, much like the mirroring of mother with baby. The calming and organizing effect of nature on the nervous system is evident because the residents are more accessible and able to reciprocate in the midst of nature than when they are inside.

On the other side of a high hedge there is another therapeutic garden, which belongs to the Tager Centre next door. The contrast could not be greater. This garden, also designed by Katy Bott, is stark and rectilinear and devoid of sensory richness. The residents here suffer from severe autism, so severe that nature is not calming for them, rather the opposite: the very changeability of the natural world can provoke extreme anxiety. The need for a high level of predictability means there are no flowers, no berries, no leaves that change color and drop, or anything else that might alter overnight. The setting indoors may be more predictable, but it is not necessarily calmer. The residents easily feel confined and become agitated, pacing up and down for long periods of time. The evergreen space of the garden is the best place for them to be at times like this. The open air helps their negative energy disperse, and having exercised on the swings or seesaws, for a brief period of time they are able to be still.

The Tager Centre garden is an exception to the general rule for therapeutic gardens, which is that a higher level of natural complexity in a garden is associated with greater restorative potential. The ratio of green to hard surface is also important: about 7:3 works best. If there is too little greenery, a garden is not as relaxing or beneficial. Natural complexity also helps to bring wildlife to a garden and maximizes the therapeutic effects of the garden as a microcosm.

I had my own experience of this when, following surgery, which thankfully went well, I was discharged home from the hospital. The feeling of relief to return to the familiar and the loved was huge, but with my mobility temporarily restricted, the compass of my physical world was radically diminished. The grounds that I used to stride freely around now seemed like another continent. Each day, instead, I installed myself in a sheltered spot close to the house. To my surprise, although the plants gave me pleasure, they were not its main source—it was the birds that brought me real delight.

As I sat and enjoyed the late autumn sun, the small birds, mainly blue tits and coal tits, would begin to ignore me. The more they did so, the more absorbed in them I became. The birds would approach our bird feeders with caution, first perching on branches nearby. I would watch their eyes darting, checking out their surroundings before leaving the safety of the tree and flying toward the food. The mystery of this decision-making process was compelling. Each bird behaved slightly differently—some seemed more hesitant than others, but they all took care. For a time, I was able to lose myself in their world.

Soon my mobility improved and I could begin to explore the rest of the garden, but I needed crutches, and like the birds, I was cautious. One day, I ventured out to the greenhouse and on opening the door was met by an unexpected sight. There, lined up on the staging were some saffron crocuses in full flower. Instantly, the memory of buying the bulbs, only a few weeks before my accident, flooded back to me. I had made a spur-of-the-moment decision to purchase them at a plant fair, inspired by the prospect of growing saffron. So much had intervened since then that I had forgotten all about them. A most welcome surprise! Their lilac and purple petals, which were gorgeous, were at their peak, but it was the vivid red of their long stigmas trailing like ribbons that truly astonished me. A few days later, I returned and set about harvesting those precious crimson threads. The methodical work was calming, and for the first time since my accident I felt that I was doing something worthwhile. That evening I used some of the strands in a delicious saffron risotto—making it even more worthwhile.

While I had felt excited and happy to be reunited with friends and family on my return, these encounters inevitably involved relating details of my fall—an event that I was only just beginning to process myself. In the greenhouse, by contrast, there was no telling involved and no disturbance of memory or feelings to contend with. I found restorative solitude—alone but not alone—just me and the flowers. Discovering the crocuses and harvesting the saffron gave me joy; pure and simple joy.

CHAPTER 13

Green Fuse

The Barn Garden meadow.

The force that through the green fuse drives the flower
Drives my green age

Dylan Thomas (1914–1953)

The month of May is always the greenest in our garden. All the trees and grasses seem to radiate the great pulse of life as it surges up from the earth. Never have I felt more alive to this effect than when I returned from visiting a charity project in a remote part of northern Kenya.

Tom and I had spent two weeks in Turkana visiting a new initiative called Furrows in the Desert, a remarkable collaboration between a community of Spanish and Kenyan missionaries and a team of Israeli agrologists who have pioneered techniques for sustainable cultivation in arid areas. During the fortnight we were there, we worked on the productive fruit and vegetable gardens known in that part of the world as *shamba* gardens.

The Turkana people have a history of extraordinary resilience. They are tall and physically distinctive, and the women wear wide, high collars of tiny multicolored beads. Their songs and their dances have been handed down over countless generations, as has their way of life as nomadic pastoralists. This traditional lifestyle has long been a marginal one, but it is increasingly difficult to sustain because the land is suffering the effects of climate change. The weather patterns have altered; seasonal rains can no longer be relied on, and there is a shortage of vegetation for the animals to graze on. No rain had fallen for nearly a year when we arrived. Many of the children we encountered in the villages were visibly malnourished, and dead goats lay scattered along the waysides. It was hard to believe that this part of the Great Rift Valley had once formed such an ideal landscape for our early ancestors. Sometimes referred to as the cradle of humankind, here, on the border with Ethiopia, near the Omo River, is where some of the oldest human remains have been found.

Now that the nomadic way of life has become hard to sustain, people have settled in communities, where they continue to live in their traditional brushwood huts but are to some extent dependent on food aid. Ancient as these lands are, they have never seen cultivation. From time immemorial, people survived by tending their herds and foraging, but in the newly created *shamba* gardens, men and women are being trained to grow edible plants.

There are now 150 gardens and small farms in thirty different communities, with more planned, all using water brought to the surface by solar or wind pump and sparingly distributed by drip irrigation. The terrain is mountainous and rocky and with temperatures of 104°F and strong, dry winds, it is a hostile environment for growing food. The success of this project is largely down to the combination of Israeli expertise in desert cultivation, the building of the water infrastructure, and the local knowledge of the missionary community, which has been working here for more than twenty-five years.

Inside the gardens, produce such as kale, spinach, beans, tomatoes, and watermelons grow vigorously; the contrast with the expanse of burned-out landscape beyond could hardly be greater. To witness the work that was going on in such harsh conditions was life-affirming and inspiring. Toward the end of our stay, everyone's hopes were raised when clouds started building up in the sky, but the desperately needed rain didn't come.

With a strange feeling of still being in transit, I arrived back home and walked out into the garden. Our enclosures of high hornbeam hedges are like calm, green rooms on even the most overcast of days, but that morning the sun had set their leaves aglow. I wandered along the grass paths and around the beds, as if in a trance while my eyes drank in the great greenness of it all.

Is this, I wondered, what the ancient nomads felt when after crossing the desert, they reached an oasis with palm trees and a paradise garden—a whole place proclaiming the greening power of the earth? To have witnessed the land so parched and cracked had a profound effect on me. I could see why Hildegard of Bingen placed such emphasis on the life-defying quality of *dryness*, and for the first time I understood, really understood, the power of her green fuse, *viriditas*—and what it means to lack it. The longed-for rains finally started falling in Turkana a few days later, and the dormant life that lay hidden within the parched earth was ready to respond. In less than a week, the desolate landscape was turning from brown to green, but many months of recovery lay in store and long periods of drought have continued to occur.

In this age of climate crisis and separation from nature, we can no longer escape the connection between human nature and green nature, between human health and the health of the planet. How did it ever happen that we did? In ages gone by, people spent time meditating on such truths. They reflected on the mystery of life, and they often did it in a garden. Indeed, the origin of the garden goes back to ancient Persia when gardens provided respite from the desert heat and dust and were designed to nurture life spiritually as well as physically. The dramatic contrast with the harsh, arid surroundings was part of the effect. To sit in the restful shade of a garden accompanied by flowing water and vibrant greenery is an experience of peaceful plenitude that cannot fail to bring with it a sense of gratitude for the flourishing of the earth.

Since ancient times, gardens have helped people bridge the gap between *doing* on the one hand and *being* on the other. Achieving a healthy balance between these two states seems perennially to evade us in modern times. Furthermore, as the maker and shaper of a miniature world, the gardener can overlook the extent to which a garden has a life of its own. When I first started growing plants, I was hooked on productivity. This meant that whenever I went outside, I would automatically inspect the beds to see what needed to be done, constructing a mental list as I did so. I began to realize I was falling into the trap of always *doing*, and I learned to value times when I could just *be* in, or with, the garden.

My favorite part of the day for this is early in the morning, walking out barefoot onto the dew-covered grass. The flowers and hedges have been growing throughout the night (for this is the unseen interval in which plants do their growing), and somehow in the first light the garden feels more their place than mine. Even if the weeds start popping into focus, weeding can justifiably be postponed, for there is still plenty of time to claim the day, and all the rest of the hours to *do* things in. At night too there is something animistic in the ambiguity of the shadows, which imbues the place with a different sense of life, and you can't see the weeds or *do* any gardening in the dark.

The outer reaches of our garden are entirely meadow and involve a different kind of gardening, cultivation that largely consists of stepping back and letting nature unfold. One of the tragedies of the English countryside is the loss of wildflower meadows, 97 percent of which have disappeared during the last seventy years. Establishing a meadow is about creating conditions for sustainable regeneration; in other words, interfering as little as possible. Apart from cutting the meadow once a year, the only other intervention after the initial seeding thirty years ago has been to introduce the yellow rattle plant. Colloquially known as the farmer's enemy, it saps the strength of powerful grasses that would otherwise take out the flowers and reduce the variety of vegetation within the meadow. Ragged robin, knapweed, scabious, mallow, stitchwort are only a small part of that variety, but the real wonder of the meadow is that it's such a desirable habitat.

Over time, a bleak, treeless wheat field that was never particularly productive has become a haven for wildlife. In summer, the insect population explodes. The meadow attracts marbled white butterflies, which float and flutter about in large numbers in the air. Then there are the eye-catching burnet moths, with brilliant red spots on their dark wings, and the exquisite, vividly colored common blue butterflies, sadly not so common now, although multiplying here. Woodpeckers visit frequently to sample the many colonies of ants. Partridges and pheasants build their nests, safe in the meadow's cover.

This kind of gardening is a form of husbandry that is less focused on *doing*, more on letting nature be. Gardening, of course, is not always about protecting resources or being environmentally friendly, and the history of the garden reflects this. The evolution of humankind's ideas concerning man's dominion over nature are writ large in the history of the garden. In different eras we find nature tamed and restrained or nature enhanced and perfected, and then with the advent of the water-guzzling, herbicide-soaked green lawn, we find nature consumed. These days, with the crisis of nature that is unfolding around us, the reparative aspect of gardening has come to the fore, so that gardens are less about dominion and more about salvage and restoration.

At the same time, a paradigm shift is taking place in how we understand and portray nature. Ideas like "red in tooth and claw," "survival of the fittest," and "the selfish gene" have hitherto shaped our thinking about the natural world. Those narratives have perhaps suited the times and meant that other forces that promote coexistence were relatively overlooked. Now, however, ideas that were previously considered offbeat are beginning to enter the mainstream. For example, a whole new area of botanical science about plant communication is being revealed. Trees, we are learning, form communities and collaborate with one another through underground fungal networks; plants warn other plants to defend themselves against threats from insects and other pests; and sunflowers go out of their way to accommodate their root systems to their neighbors'—in all sorts of ways the plant world organizes itself to enhance collective survival. And collective survival is the pressing issue of our day.

The crisis of climate is also a crisis of biodiversity. Reports in the national press about the dwindling numbers of birds, butterflies, and bees reflect only a tiny fraction of the depletion of nature that is taking place. A combination of rising temperatures, loss of habitats, and excessive use of agrochemicals, as well as the damaging effects of other pollution, has grievously damaged the interconnected web of life that underpins the health of the planet. Recently, ecologists have started monitoring the life of domestic gardens and have found they can act like hotspots of biodiversity, harboring a wealth of species, far greater than that found in the surrounding countryside. Yet, at the same time, in the UK, the front garden is disappearing to make way for car parking with a result that one in three front gardens now has no plants in it at all.

Gardens, even small ones, contain a wide range of potential habitats for all manner of wildlife. They are in effect operating as a safe house for nature, a shelter from depleted rural landscapes on the one hand and harsh townscapes on the other. The density of birds in city gardens has been found to be six times the average for the countryside in the UK, and the wide variety of flowering plants within them attracts many different kinds of pollinators. Neglected corners with piles of twigs, rotting leaves, and stumps of deadwood all provide a haven for insects such as ants, woodlice, and beetles.

The soil found in many gardens supports a healthy diversity of microbes, fungi, worms, and all the other creatures for whom the ground is a habitat. In contrast, the soil on agricultural land tends to be thin and impoverished. Decades of industrial farming techniques that have taken from the land and failed to replenish it mean that over a third of all the topsoil around the world has been lost since the Second World War. Topsoil is a precious resource; without it nothing will grow, and once lost, it takes five hundred to a thousand years to re-form. The degradation of soil through a failure of care plagued the ancient Sumerians. The ancient Romans likewise disregarded the needs of the land, and the consequent failure of their crops contributed to their downfall. More recent times have seen the destruction of the North American prairies in the dust bowl disaster of the 1930s. The same mistake is happening now, only on a much larger, worldwide scale.

The vast and spiraling problem of the state of the planet inevitably engenders feelings of helplessness, giving rise to what's been called climate grief or environmental melancholia. In response to this, we can feel caught between minimizing the problem and hoping for the best on the one hand or succumbing to despair and paralysis on the other. Either way, losing touch with the earth as a basic source of goodness has psychological consequences and can make it hard to enjoy natural beauty or feel gratitude for its flourishing. The environmentalist Naomi Klein has described how in the aftermath of the BP oil spill in the Gulf of Mexico, she lost her ability to feel joy in nature. She writes: "The more beautiful and striking the experience, the more I found myself grieving its inevitable loss—like someone unable to fall fully in love because she can't stop imagining the inevitable heartbreak." In her mind nature was already beyond repair: "Looking out at an ocean bay on British Columbia's Sunshine Coast, a place teaming with life, I would suddenly picture it barren." It was, she writes, like living in a constant state of "pre-loss," which meant that in a true melancholic state, she was cut off from the one thing that might replenish her.

Just as the state of the planet is unsustainable, so our lifestyles have become psychologically unsustainable. Depression has recently overtaken respiratory illnesses to become the leading cause of ill health and disability worldwide. While this rise is not directly linked to climate grief, it is not unrelated to it either, because the problems are so wrapped up in each other. Neglecting what people need in order to thrive is a symptom of the same mindset that has failed to help nature thrive. And that issue takes us to the heart of what it means to cultivate.

Voltaire's timeless injunction "*Il faut cultiver notre jardin*" ("We must cultivate our garden") is the conclusion of his novella *Candide*. Written more than 250 years ago, the story speaks directly to our times. *Candide* was written in the wake of what has been called the first modern disaster, the great Lisbon earthquake—a tragedy that shattered widely held cultural assumptions.

The city of Lisbon, which then was one of the wealthiest and most populated cities in the world, was completely destroyed in

1755 by one of the deadliest earthquakes in history. The seismic waves triggered a tsunami, which was followed by an outbreak of firestorms that ravaged the countryside. The scale of the devastation called into question a belief in the smooth running of a clockwork universe, a notion that Newtonian physics had given rise to and which underpinned eighteenth-century thought. The model of a clockwork universe might seem absurd to us now, but it is an example of the pervasiveness of machine as metaphor in Western thought. The equivalent in our own time is the brain-as-computer metaphor, in which we find the same mismatch between machine and nature. Metaphors are powerful; as much as they can deepen our thinking, they can also limit or distort it. The perilous state of the biosphere has arisen through humankind's failure to respect nature as a living system, and in that sense, we are witnessing the far-reaching consequences of a clockwork universe.

Voltaire vehemently opposed the philosophical and religious beliefs associated with the idea of that smooth-running universe, and he satirized them through the story of Candide. As a result, the book was immediately banned and then became a massive best seller. Voltaire's main target in the story is a form of blind optimism (a version of the philosophy of Leibniz), which tenaciously assumes the best and minimizes, or takes flight from, anything bad, with a result that uncomfortable realities are avoided. The narrative reflects this with its fast-unfolding events and impossible turns of plot, in which characters who have been brutally killed or injured in one part of the book suddenly reappear in another. As a result, it reads like a forerunner of magical realism.

As we follow Candide on his adventures, it becomes progressively impossible to ignore the extent to which this type of optimism protects the characters in the story from feeling disturbed about anything horrible in the world. Candide finally understands this himself when he encounters the plight of a horribly mutilated sugar plantation slave. The appalling human cost of sugar production is a shocking revelation, and for the first time he acknowl-edges that optimism is a "mania for insisting that all is well when all is by no means well." The problem for him is that without his blind optimism to protect him, he is consumed by the thought that evil will always triumph, and he falls into a state of helpless melancholy. The only alternative to the mania of denial, it seems, is pessimism—a depressive turn of mind in which there is no point in trying to change the world or anything in yourself because it is all too large and too difficult to address.

The end of the story finds Candide coming ashore from a boat on the Sea of Marmara, the very place where my grandfather was taken prisoner. While this coincidence takes my associations to Ted's experience of the First World War and brings this book full circle, for Voltaire's readers the associations would have been very different. In the popular imagination of that era, Turkey was an exotic place, associated with flowers and gardens, both the mag-nificent gardens of the Sultans and the traditional *bostan* gardens, small productive vegetable plots that were widespread.

Somewhere in the countryside near Constantinople, Candide encounters "a worthy old man" living with his sons and daughters on a small farm. The old man welcomes Candide and his com-panions into his home and offers them fruits from his garden. Together, they feast on oranges, pineapples, and pistachios, along with homemade sorbets and spiced cream. Candide is amazed to discover that this simple farm is so flourishing. He and his friends have been spending their time in drawn-out philosophical dis-cussions that have left them feeling bored, restless, and anxious. Instead, Candide realizes, they need to cultivate their garden.

Voltaire's optimism and pessimism, albeit in different guises, dominate our lives today. Pessimism is all around us, not least in the current epidemic of depression and anxiety and in widespread feelings of passivity and helplessness about the state of the world, about the climate crisis, about wars and violence and the relentless exploitation of nature and people. As in the time of Candide, it seems we live in a bipolar world, in which we either suffer overwhelming gloom about the direction we are heading in or live in a state of denial and assume "all will be well," while continuing to gaze into a screen that takes us to another realm.

The garden is perhaps the best metaphor we have for life, but it is also much more than a metaphor. So it was for Voltaire. Following the publication of *Candide*, in the last twenty years of his life, he lived out his message and devoted much time and energy to cultivating the land. He took on a neglected estate at Ferney, where, in a rejection of the French fashion for formal design, he created a productive fruit and vegetable garden. He kept bees and planted thousands of trees, many with his own hands. He once wrote: "I have only done one sensible thing in my life—to cultivate the ground. He who tills a field, renders a better service to mankind than all the scribblers in Europe." Voltaire's idea of the garden is not a retreat: it is a deeply pragmatic approach that contributes to the common good.

"*Il faut cultiver notre jardin*" means accepting that life has to be nourished and that we can do that best through shaping our own lives, our communities, and the environments we inhabit. The moral of Voltaire's tale is to stop chasing an idealized version of life while turning a blind eye to the problems of this one; make the most of what you have around you and get stuck into something real.

In this era of virtual worlds and fake facts, the garden brings us back to reality; not the kind of reality that is known and predictable, for the garden always surprises us and in it we can experience a different kind of knowing, one that is sensory and physical and which stimulates the emotional, spiritual, and cognitive aspects of our being. Gardening is, in this sense, simultaneously ancient and modern. Ancient because of the evolutionary fit between brain and nature, and also ancient as a way of life that lies between foraging and farming, that expresses our deeply inscribed need to attach to place. Modern because the garden is intrinsically forward-looking and the gardener is always aiming for a better future.

Cultivation works both ways—it is inward as well as outward—and tending a garden can become an attitude toward life. In a world that is increasingly dominated by technology and consumption, gardening puts us in a direct relationship with the reality of how life is generated and sustained and how fragile and fleeting it can be. Now, more than ever, we need to remind ourselves that first and foremost, we are creatures of the earth.

Acknowledgments

Ted May with some of his orchids, late 1960s.

Many of the ideas in *The Well-Gardened Mind* have grown from a talk that I gave at the first of the Garden Museum's summer literary festivals in 2013. I am forever grateful to Christopher Woodward, the inspirational director of the museum, for suggesting that I speak at that event.

One strand of this book is about family history, specifically that of my grandfather Ted May. I could not have explored his wartime experiences or his love of horticulture without help and support from my mother, Judy Roberts, my brother, Nigel Evans, and my cousin Roger Cornish. To them, huge thanks. Another strand concerns the making of the Barn Garden at Serge Hill with my husband, Tom, none of which could have happened without the generosity of my parents-in-law, Joan and Murray Stuart-Smith, who helped to shape our lives at the Barn in countless wonderful ways. Family support for the book has also come from Bella, Mark, and Kate Stuart-Smith. Kate also devoted time and effort to editing the final manuscript, and I am grateful for her perceptive reading of the text.

The following people shared with me their experiences of being helped through gardens and gardening. In speaking with passion and eloquence from direct experience, these participants offered key insights, and the book would not be what it is without their contributions: Andrew Albright, Shakim Allen, José Althia, Ian Belcher, Dagmara Bernoni, Juan Bran, Tiffany Champagne, José Diaz, Vanessa Eranzo, Hussein Ershadi, Harry Gaved, David Golden, Darrin Haynes, Christian Howells, Glenn Johnson, Velvet Johnson, Valerie Leone, David Maldonado, Jack Mannings, José Mota, Wilmer Osibin, Hiro Perulta, Caroline Ralph, Juan Rodas, José Rodriguez, Frank Ruiz, Jane Shrimpton, Albert Silvagnoli, Sharon Tizzard, Angel Vega, Richard Warren, Holland Williams, and Kevin Williams.

I am grateful for assistance from the Royal Horticultural Society, particularly Fiona Davison at the Lindley Library and Alistair Griffiths, director of science and collections. At Thrive, I would like to thank Shirley Charlton, Penny Cooke, Nathan Dippie, Steve Humphries, Kathryn Rossiter, and Sally Wright. The New York Botanical Garden was tremendously helpful with my research in the US: Ursula Chanse, Barbara Corcoran, and Gregory Long went out of their way to assist me in various ways and linked me up with interesting projects. The Chicago Botanic Garden, likewise, arranged visits and provided me with contacts. I particularly want to thank Eliza Fournier, Rachel Kimpton, and Barbara Kreski.

Many people involved in running community projects and horticultural therapy programs in different countries gave up their time to speak to me. I want to pay tribute to their deep understanding of the transformative potential of working with nature. I have tried to be inclusive, but if I have missed anyone out, I can only apologize: Kurt Ackerman, Anna Adevi, Shaniece Alexander, Or Algazi, Barbara Barbieri, Isobel Barnes, Monica Bazanti, Leahanne Black, Natalie Brickajlik, Estelle Brown, Heather Budge-Reid, Ahmet Caglar, Pat Callaghan, Olivia and David Chapple, Keely Siddiqui Charlick, Mary Clear, Paula Conway, Kyle Cornforth, Anna Baker Cresswell, Phyllis D'Amico, Pino D'Aquisito, Elizabeth Diehl, Mike Erickson, Maque Falgás, Christian Fernández, Ron Finlay, Gwenn Fried, Darrie Ganzhorn, Andreas Ginkell, Patrik Grahn, Edwina Grosvenor, Rex Haigh, Mark Harding, Sonya Harper, Paul Hartwell, Teresia Hazen, Qayyum Johnson, Hilda Krus, Jean Larson, Adam Levin, Ruth Madder, Susanna Magistretti, Orin Martin, Marianna Merisi, Tiziano Monaco, Cara Montgomery, Alfonso Montiel, Kai Nash, Konrad Neuberger, John Parker, Keith Petersen, Harry Rhodes, Anne and Jean-Paul Ribes, Jay Stone Rice, Liz Rothschild, Cecil-John Roussow, Carol Sales, Albert Salvans, Rebekah Silverman, Cathrine Sneed, Malin Strand, Lindsay Swan, Mike Swinburne, Paul Taliaard, Phoebe Tanner, Alex Taylor, Julie and John Tracy, Clare Trussler, Lucy Voelker, and Beth Waitkus.

The following academics, physicians, and authors generously shared their expertise with me and have informed the book, even when not directly cited: William Bird, David Buck, Paul Camic, Chris Cullen, Robyn Francis, Dorian Fuller, Richard Fuller, Charles Guy, Jan Hassink, Teresia Hazen, Kenneth Helphand, Glynis Jones, Rachel Kelly, Kelly Lambert, Christopher Lowry, Annie Maccoby, Alan McLean, Andreas Meyer-Lindenberg, David Nutt, Matthew Patrick, Jules Pretty, Jenny Roe, Edward Rosen, Joe Sempik, Philip Siegel, Matilda van den Bosch, and Peter Whybrow. In addition, the designers Katy Bott, Gayle Souter-Brown, and Cleve West illuminated my understanding of what is involved in creating a therapeutic garden.

Deborah Pursch helped me with some of the research, ingeniously seeking out sources and information that had eluded me. Sally Miller from the Hampshire Gardens Trust explored the county archives and uncovered the material about Sarisbury Court in Chapter 9. I also thank Bryony Davies at the Freud Museum picture library and Frances Wharton for her translation of the Freud letter from the Torre del Gallo, quoted in Chapter 10.

At Scribner, Colin Harrison's editorial input shaped the book in many different ways, and his compassionate and clear-sighted attention to the text taught me a great deal about the craft of writing. The making of a book involves many people, and I am indebted to a whole team at Scribner who have helped to lift the book to another level: Erich Hobbing, Roz Lippel, Sarah Goldberg, Nan Graham, Mark LaFlaur, and Rick Willett.

I also need to thank Arabella Pike, my editor at HarperCollins, for her discerning reading and commitment to the book. Vanessa Beaumont helped me with the structuring of the early chapters, and in the closing stages of the book's production, my devoted friend Caroline Oulton took on an intense burst of editing with dedication and humor, deploying her keen intelligence to help me prune and weed the manuscript.

Friends, family, and colleagues have read some or all of the chapters at various stages. I particularly want to thank Cyril Couve, Tony Garelick, Susie Godsil, Karen Jenkinson, Anna Ledgard, Neil Morgan, and Purdy Rubin for their comments and insights. At home, I need to thank Julia Maslin for administrative support and Jenny Levy for looking after the vegetable garden when the book kept me at my desk. For hospitality in the US, I am grateful to Za Bervern, John Fornengo, Elizabeth Louis, and Martha Pichey.

My great friend Nici Dahrendorf helped set the book in motion by introducing me to my agent Felicity Bryan. Felicity's tremendous belief in the project from the outset allowed me to develop and deepen my thinking about gardening for the mind, and her commitment and energy has never wavered. My thanks also to my US agent, Zoë Pagnamenta, for everything she has done.

I have received all manner of encouragement and help from friends and colleagues, particularly from: Phil Athill, Jinny Blom, Madeleine Bunting, Tania Compton, Alex Coulter, Sarah Draper, Helena Drysdale, Susannah Fiennes, Francis Hamel, Beth Heron, Michael Hue-Williams, Marilyn Imrie, Anna-Maria Ivstedt, Ali Joy, Joseph Koerner, Todd Longstaffe-Gowan, Adam Lowe, Martin Lupton, Rebecca Nicolson, Jo O'Reilly, Rosie Pearson, James Runcie, Agnes Schmitz, Kate Sebag, and Robin Walden. Along the way I have been touched by the thoughtfulness of many other friends who have alerted me to news items or research projects relevant to the book.

As Goethe wrote: "The sum which two married people owe to one another defies calculation." So it is with my husband, Tom, with whom I am lucky to share my life. Thanks beyond measure for being a constant companion, for reading and editing, for keeping up my morale when it flagged, and above all for being such a powerful source of inspiration. Finally, the enthusiasm and crucial doses of support provided by Rose, Ben, and Harry, our three children, who grew up alongside the garden, have accompanied me in the making of this book.

Selected General Sources on Nature, Gardens, and Health

Bailey, D. S. (2017). "Looking back to the future: the re-emergence of green care." *British Journal of Psychiatry International* 14(4): 79. doi: 10.1192/s205647400000204x.

Barton, J., et al. (2016). *Green Exercise*. Abingdon, UK: Routledge.

Borchardt, R. (2006). *The Passionate Gardener*. Kingston, NY: McPherson & Company.

Bowler, D. E., et al. (2010). "A systematic review of evidence for the added benefits to health of exposure to natural environments." *BMC Public Health* 10(1). doi:10.1186/1471-2458-10-456.

Bragg, R., and Leck, C. (2017). *Good practice in social prescribing for mental health: The role of nature-based interventions*. Natural England Commissioned Reports, Number 228. York.

Buck, D. (May 2016). *Gardens and Health: Implications for Policy and Practice*. The Kings Fund, report commissioned by the National Gardens Scheme. https://www.kingsfund.org.uk/sites/default/files/field/field_publication_file/Gardens_and_health.pdf.

Burton, A. (2014). "Gardens that take care of us." *Lancet Neurology* 13(5): 447–448. doi:10.1016/s1474-4422(14)70002-x.

Cooper, D. E. (2006). *A Philosophy of Gardens*. Oxford: Clarendon Press.

Cooper Marcus, C. C., and N. A. Sachs (2013). *Therapeutic Landscapes: An Evidence-Based Approach to Designing Healing Gardens and Restorative Outdoor Spaces*. Hoboken, NJ: John Wiley & Sons.

Francis, M., and Hester, R. T. (eds.) (1995). *The Meaning of Gardens: Idea, Place and Action*. Cambridge, MA: MIT Press.

Frumkin, H., et al. (2017). "Nature contact and human health: a research agenda." *Environmental Health Perspectives* 125(7): 075001. doi: 10.1289/ehp1663.

Goulson, D. (2019). *The Garden Jungle: Or Gardening to Save the Planet*. London: Jonathan Cape.

Haller, R. L., K. L. L. Kennedy, and C. L. Capra (2019). *The Profession and Practice of Horticultural Therapy*. Boca Raton, FL: CRC Press.

Harrison, R. P. (2009). *Gardens: an Essay on the Human Condition*. Chicago: University of Chicago Press.

Hartig, T., M. Mang, and G. W. Evans (1991). "Restorative effects of natural environment experiences." *Environment and Behavior* 23(1): 3–26. doi: 10.1177/0013916591231001.

Jordan, M., and J. Hinds (2016). *Ecotherapy: Theory, Research and Practice* London: Palgrave.

Kaplan, R. (1973). "Some psychological benefits of gardening." *Environment and Behavior* 5(2): 145–162. doi: 10.1177/001391657300500202.

Lewis, C. A. (1996). *Green Nature/Human Nature: The Meaning of Plants in Our Lives.* Champaign, IL: University of Illinois Press.

Louv, R. (2010). *Last Child in the Woods: Saving Our Children from Nature-Deficit Disorder.* London: Atlantic Books.

Mabey, R. (2008). *Nature Cure.* New York: Vintage Books.

McKay, G. (2011). *Radical Gardening: Politics, Idealism & Rebellion in the Garden.* London: Francis Lincoln.

Olds, A. (1989). "Nature as healer." *Children's Environments Quarterly* 6(1): 27–32.

Relf, D. (1992). *The Role of Horticulture in Human Well-Being and Social Development: A National Symposium.* Portland, OR: Timber Press.

Ross, S. (2001). *What Gardens Mean.* Chicago: University of Chicago Press.

Roszak, T., M. E. Gomes, and A. D. Kanner (eds.) (1995). *Ecopsychology: Restoring the Earth, Healing the Mind.* San Francisco: Sierra Club Books.

Sempik, J. (2010). "Green care and mental health: Gardening and farming as health and social care." *Mental Health and Social Inclusion* 14(3): 15–22. doi:10.5042/mhsi.2010.0440.

Souter-Brown, G. (2015). *Landscape and Urban Design for Health and Well-Being: Using Healing, Sensory, Therapeutic Gardens.* Abingdon, UK: Routledge.

Sternberg, E. M. (2010). *Healing Spaces.* Cambridge, MA: Harvard University Press.

Townsend, M., and R. Weerasuriya (2010). *Beyond Blue to Green: The Benefits of Contact with Nature for Mental Health and Wellbeing.* Melbourne: Beyond Blue Ltd.

Wellbeing Benefits from Natural Environments Rich in Wildlife: A Literature Review for The Wildlife Trusts. (2018). Colchester, UK: The University of Essex.

Williams, F. (2017). *The Nature Fix: Why Nature Makes Us Happier, Healthier, and More Creative.* New York: W. W. Norton.

Notes

SE: The Standard Edition of the Complete Psychological Works of Sigmund Freud, 24 vols. James Strachey, trans. London: Hogarth Press, 1953–1974.

Abbreviation Used in the Notes

Chapter 1: Beginnings

1   William Wordsworth quotation from "The Tables Turned" *in Lyrical Ballads*, 1798.

5   *the poet who himself had learned:* From "Lines Composed a Few Miles Above Tintern Abbey (1798/1994)," *The Collected Poems of William Wordsworth* (Ware, Hertfordshire: Wordsworth Editions Ltd.).

13   *the chemical factory* at *Seveso:* On July 10, 1976, an explosion at an Italian chemical plant released a cloud of dioxin that settled on the town of Seveso, north of Milan. First, animals began to die; four days later people began to feel ill effects, and it took weeks for the town to be evacuated.

14   *rates of depression and anxiety:* In 2013, according to WHO, depression was the second leading cause of years lived with disability worldwide. In 2014, 19.7 percent of people in the UK aged sixteen and older showed symptoms of anxiety or depression—a 1.5 percent increase from 2013. Mental Health Foundation report, 2016: "Instances of common mental disorders such as depression and anxiety in people aged 16–74 years rose from 16.2% in 2007 to 17% in 2014" (Office of National Statistics, 2016). *Adult psychiatric morbidity in England, 2014: results of a household survey.*

14   *forerunner of psychoanalytic thinking:* R. D. McGhee (1993), *Guilty Pleasures: William Wordsworth's Poetry of Psychoanalysis* (Albany, NY: Whitston Publishing Co.), and M. Harris Williams and M. Waddell (1991), *The Chamber of Maiden Thought: Literary Origins of the Psychoanalytic Model of the Mind* (Abingdon, UK: Routledge).

14   *modern neuroscience confirms:* See V. S. Ramachandran and S. Blakeslee (2005), *Phantoms in the Brain: Human Nature and the Architecture of the Mind* (New York: Harper Perennial).

15   *for Wordsworth and his sister, Dorothy:* D. Wordsworth (1991), *The Grasmere Journals* (Oxford University Press) and F. Wilson (2008), *The Ballad of Dorothy Wordsworth* (London: Faber & Faber).

15   *"nook of mountain-ground":* From Wordsworth's poem "A Farewell," 1802.

15   *"emotion recollected in tranquillity":* Wordsworth's Preface to *Lyrical Ballads.*

15   *a lifelong habit:* Buchanan, in *Wordsworth's Gardens*, p. 35, writes: "All his life he wrote his poetry in the garden, pacing out rhythms and chanting verses aloud as he strode along the paths."

15 *Wordsworth's love of horticulture:* See P. Dale and B. C. Yen (2018), *Wordsworth's Gardens and Flowers: The Spirit of Paradise* (New York: ACC Art Books). Also: C. Buchanan and R. Buchanan (2001), *Wordsworth's Gardens* (Lubbock, TX: Texas Tech University Press).

16 *The purpose of a garden:* Wordsworth's letter to George Beaumont, quoted in Buchanan, *Wordsworth's Garden*, p. 30.

16 *Winnicott called a "transitional" area of experience:* D. W. Winnicott, (1953), "Transitional objects and transitional phenomena," *International Journal of Psychoanalysis* 34(2): 89–97.

16 *his understanding of the mind:* For an overview, see Lesley Caldwell and Angela Joyce (2011), *Reading Winnicott* (Abingdon, UK: Routledge).

17 *Winnicott believed that play:* D. W. Winnicott (1971), *Playing and Reality* (London: Tavistock Publications).

17 *"alone in the presence of the mother":* D. W. Winnicott (1958), "The capacity to be alone," *International Journal of Psychoanalysis* 39: 416–420.

18 *The field of attachment theory:* See J. Holmes (2014), *John Bowlby and Attachment Theory* (2nd ed.) (Abingdon, UK: Routledge).

18 *animals do not roam about at random:* J. Bowlby (1971), *Attachment and Loss, Vol.2: Separation* (London: Pimlico), pp. 177–178.

18 *Attachment to place:* See L. C. Manzo and P. Devine-Wright (2014), *Place Attachment: Advances in Theory, Methods and Applications* (Abingdon, UK: Routledge). Also: M. Lewicka (2011), "Place attachment: How far have we come in the last 40 years?," *Journal of Environmental Psychology* 31: 207–230.

19 *Research shows that when children are upset:* L. Chawla (1992), "Childhood place attachments," in I. Altman and S. M. Low (eds.), *Place Attachment* (New York: Plenum Press), pp. 63–86.

19 *"Nature mourns with the mourner":* M. Klein, (1940/1998), "Mourning and its relation to manic-depressive states," in *Love, Guilt and Reparation and Other Works 1921–1945* (London: Vintage Classics).

20 *metaphors that have profoundly shaped:* See G. Lakoff and M. Johnson (1980), *Metaphors We Live By* (University of Chicago Press).

21 *"It is when the world within us":* H. Segal (1981), *The Work of Hanna Segal: A Kleinian Approach to Clinical Practice* (London: J. Aronson), p. 73.

Chapter 2: Green Nature: Human Nature

23 George Herbert quotation from "The Flower," 1633.

24 *Kay rented a flat:* Names and certain characteristics of people in the case studies presented in this and subsequent chapters have been changed. Interview material that is quoted is in the participants' own words.

26 *The story of St. Maurilius:* See C. Thacker (1994), *The Genius of Gardening* (London: Weidenfeld & Nicolson) and G. Jones (2007), *Saints in the Landscape* (Cheltenham, UK: Tempus Publishing).

27 *Maurilius's seven years of gardening:* A. Butler (1985), *Butler's Lives of the Saints* (London: Burns & Oates).

27 *Benedictine's Rule:* C. Brooke (2003), *The Age of the Cloister: The Story of Monastic Life in the Middle Ages* (Mahwah, NJ: Paulist Press).

28 *St. Bernard's account of the hospice gardens:* Quoted in N. Gerlach-Spriggs, R. E. Kaufman, and S. B. Warner (2004), *Restorative Gardens: The Healing Landscape* (New Haven: Yale University Press), p. 9.

29 *viriditas:* M. Fox (2012), *Hildegard of Bingen: A Saint for Our Times.* (Vancouver, Canada: Namaste).

29 *The emotional significance of reparation:* M. Klein (1998), *Love, Guilt and Reparation and Other Works: 1921–1945* (London: Vintage Classics).

30 *L'Enfant et les Sortilèges:* See Klein's 1929 paper "Infantile anxiety situations reflected in a work of art and in the creative impulse," *in Love, Guilt and Reparation,* pp. 210–218.

32 *Naomi Klein recently observed:* Interview, *New Statesman* , July 2, 2017. https://www.newstatesman.com/2017/07/take-back-power-naomi-klein.

33 *the same three mathematical laws*: A. Conn et al. (2017), "A statistical description of plant shoot architecture," *Current Biology* 27(14): 2078–2088.e3. https://doi.org/10.1016/j.cub.2017.06.009.

34 *These specialist cells are highly mobile:* V. Hughes (2012), "Microglia: The constant gardeners," *Nature* 485(7400): 570–572 (doi: 10.1038/485570a) and D. P. Schafer et al. (2012), "Microglia sculpt postnatal neural circuits in an activity and complement-dependent manner," *Neuron* 74(4): 691–705 (doi: 10.1016/j.neuron.2012.03.026).

34 *Recent developments in imaging techniques:* European Molecular Biology Laboratory (March 2018), "Captured on film for the first time: Microglia nibbling on brain synapses: Microglia help synapses grow and rearrange. *ScienceDaily*, March 26, 2018. www.sciencedaily.com/releases/2018/03/180326090326.htm.

34 *the brain's "Miracle-Gro":* J. J. Ratey and E. Hagerman (2008), *Spark: The Revolutionary New Science of Exercise and the Brain.* Little, Brown.

35 *implicated in depression:* One of the therapeutic effects of antidepressants is to raise levels of BDNF. See: B. H. Lee and Y. K. Kim (2010), "The roles of BDNF in the pathophysiology of major depression and in antidepressant treatment," *Psychiatry Investigation* 7(4): 231–235.

35 *We are a grassland species:* V. Cregan-Reid (2018), *Primate Change: How the World We Made Is Remaking Us* (London: Hachette).

38 *first became prominent in the eighteenth century:* See C. Hickman (2013), *Therapeutic Landscapes* (Manchester University Press).

38 *"a quiet haven in which the shattered bark":* Quoted by Samuel Tuke in his *Description of the Retreat* (1813).

38 *observed that mental health patients: Medical Inquiries and Observations Upon the Diseases of the Mind* was published by Benjamin Rush in 1812.

39 *"Social prescribing" schemes:* A. Kilgarriff-Foster and A. O'Cathain (2015), "Exploring the components and impact of social prescribing," *Journal of Public Mental Health* 14(3): 127–134, and Rachel Bragg et al. (2017), *Good Practice in Social Prescribing for Mental Health: The Role of Nature-Based Interventions* (Natural England Report number 228).

39 *The GP William Bird:* M. van den Bosch and W. Bird (2018), *Oxford Textbook of Nature and Public Health: The Role of Nature in Improving the Health of a Population* (Oxford University Press).

39 *saved through reduced health costs:* See also N. Ireland (2013), *Social Return on Investment (SROI) Report: Gardening in Mind.* http://www.socialvalueuk.org/app/uploads/2016/04/Gardening-in-Mind-SROI-Report-final-version-1.pdf.

39 *a large-scale survey:* R. Bragg, C. Wood, and J. Barton (2013), *Ecominds Effects on Mental Wellbeing: An Evaluation for MIND.*

39 *research across the last few decades:* M. T. Gonzalez et al. (2010), "Therapeutic horticulture in clinical depression: a prospective study of active components," *Journal of Advanced Nursing* (doi: 10.1111/j.1365-2648.2010.05383.x); and H. Kamioka et al. (2014), "Effectiveness of horticultural therapy: A systematic review of randomized controlled trials," *Complementary Therapies in Medicine* 22(5): 930–943 (doi: 10.1016/j.ctim.2014.08.009).

40 *randomly allocated to a treatment:* U. K. Stigsdotter et al. (2018), "Efficacy of nature-based therapy for individuals with stress-related illnesses: randomised controlled trial," *British Journal of Psychiatry* 213(1): 404–411. doi: 10.1192/bjp.2018.2.

41 *Like the Benedictine monastic gardens:* Monastery gardens have become a template for therapeutic gardens. See G. Souter-Brown (2015), *Landscape and Urban Design for Health and Well-Being: Using Healing, Sensory and Therapeutic Gardens* (Abingdon, UK: Routledge).

41 *sublimation:* S. Freud (1930), *Civilisation and Its Discontents S.E., 21:* 79–80.

42 *Miss Havisham:* C. Dickens (1996), *Great Expectations* (London: Penguin Classics).

Chapter 3: Seeds and Self-Belief

45 T. Fuller (1732), *Gnomologia: Adages and Proverbs; Wise Sentences and Witty Sayings, Ancient and Modern, Foreign and British* (London: Barker & Bettesworth Hitch).

48 *"Then I make the big connection":* M. Pollan (1991), *Second Nature: A Gardener's Education* (New York: Atlantic Press).

48 *the psychoanalyst Marion Milner:* M. Milner (1955), "The role of illusion in symbol-formation," in M. Klein (Ed.), *New Directions in Psycho-analysis* (London: Tavistock Publications).

48 *not only is a baby the center of its own world:* See D. W. Winnicott (1988), *Human Nature* (London: Free Association Books). Winnicott writes: "The infant has the illusion that what is found is created."

49 *"the joy in being a cause":* The quotation is from Karl Groos's *The Play of Man,* E. L. Baldwin, trans., originally published in 1901. Groos's thinking influenced Winnicott.

49 *the "good enough mother":* D. W. Winnicott (1953), "Transitional objects and transitional phenomena, *International Journal of Psychoanalysis* 34(2): 89–97.

49 *"The mother's eventual task":* D. W. Winnicott (1973), *The Child, the Family, and the Outside World* (London: Penguin Books).

50 *"One felt that if he were growing a daffodil":* S. Grolnick (1990), *The Work & Play of Winnicott* (London: Jason Aronson), p. 20.

51 *Royal Horticultural Society (RHS) has been running a campaign:* RHS Gardening *in Schools: A Vital Tool for Children's Learning* (2010) (London: Royal Horticultural Society). www.rhs.org.uk/schoolgardening.

53 *the re-offending rate:* Rikers rates are comparable to similar programs. S. Seevan der Linden (2015), "Green prison programmes, recidivism and mental health: A primer," *Criminal Behaviour and Mental Health* 25(5): 338–342.

60 *how much a bird like that cost:* J. Jiler (2006), *Doing Time in the Garden* (New York: Village Press).

61 *research conducted in Liverpool:* S. Maruna (2013), *Making Good: How Ex-convicts Reform and Rebuild Their Lives* (Washington, DC: American Psychological Association).

62 *an evaluation of the program:* Carried out by Lisa Benham in 2002 for the Insight Garden Program.

63 *the average child spends less time outside:* As a result of not playing outdoors, up to 70 percent of children are insufficient in vitamin D. See Voortman et al. (2015), "Vitamin D deficiency in school-age children is associated with sociodemographic and lifestyle factors," *Journal of Nutrition* 145(4): 791–798. The Play in Balance survey involved twelve thousand parents in ten countries with children aged 5–12 and found that 70 percent of children spend less than sixty minutes outdoors each day and 30 percent under thirty minutes. The study was commissioned in 2016 by Persil. See also: R. Benwell et al. (2014), "A Nature and Wellbeing Act: A green paper from the Wildlife Trusts and the RSPB" (retrieved from http://www.wildlifetrusts.org/sites/default/files/green_paper_nature_and_wellbeing_act_full_final.pdf) and S. Moss (2012), *Natural Childhood* (Wiltshire, UK: National Trust Publications).

63 *"delinquency as a sign of hope":* D. W. Winnicott (1990), *Deprivation and Delinquency* (Abingdon, UK: Routledge).

64 *sensori-motor learning:* J. Piaget (1973), *The Child's Conception of the World* (Abingdon, UK: Routledge). See also: D. G. Singer and T. A. Revenson (1978), *A Piaget Primer* (New York: Plume Books).

65 *"knitted" into our being:* M. Milner (2010), *On Not Being Able to Paint.* (Abingdon, UK: Routledge).

65 *"a form of alchemy":* M. Pollan (2002), *The Botany of Desire: A Plant's-Eye View of the World* (London: Bloomsbury).

Chapter 4: Safe Green Space

67 Erik Erikson quotation from E. Erikson (1958), *Young Man Luther: A Study on Psychoanalysis and History* (New York: W. W. Norton), p. 266.

69 *Harold Searles observed that patients:* H. F. Searles (1960), *The Nonhuman Environment in Normal Development and in Schizophrenia* (Madison, CT: International Universities Press).

69 *autobiography of the writer:* G. Rees (1960), *A Bundle of Sensations: Sketches in Autobiography* (London: Chatto & Windus) pp. 205–240.

69 *"The infant falls to pieces":* D. W. Winnicott, (1988), *Human Nature* (London: Free Association Books), p. 117.

70 *the rhyme's universal appeal:* Winnicott, *Human Nature*, p. 118.

70 *"habitat theory":* J. Appleton (1975), *The Experience of Landscape* (New York: John Wiley & Sons).

71 *a "nested hierarchy":* J. Panksepp (1998), *Affective Neuroscience: The Foundations of Human and Animal Emotions* (New York: Oxford University Press).

72 *trauma cannot be integrated:* B. van der Kolk (2000), "Posttraumatic stress disorder and the nature of trauma," *Dialogues in Clinical Neuroscience* 2(1): 7–22.

72 *first step of any trauma treatment:* J. Herman (1997), *Trauma and Recovery: The Aftermath of Violence—from Domestic Abuse to Political Terror* (New York: Basic Books).2

73 *in horticultural therapy:* For further studies on veterans, see S. Westlund (2014), *Field Exercises* (Gabriola Island, Canada: New Society Publishers) and J. Wise (2015), *Digging for Victory* (London: Karnac Books).

74 *olfactory triggers:* N. Kline and J. Rausch (1985), "Olfactory precipitants of flashbacks in post traumatic stress disorder: Case reports," *Journal of Clinical Psychiatry* 46: 383–384.

74 *the color green:* E. M. Sternberg (2010), *Healing Spaces* (Cambridge, MA: Harvard University Press).

74 *pioneered research:* See for example: R. S. Ulrich (1981), "Natural versus urban scenes: Some psycho-physiological effects," *Environmental Behavior* 13: 523–556, and R. S. Ulrich et al. (1991), "Stress recovery during exposure to natural and urban environments," *Journal of Environmental Psychology* 11(3): 201–230. doi: 10.1016/s0272-4944(05)80184-7.

75 *changes in heart rate and blood pressure:* V. F. Gladwell et al. (2012), "The effects of views of nature on autonomic control," *European Journal of Applied Physiology* 112(9): 3379–3386. doi: 10.1007/s00421-012-2318-8.

75 *levels of the stress hormone cortisol:* A. E. van den Berg and M. H. Custers, (2010), "Gardening promotes neuroendocrine and affective restoration from stress," *Journal of Health Psychology* 16(1): 3–11. doi: 10.1177/1359105310365577.

76 *Practicing mindfulness:* M. Williams and D. Penman (2011), *Mindfulness: A Practical Guide to Finding Peace in a Frantic World* (London: Piatkus) and J. Kabat-Zinn (2013), *Full Catastrophe Living* (London: Piaktus).

76 *restore a more integrated state:* N. A. S. Farb, A. K. Anderson, and Z. V. Segal (2012), "The mindful brain and emotion regulation in mood disorders," *Canadian Journal of Psychiatry* 57(2): 70–77. doi: 10.1177/070674371205700203.

77 *"the desire to see without being seen":* J. Appleton (1975), *The Experience of Landscape* (New York: John Wiley & Sons).

78 *light is a form of nourishment:* G. Lambert et al. (2002), "Effect of sunlight and season on serotonin turnover in the brain," *Lancet* 360 (9348): 1840–1842. doi: 10.1016/s0140-6736(02)11737-5.

78 *dysfunction of the serotonin system:* A. Frick et al. (2015), "Overlapping expression of serotonin transporters and neurokinin-1 receptors in posttraumatic stress disorder: A multi-tracer PET study," *Molecular Psychiatry* 21(10): 1400–1407. doi: 10.1038/mp.2015.180.

79 *another beneficial effect of exercise:* C. Cotman (2002), "Exercise: A behavioral

intervention to enhance brain health and plasticity," *Trends in Neurosciences* 25(6): 295–301. doi: 10.1016/s0166-2236(02)02143-4; M. P. Mattson, S. Maudsley, and B. Martin (2004), "BDNF and 5-HT: A dynamic duo in age-related neuronal plasticity and neurodegenerative disorders," *Trends in Neurosciences* 27(10): 589–594. doi: 10.1016/j.tins.2004.08.001; N. Sayal (2015), "Exercise training increases size of hippocampus and improves memory," *Annals of Neurosciences* 22(2). doi: 10.5214/ans.0972.7531.220209.

79 *When we use the large muscles:* L. Z. Agudelo et al. (2014), "Skeletal muscle pgc-1-1 modulates kynurenine metabolism and mediates resilience to stress-induced depression," *Cell* 159(1): 33–45. doi: 10.1016/j.cell.2014.07.051.

79 *turning "passive to active":* R. M. Sapolsky (2004), *Why Zebras Don't Get Ulcers* (New York: St. Martin's Press).

79 *Exercising outdoors is better still:* J. Barton and J. Pretty (2010), "What is the best dose of nature and green exercise for improving mental health? A multi-study analysis." *Environmental Science & Technology* 44(10): 3947–3955. doi: 10.1021/es903183r.

79 *geosmin:* K. F. Chater (2015), *The Smell of the Soil*, available at https://microbio logysociety.org/publication/past-issues/soil/article/the-smell-of-the-soil.html. Also E. H. Polak and J. Provasi (1992), "Odor sensitivity to geosmin enantiomers," *Chemical Senses* 17. doi: 10.1093/chemse/17.1.23.

79 *boost serotonin levels and help regulate the immune system:* C. A. Lowry et al. (2016), "The microbiota, immunoregulation, and mental health: implications for public health," *Current Environmental Health Reports* 3(3): 270–286 (doi:10.1007/s40572-016-0100-5) and D. M. Matthews and S. M. Jenks (2013), "Ingestion of mycobacterium vaccae decreases anxiety-related behavior and improves learning in mice," *Behavioural Processes* 96: 27–35 (doi: 10.1016/j. beproc.2013.02.007).

80 *other strains of bacteria:* S. C. Anderson, with J. F. Cryan and T. Dinan (2017), *The Psychobiotic Revolution* (New York: National Geographic) and Ed Yong, (2016), *I Contain Multitudes* (London: The Bodley Head).

81 *veterans project in Denmark:* D. V. Poulsen et al. (2016), "Everything just seems much more right in nature: How veterans with post-traumatic stress disorder experience nature-based activities in a forest therapy garden," *Health Psychology Open* 3(1): 205510291663709. doi: 10.1177/2055102916637090.

82 *ancient rites involved in tree worship:* J. G. Frazer (1994), *The Golden Bough* (Oxford University Press).

86 *"brings the individual close to the soil":* Menninger quotation is from P. D. Relf, "Agriculture and health care: The care of plants and animals for therapy and rehabilitation in the United States," in Jan Hassink and Majken van Dijk (eds.) (2006), *Farming for Health: Green-Care Farming Across Europe and the United States of America* (New York: Springer), pp. 309–343.

Chapter 5: Bringing Nature to the City

87 Frederick Law Olmsted quotation in F. L. Olmsted (1852), *Walks and Talks of an American Farmer in England* (New York: G.P. Putnam & Co.).

89 *Plans of Uruk, one of the very first cities:* S. N. Kramer (1981), *History Begins at Sumer: Thirty-Nine Firsts in Man's Recorded History* (3rd ed.) (Philadelphia: University of Pennsylvania Press).

89 *The great seventeenth-century essayist:* Evelyn's Fumifugium of 1661 is quoted in W. Cavert (2016), *The Smoke of London: Energy and Environment in the Early Modern City* (Cambridge University Press), p. 181.

91 *"employs the mind without fatigue":* F. Olmsted and R. Nash (1865), *The Value and Care of Parks,* Report to the Congress of the State of California, reprinted in *The American Environment* (Hillsdale, NJ), pp. 18–24.

92 *"a prophylactic and therapeutic agent of value":* In C. Beveridge (ed.) (2016), *Frederick Law Olmsted: Writings on Landscape, Culture, and Society* (New York: Library of America), p. 426.

92 *George Miller Beard, the American physician:* M. Gijswijt-Hofstra and R. Porter, R. (2001), *Cultures of Neurastheni* (London: The Wellcome Trust).

93 *rates of both of these are higher in urban settings:* S. McManus et al. (2009), *Adult Psychiatric Morbidity in England, 2007: Results of a Household Survey.* 10.13140/2.1.1563.5205; J. Peen et al. (2010), "The current status of urban-rural differences in psychiatric disorders," *Acta Psychiatrica Scandinavica* 121(2): 84–93. doi: 10.1111/j.1600-0447.2009.01438.x.

93 *A recent UK study:* J. Newbury et al. (2017), "Cumulative effects of neighborhood social adversity and personal crime victimization on adolescent psychotic experiences," *Schizophrenia Bulletin* 44(2): 348–358. doi: 10.1093/schbul/sbx060.

93 *we pay a price:* F. Lederbogen et al. (2011), "City living and urban upbringing affect neural social stress processing in humans," *Nature* 474(7352), 498–501. doi: 10.1038/nature10190; E. Vassos et al. (2012), "Meta-analysis of the association of urbanicity with schizophrenia," *Schizophrenia Bulletin* 38(6): 1118–1123. doi: 10.1093/schbul/sbs096.

93 *Health surveys of commuters reveal:* Office for National Statistics Commuting and Personal Well-being, 2014.

94 *Proximity to green space has been shown:* T. Hartig (2008), "Green space, psychological restoration, and health inequality," *Lancet* 372(9650): 1614–1615 (doi:10.1016/s0140-6736(08)61669-4); J. Roe et al. (2013), "Green space and stress: Evidence from cortisol measures in deprived urban communities," *International Journal of Environmental Research and Public Health* 10(9): 4086–4103 (doi: 10.3390/ijerph10094086); L. Keniger et al. (2013), "What are the benefits of interacting with nature?," *International Journal of Environmental Research and Public Health* 10(3): 913–935 (doi: 10.3390/ijerph10030913); D. F. Shanahan et al. (2015), "Toward improved public health outcomes from urban nature," *American Journal of Public Health* 105(3): 470–477. doi: 10.2105/ajph.2014.302324.

94 *A study led by the ecologist:* R. A. Fuller et al. (2007), "Psychological benefits of greenspace increase with biodiversity," *Biology Letters* 3(4): 390–394. doi: 10.1098/rsbl.2007.0149.

95 *Recent research carried out by Fuller in Brisbane:* D. F. Shanahan et al. (2016), "Health benefits from nature experiences depend on dose," *Scientific Reports* 6(28551): 1–10.

95 *study carried out at the Centre for Research on Environment:* R. J. Mitchell et al. (2015), "Neighborhood environments and socioeconomic inequalities in mental well-being," *American Journal of Preventive Medicine* 49(1): 80–84. doi: 10.1016/j.amepre.2015.01.017.

96 *presence of street trees:* O. Kardan et al. (2015), "Neighborhood greenspace and health in a large urban center," *Scientific Reports* 5(1). doi:10.1038 /srep11610.

96 *a number of influential studies:* F. E. Kuo et al. (1998). "Fertile ground for community: inner-city neighborhood common spaces," *American Journal of Community Psychology* 26(6): 823–851 (doi:10.1023/a:1022294028903); F. E. Kuo (2001), "Coping with poverty," *Environment and Behavior* 33(1): 5–34 (doi:10. 1177/00139160121972846); F. E. Kuo and W. C. Sullivan (2001), "Aggression and violence in the inner city," *Environment and Behavior* 33(4): 543–571 (doi:1 0.1177/00139160121973124); F. E. Kuo and W. C. Sullivan (2001), "Environment and crime in the inner city," *Environment and Behavior* 33(3): 343–367 (doi:10.1177/0013916501333002).

97 *associated with changes in the brain:* G. N. Bratman, J. P. Hamilton, and G. C. Daily (2012), "The impacts of nature experience on human cognitive function and mental health," *Annals of the New York Academy of Sciences* 1249(1): 118– 136. doi:10.1111/j.1749-6632.2011.06400.x.

98 *"Put human history into one week":* J. Pretty (2007), *The Earth Only Endures* (Abingdon, UK: Earthscan), p. 217.

98 *a series of experiments carried out in the 1980s:* R. Kaplan and S. Kaplan (1989), *The Experience of Nature: A Psychological Perspective* (Cambridge University Press).

98 *"Attention Restoration":* R. Berto (2005), "Exposure to restorative environments helps restore attentional capacity," *Journal of Environmental Psychology* 25(3), 249–259 (doi:10.1016/j.jenvp.2005.07.001); K. E. Lee et al. (2015), "40-second green roof views sustain attention: The role of micro-breaks in attention restoration," *Journal of Environmental Psychology* 42: 182–189 (doi:10.1016/j.jenvp.2015.04.003).

98 *students who walked:* M. G. Berman, J. Jonides, and S. Kaplan (2008), "The cognitive benefits of interacting with nature," *Psychological Science* 19(12): 1207– 1212. doi:10.1111/j.1467-9280.2008.02225.x.

99 *the relationship between the right and left hemispheres of the brain:* Quotations in this section are from I. McGilchrist (2010), *The Master and His Emissary* (New Haven: Yale University Press).

100 *innate "emotional affiliation":* E. O. Wilson (1984), *Biophilia* (Cambridge, MA: Harvard University Press).

100 *Two research studies at the Institute of Psychiatry:* L. Ellett, D. Freeman, and P. A. Garety (2008), "The psychological effect of an urban environment on individuals with persecutory delusions: The Camberwell walk study," *Schizophrenia Research* 99(1–3): 77–84 (doi:10.1016/j.schres.2007.10.027); D. Freeman et al. (2014), "The stress of the street for patients with persecutory delusions: A test of the symptomatic and psychological effects of going outside into a busy urban area," *Schizophrenia Bulletin* 41(4): 971–979 (doi:10.1093/schbul/sbu173).

104 *many different therapeutic aspects:* See S. Roberts and A. J. Bradley (2011),

"Horticultural therapy for schizophrenia," *Cochrane Database of Systematic Reviews,* Issue 11.

104 *complex environmental stimulation:* E. L. Burrows et al. (2015), "Environmental enrichment ameliorates behavioral impairments modeling schizophrenia in mice lacking metabotropic glutamate receptor 5," *Neuropsychopharmacology* 40(8): 1947–1956. doi:10.1038/npp.2015.44.

104 *enriched environments:* G. Kempermann, H. G. Kuhn, and F. H. Gage (1997), "More hippocampal neurons in adult mice living in an enriched environment," *Nature* 386(6624): 493–495 (doi:10.1038/386493a0); A. M. Sirevaag, and W. T. Greenough (1987), "Differential rearing effects on rat visual cortex synapses," *Brain Research* 424(2): 320–332 (doi:10.1016/0006-8993(87)91477-6).

105 *a third type of cage:* K. Lambert et al. (2016), "Natural-enriched environments lead to enhanced environmental engagement and altered neurobiological resilience," *Neuroscience* 330: 386–394 (doi:10.1016/j.neuroscience.2016.05.037); K. G. Lambert et al. (2015), "Brains in the city: Neurobiological effects of urbanization," *Neuroscience & Biobehavioral Reviews* 58: 107–122 (doi:10.1016/j.neubiorev.2015.04.007).

106 *It has been reported that Americans:* U.S. Environmental Protection Agency, 1989, Report to Congress on indoor air quality: Volume 2, EPA/400/1-89/001C, Washington, DC.

107 *sociability effect of green vegetation on people:* K. Yamane et al. (2004), "Effects of interior horticultural activities with potted plants on human physiological and emotional status," *Acta Horticulturae* (639): 37-43. (doi:10.17660/actahortic.2004.639.3); N. Weinstein, A. K. Przybylski, and R. M. Ryan, (2009), "Can nature make us more caring? Effects of immersion in nature on intrinsic aspirations and generosity," *Personality and Social Psychology Bulletin* 35(10): 1315–1329 (doi:10.1177/0146167209341649); J. M. Zelenski, R. L. Dopko, and C. A. Capaldi (2015), "Cooperation is in our nature: Nature exposure may promote cooperative and environmentally sustainable behavior," *Journal of Environmental Psychology* 42: 24–31 (doi:10.1016/j.jenvp.2015.01.005).

107 *activated parts of the brain involved in generating empathy:* G. Kim et al. (2010), "Functional neuroanatomy associated with natural and urban scenic views in the human brain: 3.0T Functional MR imaging," *Korean Journal of Radiology* 11(5): 507. doi:10.3348/kjr.2010.11.5.507.

107 *human connection:* J. Maas et al. (2009), "Social contacts as a possible mechanism behind the relation between green space and health," *Health & Place* 15(2): 586–595. doi:10.1016/j.healthplace.2008.09.006.

Chapter 6: Roots

109 Henry David Thoreau quotation is from Henry David Thoreau, *Walden* (1854), Chapter Twelve.

111 *The influential archaeologist V. Gordon Childe:* V. G. Childe (1948), *Man Makes Himself* (London: Thinker's Library).

112 *Rather than being a revolution:* P. Bellwood, (2005), *First Farmers* (Hoboken, NJ: Blackwell).

112 *the first farmers were drawing on:* D. Q. Fuller, G. Willcox, and R. G. Allaby (2011), "Early agricultural pathways: moving outside the 'core area' hypothesis in Southwest Asia," *Journal of Experimental Botany* 63(2): 617–633 (doi:10.1093/jxb/err307); Bob Holmes (October 28, 2015), "The real first farmers: How agriculture was a global invention," *New Scientist.*

113 *the first plants that people grew were highly desirable or scarce:* I. S. Farrington and J. Urry (1985), "Food and the early history of cultivation," *Journal of Ethnobiology* 5(2): 143–157.

113 *started with growing luxuries:* A. Sherratt (1997), "Climatic cycles and behavioural revolutions: The emergence of modern humans and the beginning of farming," *Antiquity* 7 (272).

113 *Settlement sites by lakes:* B. D. Smith (2011), "General patterns of niche construction and the management of 'wild' plant and animal resources by small-scale pre-industrial societies," *Philosophical Transactions of the Royal Society of London, Biological Sciences* 366(1566): 836–848.

113 *hunter-gatherer camp known as Ohalo II:* A. Snir et al. (2015), "The origin of cultivation and proto-weeds, long before neolithic farming," *PLOS ONE* 10(7): e0131422. doi:10.1371/journal.pone.0131422.

114 *proactive foraging:* B. D. Smith (2011), "General patterns of niche construction and the management of 'wild' plant and animal resources by small-scale pre-industrial societies," *Philosophical Transactions of the Royal Society of London, Biological Sciences* 366(1566): 836–848; P. Rowley-Conwy and R. Layton (2011), "Foraging and farming as niche construction: Stable and unstable adaptations," *Philosophical Transactions of the Royal Society of London, Biological Sciences* 366(1566): 849–862 (doi:10.1098/rstb.2010.0307).

114 *"vast and diverse middle ground":* B. D. Smith (2001), "Low-Level food production," *Journal of Archaeological Research* 9: 1–43.

114 *the earliest forms of gardening on the planet:* Bob Holmes, "The real first farmers: How agriculture was a global invention," *New Scientist*, October 28, 2015: https://www.newscientist.com/article/mg22830450-700-the-real-first-farmers-how-agriculture-was-a-global-invention/

115 *what ecologists call a "niche":* Bruce D. Smith (2007), "Niche construction and the behavioral context of plant and animal domestication," *Evolutionary Anthropology: Issues, News, and Reviews* 16(5): 188–199.

115 *the long-spined limpets:* C. D. McQuaid and P. W. Froneman (1993), "Mutualism between the territorial intertidal limpet Patella longicosta and the crustose alga Ralfsia verrucosa," *Oecologia* 96(1): 128–133. doi:10.1007/bf00318040.

116 *discovered to plant seeds of Squamellaria:* G. Chomicki et al. (2019), "Squamellaria: Plants domesticated by ants," *Plants, People, Planet* 1(4): 302–305. doi:10.1002/ppp3.10072.

116 *a seed-planting worm:* Zhenchang Zhu et al., "Sprouting as a gardening strategy to obtain superior supplementary food: evidence from a seed-caching marine worm," October 3, 2016, *Ecology* 97:12 (December 2016), pp. 3278–3284;

Sandrine Ceurstemont, "Worms seen farming plants to be eaten later for the first time," *New Scientist* (October 14, 2016): https://www.newscientist.com /article/2109058-worms-seen-farming-plants-to-be-eaten-later-for-the-first-time/

116 *"involved both human intentionality":* V. K. Flannery (ed.) (1986), *Guilá Naquitz: Archaic Foraging and Early Agriculture in Oaxaca, Mexico* (Bingley, UK: Emerald Group Publishing Ltd.).

117 *The "dump heap theory":* E. Anderson (1954), *Plants, Man & Life* (New York: Anchor Books).

117 *concerns the origin of a different kind of garden:* C. B. Heiser (1985), *Of Plants and People* (Norman, OK: University of Oklahoma Press), pp. 191–220; Charles Heiser (1990), *Seed to Civilization: The Story of Food* (Cambridge, MA: Harvard University Press), pp. 24–26.

119 *One of the defining works on the practice of ritual:* B. Malinowski (2013), *Coral Gardens and Their Magic, Volume 1: The Description of Gardening* (Severus).

120 *"Trobriand garden as an artist's canvas":* A. Gell (1992), "The technology of enchantment and the enchantment of technology," in *Anthropology, Art and Aesthetics,* J. Coote and A. Shelton, eds. (Oxford, UK: Clarendon Press), pp. 60–63.

120 *"The belly of my garden":* Malinowski, *Coral Gardens*, p. 98.

121 *living among the Achuar:* P. Descola (1994), *In the Society of Nature*, N. Scott, trans. (Cambridge University Press).

121 *believe in garden magic:* Descola, *In the Society of Nature*, pp. 136–220.

122 *"horticultural mothering":* P. Descola (1997), *The Spears of Twilight: Life and Death in the Amazon Jungle*, J. Lloyd, trans. (Flamingo), pp. 92–94.

123 *"simple social relationship":* N. Humphrey (1984), *Consciousness Regained* (Oxford University Press), pp. 26–27.

123 *"Caring for an environment":* T. Ingold (2000), *The Perception of the Environment* (Abingdon, UK: Routledge), pp. 86–87.

124 *The British-born explorer James Douglas:* Quoted in J. Ringuette (2004), *Beacon Hill Park History, 1842–2004* (Victoria, Canada), p. 25.

125 *Lekwungen families cared for their own plots:* W. Suttles (1987), *Coast Salish Essays*, in D. D. Talonbooks and N. J. Turner (eds). (2005), *Keeping It Living: Traditions of Plant Use and Cultivation on the Northwest Coast of North America* (Seattle, WA: University of Washington Press).

126 *the Garry oaks to dwindle:* M. Acker (2012), *Gardens Aflame* (Vancouver, Canada: New Star Books).

127 *untended to simulate camas:* N. J. Turner et al. (2013), "plant management systems of British Columbia's first peoples," *BC Studies: The British Columbian Quarterly* (179): 107–133.

127 *the phrase "agricultural mindset":* G. Jones (2005), "Garden cultivation of staple crops and its implications for settlement location and continuity," *World Archaeology* 37(2): 164–176.

127 *descended from a long line of gardening people:* E. Best (1987), *Maori Agriculture* (AMS Press).

129 *"The Gardener's Mortal Sin":* As translated by S. N. Kramer (1981), In *History Begins at Sumer: Thirty-Nine Firsts in Man's Recorded History* (3rd ed.) (Philadelphia: University of Pennsylvania Press).

130 *"Plow my vulva":* Kramer, *History Begins at Sumer*, p. 306.

130 *Sumerian seal:* K. Tharoor and M. Maruf (March 11, 2016), "Museum of lost objects: Looted Sumerian seal," *BBC News Magazine.*

131 *natural world is a living continuum:* All the Jung quotations are from Meredith Sabini (2002), *The Earth Has a Soul: C. G. Jung's Writings on Nature, Technology and Modern Life* (Berkeley, CA: North Atlantic Books).

133 *the root of gardening's power:* R. Dash (2000), *Notes from Madoo: Making a Garden in the Hamptons* (New York: Houghton Mifflin), p. 234.

Chapter 7: Flower Power

135 Claude Monet quotation can be found at https://fondation-monet.com/en/claude-monet/quotations/.

136 *"freely and on their own account":* I. Kant (1790/2008), *Critique of Judgement*, N. Walker, ed., and J. C. Meredith, trans. (Oxford, UK: Oxford World's Classics), p. 60.

137 *"I perhaps owe having become a painter to flowers":* https://fondation-net.com/en/claude-monet/quotations/.

137 *collecting rare plants and flower specimens:* A. Freud Bernays (1940), "My brother, Sigmund Freud," in H. M. Ruitenbeek (ed.) (1973), *Freud as We Knew Him* (Detroit, MI: Wayne State University Press), p. 141.

137 *"unusual familiarity with flowers":* E. Jones (1995), *The Life and Work of Sigmund Freud, Vol.1: The Young Freud (1856–1900)* (London: Hogarth Press).

137 *"The enjoyment of beauty":* S. Freud (1930), *Civilisation and Its Discontents*, SE 21, pp. 59–145.

137 *Semir Zeki, London-based professor of neurosaesthetics:* See S. Zeki et al. (2014), "The experience of mathematical beauty and its neural correlates," *Frontiers in Human Neuroscience* 8. doi:10.3389/fnhum.2014.00068.

138 *part of our pleasure and reward pathways:* K. C. Berridge and M. L. Kringelbach (2008), "Affective neuroscience of pleasure: reward in humans and animals," *Psychopharmacology* 199(3): 457–480. doi:10.1007/s00213-008-1099-6.

138 *The simple geometries we find in nature:* See K. Crithlow (2011), *The Hidden Geometry of Flowers* (Edinburgh, UK: Floris Books).

139 *Charles Darwin was sent a specimen:* J. Ardetti et al. (2012), "'Good Heavens what insect can suck it'—Charles Darwin, *Angraecum sesquipedale* and *Xanthopan morganii praedicta*," *Botanical Journal of the Linnean Society* 169: 403–432.

140 *bees will cease looking for nectar:* C. J. Perry, L. Baciadonna, and L. Chittka (2016), "Unexpected rewards induce dopamine-dependent positive emotion-like state changes in bumblebees," *Science* 353(6307): 1529–1531 (doi:10.1126/science.aaf4454). For general overview: C. J. Perry and A. B. Barron (2013), "Neural mechanisms of reward in insects," *Annual Review of Entomology* 58(1): 543–562 (doi:10.1146/annurev-ento-120811-153631). Also, nectar that contains small amounts of nicotine or caffeine helps to keep bees loyal: J. D. Thomson, M. A. Draguleasa, and M. G. Tan (2015), "Flowers with caffeinated nectar receive more pollination" *Arthropod-Plant Interactions* 9(1): 1–7 (doi:10.1007/s11829-014-9350-z).

141 *"orchids in all colours and descriptions":* H. Sachs (1945), *Freud: Master & Friend* (London: Imago), p. 165.

141 *this little flower had "pride of place":* M. Freud (1957), *Glory Reflected: Sigmund Freud–Man and Father* (London: Angus & Robertson).

141 *The American poet:* H. Doolittle (1971), *Tribute to Freud* (New York: New Direction Books).

142 *Lavender, long known:* L. R. Chioca et al. (2013), "Anxiolytic-like effect of lavender essential oil inhalation in mice: Participation of serotonergic but not GABAA/benzodiazepine neurotransmission, *Journal of Ethnopharmacology* 147(2): 412–418 (doi:10.1016/j.jep.2013.03.028); V. López et al. (2017), "Exploring pharmacological mechanisms of lavender (*Lavandula angustifolia*) essential oil on central nervous system targets," *Frontiers in Pharmacology* 8 (doi:10.3389/fphar.2017.00280).

142 *rosemary is stimulating:* M. Moss and L. Oliver (2012), "Plasma 1,8-cineole correlates with cognitive performance following exposure to rosemary essential oil aroma," *Therapeutic Advances in Psychopharmacology* 2(3): 103–113. doi:10.1177/2045125312436573.

142 *Citrus blossoms are uplifting:* C. A. Costa et al. (2013), "Citrus aurantium L. essential oil exhibits anxiolytic-like activity mediated by 5-HT1A-receptors and reduces cholesterol after repeated oral treatment," *BMC Complementary and Alternative Medicine* 13(1). doi:10.1186/1472-6882-13-42.

142 *The smell of roses:* H. Ikei et al. (2014), "The physiological and psychological relaxing effects of viewing rose flowers in office workers," *Journal of Physiological Anthropology* 33(1): 6. doi:10.1186/1880-6805-33-6.

142 *indicated future food supplies:* S. Pinker (1998), *How the Mind Works* (New York: Penguin Books).

143 *The Ohalo II site on the shore of the Sea of Galilee:* E. Weiss, et al. (2008), "Plant-food preparation area on an Upper Paleolithic brush hut floor at Ohalo II, Israel, *Journal of Archaeological Science* 35(8): 2400–2414. doi:10.1016/j.jas.2008.03.012.

143 *humans are thought to have started cultivating flowers:* J. Haviland-Jones et al. (2005), "An environmental approach to positive emotion: Flowers," *Evolutionary Psychology* 3(1). doi:10.1177/147470490500300109.

144 *The ancient Egyptians, in particular, regarded flowers as divine messengers:* J. Goody (1993), *The Culture of Flowers* (Cambridge University Press), p. 43.

145 *Why didn't I become a gardener instead of a doctor:* Letter to Martha Bernays (July 13, 1883) in E. L. Freud (ed.) (1961), *Letters of Sigmund Freud 1873–1913*, T. Stern and J. Stern, trans. (London: The Hogarth Press), p. 165.

145 *Freud was interested in how images of plant life:* S. Freud, *The Interpretation of Dreams, SE* 4 and 5.

146 *Sergei Pankejeff:* M. Gardiner (ed.) (1973), *The Wolf-Man and Sigmund Freud* (New York: Penguin Books), p. 139.

146 *Oskar Pfister, a pastor who went on to become a psychoanalyst:* Quotation from L. Appignanesi and J. Forrester (1992), *Freud's Women* (New York: Basic Books), p. 29.

147 *"the illusion of splendour and glowing sunshine":* Letter dated May 8, 1901, in G. Masson (ed.) (1986), *The Complete Letters to Wilhelm Fliess, 1887–1904* (Cambridge, MA: Harvard University Press), p. 440.

147 *He once referred to it as "a medicine":* Letter to Martha Bernays dated April 28, 1885, in E. L. Freud (ed.) (1961), *Letters of Sigmund Freud 1873–1913*, T. Stern and J. Stern, trans. (London: The Hogarth Press), p. 152.

147 *A conversation took place on one of Freud's mountain walks:* S. Freud (1915), "On Transience," *SE* 14, pp. 305–307.

149 *war had destroyed "the beauty of the countrysides":* Freud, "On Transcience."

150 *"The rain today didn't stop me from going to a special place":* I. Meyer-Palmedo (ed.) (2014), *Sigmund Freud & Anna Freud Correspondence 1904 –1938*, N. Somer, trans. (Cambridge, UK: Polity Press).

150 *The theory of Eros and Thanatos:* S. Freud, *Beyond the Pleasure Principle*, *SE* 18, pp. 7–64.

150 *he quoted Goethe's Faust: Civilisation and Its Discontents*, *SE* 21, pp. 59–145.

150 *The psychoanalyst and social psychologist Erich Fromm:* See L. J. Friedman (2013), *The Lives of Erich Fromm* (New York: Columbia University Press), p. 302.

150 *"the passionate love of life":* E. Fromm (1973), *The Anatomy of Human Destructiveness* (New York: Holt, Rinehart & Winston), p. 365.

150 *"The soil, the animals, the plants are still man's world":* E. Fromm (1995), *The Art of Loving* (London: Thorsons).

150 *The term "biophilia" was used again:* E. O. Wilson (1984), *Biophilia* (Cambridge, MA: Harvard University Press).

151 *the brain has been called a "relational organ":* T. Fuchs (2011), "The brain— A mediating organ," *Journal of Consciousness Studies* 18: 196–221.

Chapter 8: Radical Solutions

157 Mahatma Gandhi quotation is from Richard Attenborough, *The Words of Gandhi.*

159 *There was a long tradition of working men cultivating auriculas:* Patricia Cleveland-Peck (2011), *Auriculas Through the Ages* (Marlborough, UK: The Crowood Press).

160 *Florist societies brought . . . Gooseberry growing was popular too:* See Margaret Willes (2014), *The Gardens of the British Working Class* (New Haven: Yale University Press).

160 *When the physician and author William Buchan:* Willes, *Gardens of the British.* The eighteenth-century physician William Buchan wrote a best-selling book called *Domestic Medicine*, in which he extolled the virtues of gardening.

161 *study of botany . . . held eight a year:* J. M. Uings (April 2013), *Gardens and Gardening in a Fast-Changing Urban Environment: Manchester 1750–1850*, thesis submitted to Manchester Metropolitan University, UK, for the degree of doctor of philosophy.

161 *"Alas! there are no flowers":* E. Gaskell (1848/1996), *Mary Barton: A Tale of Manchester Life* (New York: Penguin Classics).

161 *as Carl Jung observed:* All quotations are in M. Sabini (2002), *The Earth Has a Soul: C. G. Jung's Writings on Nature, Technology and Modern Life* (Berkeley, CA: North Atlantic Books).

166 *plague of loneliness: Trapped in a Bubble*, report for the Co-Op and British Red Cross, December 2016.

166 *30 percent greater risk of early death:* J. Holt-Lunstad, T. B. Smith, and J. B. Layton (2010), "Social relationships and mortality risk: A Meta-analytic review," *PLoS Medicine* 7(7): e1000316. doi:10.1371/journal.pmed.1000316.

167 *urban farm at Oranjezicht:* L. Joubert (2016), *Oranjezicht City Farm,* NPC.

170 *started a movement in London:* R. Reynolds (2009), *On Guerrilla Gardening: A Handbook for Gardening Without Boundaries* (London: Bloomsbury).

172 *"gardens as a social bridge":* R. Santo, B. F. Kim, and A. M. Palmer (April 2016), *Vacant Lots to Vibrant Plots: A Review of the Benefits and Limitations of Urban Agriculture,* report for the Johns Hopkins Center for a Livable Future.

173 *Urban "cleaning and greening" projects:* M. Shepley et al. (2019). "The impact of green space on violent crime in urban environments: An evidence synthesis," *International Journal of Environmental Research and Public Health* 16(24): 5119. doi:10.3390/ijerph16245119.

173 *Philadelphia's LandCare Program:* C. C. Branas et al. (2011), "A difference-in-differences analysis of health, safety, and greening vacant urban space," *American Journal of Epidemiology* 174(11): 1296–1306 (doi:10.1093/aje/kwr273); C. C. Branas et al. (2018), "Citywide cluster randomized trial to restore blighted vacant land and its effects on violence, crime, and fear," *Proceedings of the National Academy of Sciences* 115(12): 2946–2951.

177 *the theory of "natural pedagogy":* G. Csibra, and G. Gergely, "Natural pedagogy as evolutionary adaptation," *Philosophical Transactions of the Royal Society of London, Biological Sciences* 366(1567): 1149–1157.

178 *crucial role that social bonds play in facilitating learning:* See Louis Cozolino (2013), *The Social Neuroscience of Education: Optimizing Attachment and Learning in the Classroom* (New York: W. W. Norton).

178 *"The mind has grown to its present state of consciousness":* M. Sabini (2002), *The Earth Has a Soul: C. G. Jung's Writings on Nature, Technology and Modern Life* (Berkeley, CA: North Atlantic Books).

178 *"plant blindness":* J. Wandersee and E. Schussler's paper *Toward a Theory of Plant Blindness* can be accessed at https://www.botany.org/bsa/psb/2001/psb47-1 .pdf.

180 *in ancient Greece that Priapus:* https://www.theoi.com/Georgikos/Priapus .html.

180 *"Jack and the Beanstalk":* Fairy tale origins thousands of years old: S. Silva and J. Tehrani (2016), "Comparative phylogenetic analyses uncover the ancient roots of Indo-European folktales," *Royal Society Open Science* 3: 150645.

Chapter 9: War and Gardening

183 Vita Sackville-West quotation is from V. Sackville-West (1946/2004), *The Garden* (London: Frances Lincoln).

185 *Writing in 329 BC, Xenophon:* P. Hobhouse (2009), *Gardens of Persia* (New York: W. W. Norton), p. 51.

185 *in an interview reported by the poet Siegfried Sassoon:* S. Sassoon (1945), *Siegfried's Journey 1916–1920.*(London: Faber & Faber).

185 *Churchill was serious:* See Anthony Storr (1990), *Churchill's Black Dog* (London:

Fontana) and S. Buczacki (2007), *Churchill & Chartwell.* (London: Frances Lincoln).

186 *Gardens were created by soldiers, chaplains, doctors and nurses:* See J. Lewis-Stempel (2017), *Where Poppies Blow: The British Soldier, Nature, the Great War* (London: Weidenfeld & Nicolson). Also: A. Powell (2015), *Gardens Behind the Lines: 1914–1918* (London: Cecil Woolf).

186 *Walker arrived in December 1915 . . . "Oh what sights, the multitudes":* Quotations from "Slaughter on the Somme," in M. Moynihan (ed.) (1973), *People at War 1914–18* (Exeter, UK: David & Charles), pp. 69–82.

188 *The American journalist Carita Spencer:* C. Spencer (1917), *War Scenes I Shall Never Forget* (Victoria, Australia: Leopold Classic Library), pp. 17–22.

188 *Alexander Douglas Gillespie . . . "We have a wonderful trench of Madonna lilies":* All quotations are from A. D. Gillespie (1916), *Letters from Flanders Written by Second Lieutenant A. D. Gillespie* (London: Smith, Elder).

190 *In a letter he wrote to his former headmaster:* A. Seldon and D. Walsh (2013), *Public Schools and the Great War* (Barnsley, UK: Pen & Sword Military). See also: https://www.thewesternfrontway.com/our-story/.

191 *"to hold the graces and the courtesies":* V. Sackville-West (2004), *The Garden* (London: Frances Lincoln).

191 *"Peace is not just the absence of war":* K. I. Helphand (2008), *Defiant Gardens: Making Gardens in Wartime* (San Antonio, TX: Trinity), p. 9.

191 *"it seems counter-intuitive" . . . "urgent biophilia":* K. G. Tidball and M. E. Krasny (2014), *Greening in the Red Zone* (New York: Springer), p. 54.

192 *The great war poet Wilfred Owen wrote to his mother:* J. Breen (ed.) (2014), *Wilfred Owen: Selected Poetry and Prose* (Abingdon, UK: Routledge).

192 *Owen's poem "Mental Cases":* Breen, *Wilfred Owen.*

193 *the regime at Craiglockhart . . . used the myth of Antaeus:* For quotations and descriptions, see the following papers: A. M. Crossman (2003), "The Hydra, Captain A. J. Brock and the treatment of shell-shock in Edinburgh," *Journal of the Royal College of Physicians of Edinburgh* 33: 119–123; T. Webb (2006), "'Dottyville'—Craiglockhart War Hospital and shell-shock treatment in the First World War," *Journal of the Royal Society of Medicine* 99: 342–346; D. Cantor (2005), "Between Galen, Geddes, and the Gael: Arthur Brock, modernity, and medical humanism in early twentieth century Scotland," *Journal of the History of Medicine* 60 (1).

193 *"give Nature a chance":* A. J. Brock (1923), *Health and Conduct* (London: Williams & Norgate).

193 *Scottish social reformer Patrick Geddes:* See H. Meller (1990), *Patrick Geddes: Social Evolutionist and City Planner* (Abingdon, UK: Routledge). Also: P. Boardman (1944), *Patrick Geddes Maker of the Future* (Chapel Hill: University of North Carolina Press).

195 *Owen's experience of being blasted into the air:* D. Hibberd (2003), *Wilfred Owen: A New Biography* (London: Weidenfeld & Nicolson).

196 *gave a paper on "The classification of soils" . . . Siegfried Sassoon later recalled that:* S. Sassoon (1945), *Siegfried's Journey 1916–1920* (London: Faber and Faber), p. 61.

197 *"underhand, unfair, and damned un-English":* R. MacKay (2003), *A Precarious Existence: British Submariners in World War One* (Reading, UK: Periscope Publishing Ltd.).

197 *The early submarines were extremely rudimentary:* J. Winton (2001), *The Submariners* (London: Constable).

198 *"cluttered up with gear and food for three weeks":* C. G. Brodie (1956), *Forlorn Hope, 1915: The Submarine Passage to the Dardanelles* (London: Frederick Books).

199 *As morning broke on April 17:* See account in D. Boyle (2015), *Unheard Unseen* (Scotts Valley, CA: Createspace).

200 *not well documented:* To some extent this has changed recently with publication of K. Ariotti (2018), *Captive Anzacs: Australian POWs of the Ottomans During the First World War* (Cambridge University Press).

200 *a small number of diaries kept by captured men . . . transported to the village of Belemedik:* The diary of Able Seaman John Harrison Wheat can be accessed here: http://blogs.slq.qld.gov.au/ww1/2016/05/22/diary-of-a-submariner/. The diary of Able Seaman Albert Edward Knaggs has been transcribed http://jefferyknaggs.com/diary.html. See also: J. Still (1920), *A Prisoner in Turkey* (London: John Lane). Also: M. W. D. White, "Australian submariner P.O.W.'s after the Gallipoli landing," *Journal of the Royal Historical Society of Queensland* 14(4) (1990): 136–144, University of Queensland website.

201 *By the end of the war nearly 70 percent of the Allied POWs held in Turkey had died:* Report on the Treatment of British Prisoners of War in Turkey, HMSO, 1918, https://www.bl.uk/collection-items/report-on-treatment-of-british-prisoners -of-war-in-turkey.

203 *a Swiss physician, Adolf Vischer, visited POW camps . . . joyless monotony:* A. L. Vischer (1919), *Barbed Wire Disease—A Psychological Study of the Prisoner of War* (London: John Bale & Danielsson). See also: J. Yarnall (2011), *Barbed Wire Disease* (Staplehurst, UK: Spellmount).

204 *When Sir Arthur Griffith Boscawen MP . . . "fitting our gallant soldiers to occupy a position on the land":* Reported in *Kent and Sussex Courier*, Friday, June 27, 1919, https://www.britishnewspaperarchive.co.uk.

205 *The mansion at Sarisbury Court:* Sally Miller, "Sarisbury Court and its role in the re-training of disabled ex-servicemen after the First World War," *Hampshire Gardens Trust Newsletter*, Spring 2016, http://www.hgt.org.uk/wp-content/uploads/2016/04/2016-03-HGT-Newsletter.pdf.

207 *"agriculture far above all others":* N. Fenton (1926), *Shell Shock and Its Aftermath* (St. Louis: C. V. Mosby Co.).

Chapter 10: The Last Season of Life

209 Tomb inscription is from M. L. Gothein (1966), *A History of Garden Art*, L. Archer-Hind, trans. (London: J. M. Dent), p. 20.

210 *"I want death to find me planting my cabbages":* M. de Montaigne, "That to \philosophize is to learn to die," in *Complete Essays*, D. Frame, trans. (2005) (London: Everyman), p. 74.

212 *"Thou owest Nature a Death":* S. Freud, *The Interpretation of Dreams, SE* 4 and 5, p. 204.

212 *Freud suffered from attacks of what he called "Todesangst":* E. Jones (1957), *The Life and Work of Sigmund Freud, Vol. 3: The Last Phase (1919–39)* (London: Hogarth Press), pp. 300–3011. His brother's death left a "germ of guilt in him." See M. Schur (1972), *Freud, Living and Dying* (London: Hogarth Press), p. 199.

212 *death is not necessarily recognized as a natural process:* S. Freud (1920), *Beyond the Pleasure Principle, SE* 18.

213 *Recent research at Bar Ilan University in Israel:* Y. Dor-Ziderman, A. Lutz, and A. Goldstein (2019), "Prediction-based neural mechanisms for shielding the self from existential threat," *NeuroImage* 202. doi:10.1016/j.neuroimage.2019.116080.

213 *"This was when the earth first began to be widely seen":* T. Taylor (2003), *The Buried Soul: How Humans Invented Death* (London: Fourth Estate).

214 *The Tomb of the Vines:* L. Farrar (2016), *Gardens and Gardeners of the Ancient World: History, Myth and Archaeology* (Oxford, UK: Oxbow).

214 *Tutankhamun's tomb:* Farrar, *Gardens and Gardeners.*

216 *The American poet Stanley Kunitz:* S. Kunitz, with G. Lentine (2007), *The Wild Braid* (New York: W. W. Norton).

218 *The writer Diana Athill started gardening in her sixties:* D. Athill (2009), *Somewhere Towards the End* (London: Granta).

218 *"I became hooked, and hooked":* D. Athill, "How gardening soothes the soul in later life," https://www.theguardian.com/lifeandstyle/2008/nov/29/gardening-old-age-diana-athill.

219 *"dear valiant violas":* "My grandparents' garden," a talk reprinted in *Garden Museum Journal* 28 (Winter 2013), p. 33.

219 *attribute some of their health and longevity to gardening:* A number of research studies confirm this effect. For example, L. A. Simons et al. (2006), "Lifestyle factors and risk of dementia: Dubbo Study of the elderly," *Medical Journal of Australia* 184(2): 68–70, which found a 36 percent lower risk of dementia among gardeners. doi:10.5694/j.1326–5377.2006.tb00120.x.

219 *called this phenomenon generativity:* E. H. Erikson (1998), *The Life Cycle Completed* (New York: W. W. Norton).

219 *the Harvard Grant Study:* Findings summarized in G. E. Vaillant (2003), *Aging Well* (New York: Little, Brown).

220 *continuing to ride his bicycle:* F. R. Rodman (2004), *Winnicott Life and Work* (Cambridge, MA: Da Capo Press), p. 384.

220 *"May I be alive when I die":* C. Winnicott, "D.W.W.: A reflection," in S. A. Grolnick and L. Barkin (eds.) (1978), *Between Reality and Fantasy* (Lanham, MD: Jason Aronson), p. 19.

221 *"A great deal of growing is growing downwards":* B. Kahr (1996), *D. W. Winnicott: A Biographical Portrait* (London: Karnac Book), p. 125.

222 *The Edinburgh Garden Partners program in Scotland:* S. Jackson, J. Harris, S. Sexton (no date), *Growing Friendships: A Report on the Garden Partners Project* (London: Age UK Wandsworth). https://www.ageuk.org.uk/bp-assets/globalassets/wandsworth/auw_annual-report-2013_14.pdf.

222 *creative solutions like this:* See T. L. Scott, B. M. Masser, and N. A. Pachana (2014), "Exploring the health and wellbeing benefits of gardening for older adults, *Ageing and Society* 35(10): 2176–2200. doi:10.1017/s0144686x14000865.

223 *"As people become aware of the finitude of their life"*... *Chase Memorial:* A. Gawande (2014), *Being Mortal* (London: Profile Books), pp. 123–125 and pp. 146–147.

224 *on the subject of loneliness:* M. Klein (1975/1963), "On the sense of loneliness," in *Envy and Gratitude* (London: Hogarth Press), p. 300.

224 *The philosopher Roger Scruton:* R. Scruton (2011), *Beauty: A Very Short Introduction* (Oxford University Press), p. 26.

224 *In a letter he sent to the American poet H.D.:* H. Doolittle (2012), *Tribute to Freud* (New York: New Directions Press), p.195.

224 *"One gets round to nothing in this heavenly beauty":* S. Freud *Unser Herz Zeigt Nach Dem Süden: Reisebriefe 1895–1923*, C. Tögel, ed. (Berlin: Aufbau Taschenbuch, 2003). The excerpt quoted was translated for this book by Frances Wharton.

225 *in the villa at Pötzleinsdorf:* Letter to LAS (circa July 10, 1931), in Pfeiffer, *Sigmund Freud and Lou Andreas-Salomé*, p. 194.

225 *the "idyllically quiet and beautiful" villa at Berchtesgaden:* Letter to Lou Andreas Salomé (LAS) on July 28, 1929, in E. Pfeiffer (ed.) (1985), *Sigmund Freud and Lou Andreas-Salomé, Letters* (New York: W. W. Norton).

226 *"beautiful like a fairy tale":* E. Jones (1957), *The Life and Work of Sigmund Freud: Volume 3* (London: Hogarth Press), p. 202. Also, in a letter to Princess Marie Bonaparte, May 2, 1934, Freud wrote: "It is beautiful here, like a fairy tale."

226 *His son Martin recalled:* M. Freud (1957), *Glory Reflected: Sigmund Freud—Man and Father* (Sydney: Angus & Robertson).

226 *to "die in beauty":* Letter to LAS, May 16, 1934, in Jones, *Life and Work of Sigmund Freud*, p. 202.

226 *During an interview that took place shortly after his seventieth birthday:* G. S. Viereck, *An Interview with Freud*, http://www.psychanalyse.lu/articles/Freud Interview.pdf.

227 *"dread of renewed suffering":* M. Schur (1972), *Freud, Living and Dying* (London: Hogarth Press), p. 485.

227 *he asked his friend Arnold Zweig:* Schur, *Freud, Living and Dying*, p. 491.

227 *When Sachs visited him at Grinzing:* H. Sachs (1945), *Freud: Master & Friend* (Albury, UK: Imago), p. 171.

228 *employed by Montaigne:* M. de Montaigne, "Of experience," in *Complete Essays*, D. Frame, trans. (2005) (London: Everyman), p. 1036.

229 *Freud quipped, "We are buried in flowers":* See M. Edmundson (2007), *The Death of Sigmund Freud* (London: Bloomsbury), p. 141.

229 *"It is as though we were living in Grinzing":* Letter, June 6, 1938, in E. L. Freud (ed.) (1961), *Letters of Sigmund Freud 1873–1913*, T. Stern and J. Stern, trans. (London: Hogarth Press), p 441.

230 *A home movie:* Can be viewed at https://youtu.be/SQOcf9Y-Uc8 and http://www.freud-museum.at/online/freud/media/video-e.htm.

230 *"greeted one over the walls":* H. Sachs (1945), *Freud: Master & Friend* (Albury, UK: Imago), p. 185.

230 *"All the Egyptians, Chinese and Greeks have arrived":* Letter to Jeanne Lampl de Groot, October 8, 1938, in L. Freud, E. Freud, and I. Grubrich-Simitis (1978), *Sigmund Freud: His life in Pictures and Words* (London: Andre Deutsch), p. 210.

231 *Lifton called "symbolical survival":* R. J. Lifton (1968), *Death in Life* (London: Weidenfeld & Nicolson).

231 *When Virginia Woolf paid him a visit at Maresfield Gardens:* See M. Edmundson (2007), *The Death of Sigmund Freud* (London: Bloomsbury), pp. 193–196.

232 *the role they can play in the care of the elderly and the dying:* K. Worpole, (2009), *Modern Hospice Design* (Abingdon, UK: Routledge).

232 *"sometimes in light slumber":* H. Sachs (1945), *Freud: Master & Friend* (Albury, UK: Imago), p. 187.

233 *When Lun was brought into Freud's study:* Max Schur (1972), *Freud, Living and Dying* (London: Hogarth Press), p. 526.

233 *Freud's bed was positioned so that he could gaze out at the flowers he loved:* Ernest Jones (1957), *The Life and Work of Sigmund Freud, Vol. 3: The Last Phase (1919–39)* (London: Hogarth Press), p. 262. Also in Schur, *Freud, Living and Dying*: "he could see the garden with the flowers he loved," p. 526.

233 *In a letter written the following month, Lucie records:* I. Meyer-Palmedo (ed.) (2014), *Sigmund Freud & Anna Freud Correspondence 1904 –1938*, N. Somer, trans. (Cambridge, UK: Polity Press), p. 407.

233 *Freud once wrote that dying is an achievement:* S. Freud (1915), *Thoughts for the Times on War and Death, SE* 14, pp. 175–300.

234 *"it is in vain that the old man yearns":* S. Freud, *The Theme of the Three Caskets, SE* 12.

234 *Helen Dunmore's last book of poetry:* H. Dunmore (2017), *Inside the Wave* (Eastburn, UK: Bloodaxe).

Chapter 11: Garden Time

240 *no dedicated center for perceiving it:* See M. Wittmann (2009), "The inner experience of time," *Philosophical Transactions of the Royal Society of London, Biological Sciences* 364(1525): 1955–1967.

240 *"metasensory":* D. M. Eagleman (2005), "Time and the brain: How subjective time relates to neural time," *Journal of Neuroscience* 25(45): 10369–10371. doi:10.1523/jneurosci.3487-05.2005.

243 *given the name "burnout" in 1974:* H. Freudenberger (1974), "Staff burnout," *Journal of Social Issues* 30(1): 159–165.

243 *"the Alnarp model":* U. A. Stigsdotter and P. Grahn (2002), What makes a garden a healing garden?" *Journal of Therapeutic Horticulture* 13: 60–69; A. A. Adevi, and F. Mårtensson (2013), "Stress rehabilitation through garden therapy: The garden as a place in the recovery from stress," *Urban Forestry & Urban Greening* 12(2): 230–237 (doi:10.1016/j.ufug.2013.01.007); P. Grahn et al.

(2017), "Longer nature-based rehabilitation may contribute to a faster return to work in patients with reactions to severe stress and/or depression," *International Journal of Environmental Research and Public Health* 14(11): 1310. doi:10.3390/ijerph14111310.

245 *"we have come from dwelling":* H. Searles (1972), "Unconscious processes in relation to the environmental crisis," *Psychoanalytic Review* 59(3): 368.

245 *informed the work at Alnarp:* J. Ottosson and P. Grahn (2008), "The role of natural settings in crisis rehabilitation: How does the level of crisis influence the response to experiences of nature with regard to measures of rehabilitation?," *Landscape Research* 33(1): 51–70. doi:10.1080/01426390701773813.

245 *a large "untouched stone":* J. Ottosson (2001), "The importance of nature in coping with a crisis," *Landscape Research* 26: 165–172.

247 *"the ego falls away":* M. Csikszentmihalyi (2002), *Flow: The Classic Work on How to Achieve Happiness* (New York: Rider).

248 *the symbolic meaning that can be derived:* P. Grahn et al., "Using affordances as a health promoting tool in a therapeutic garden," in C. Ward Thompson, S. Bell, and A. Aspinall (eds.) (2010), *Innovative Approaches to Researching Landscape and Health* (Abingdon, UK: Routledge) pp. 116–154.

248 *A follow-up study:* A. M. Pálsdóttir, P. Grahn, and D. Persson (2013), "Changes in experienced value of everyday occupations after nature-based vocational rehabilitation," *Scandinavian Journal of Occupational Therapy:* 1–11. doi:10.3109 /11038128.2013.832794.

248 *The Journey of Recovery:* A. Pálsdóttir et al. (2014), "The journey of recovery and empowerment embraced by nature—Clients' perspectives on nature-based rehabilitation in relation to the role of the natural environment," *International Journal of Environmental Research and Public Health* 11(7), 7094–7115. doi:10.3390/ijerph11070709.

249 *Donald Winnicott once wrote:* D. W. Winnicott (1974), "Fear of breakdown," *International Review of Psycho-Analysis* 1:103–107.

250 *"Time exists in order that":* S. Sontag (2008), *At the Same Time: Essays and Speeches* (New York: Penguin Books), p. 214.

250 *tending his potato patch:* D. Bair (2004), *Jung: A Biography* (New York: Little, Brown).

250 *"the instincts, which connect us with the soil":* M. Sabini (2002), *The Earth Has a Soul: C. G. Jung's Writings on Nature, Technology and Modern Life* (Berkeley, CA: North Atlantic Books).

251 *helps people manage subsequent stress:* V. F. Gladwell et al. (2012), "The effects of views of nature on autonomic control," *European Journal of Applied Physiology* 112(9): 3379–3386. doi:10.1007/s00421-012-2318-8.

251 *Tending their plot helped:* C. J. Wood, J. Pretty, and M. Griffin (2015), "A case–control study of the health and well-being benefits of allotment gardening," *Journal of Public Health* 38(3): e336–e344. doi:10.1093/pubmed/fdv146.

254 *"learned persistence":* K. Lambert (2008), *Lifting Depression* (New York: Basic Books).

255 *"a contingency workout":* K. Lambert (2018), *Well Grounded* (New Haven: Yale University Press).

256 *"Man feels himself isolated in the cosmos":* M. Sabini (2002), *The Earth Has a Soul: C.G. Jung's Writings on Nature, Technology and Modern Life* (Berkeley, CA: North Atlantic Books).

256 *they bring such an important sense of meaning:* J. Sempik, J. Aldridge, and S. Becker (2005), *Health, Well-Being and Social Inclusion: Therapeutic Horticulture in the UK* (Bristol, UK: The Policy Press).

Chapter 12: View from the Hospital

257 Oliver Sacks's quotation is from O. Sacks (2019), "Why We Need Gardens," in *Everything in Its Place: First Loves and Last Tales* (New York: Alfred A. Knopf), p. 245.

258 *smiled a "true smile":* J. Haviland-Jones et al. (2005), "An environmental approach to positive emotion: Flowers," *Evolutionary Psychology* 3(1). 147470490500300 .doi:10.1177/147470490500300109.

260 *light and airy hospital rooms:* F. Swain (December 11, 2013), "Fresh air and sunshine: The forgotten antibiotics," *New Scientist.*

260 *associated with shorter stays:* K. M. Beauchemin and P. Hays (1996), "Sunny hospital rooms expedite recovery from severe and refractory depressions," *Journal of Affective Disorders* 40(1–2): 49–51. doi:10.1016/0165-0327(96)00040-7.

260 *"I shall never forget the rapture of fever patients"... "fancies":* F. Nightingale (1859), *Notes on Nursing: What It Is, and What It Is Not,* Chapter V.

261 *increased psychological awareness in hospital design:* British Medical Association (2011), "The psychological and social needs of patients," *BMA Science & Education.* See also: The Planetree Model, in A. Antonovsky (2001), *Putting Patients First: Designing and Practicing Patient Centered Care* (San Francisco: Jossey-Bass).

261 *views of nature in a range of different clinical settings:* E. Huisman et al. (2012), "Healing environment: A review of the impact of physical environmental factors on users," *Building and Environment* 58: 70–80 (doi:10.1016/j.buildenv.2012.06.016); R. S. Ulrich (2001), "Effects of healthcare environmental design on medical outcomes," in: *Design and Health: Proceedings of the Second International Conference on Health and Design, Stockholm, Sweden,* pp. 49–59.

261 *first study of this kind:* R. Ulrich (1984), "View through a window may influence recovery from surgery," *Science* 224(4647): 420–421. doi:10.1126/science.6143402.

261 *randomly allocated to either type of room:* S. Park and R. H. Mattson (2008), "Effects of flowering and foliage plants in hospital rooms on patients recovering from abdominal surgery," *HortTechnology* 18(4): 563–568. doi:10.21273/horttech.18.4.563.

262 *"placebo effect":* D. Evans (2003), *Placebo: The Belief Effect* (New York: Harper-Collins).

262 *maximize the design placebo effect:* C. Jencks (2006) "The architectural placebo," in C. Wagenaar (ed.), *The Architecture of Hospitals* (Rotterdam: NAi Publishers).

263 *effects of art in hospitals:* R. S. Ulrich (1991), "Effects of health facility interior design on wellness: Theory and recent scientific research," *Journal of Health Care Design* (3): 97–109.

263 *patients recovering from heart surgery:* R. Ulrich et al. (1993), "Effects of exposure to nature and abstract pictures on patients recovering from heart surgery," thirty-third meeting of the Society for Psychophysiological Research, abstract published in *Psychophysiology* 30: 7.

263 *a semi-abstract sculpture installation of large, angular, birdlike shapes:* Roger Ulrich (2002), "Health benefits of gardens in hospitals," paper for conference *Plants for People*, Floriade, The Netherlands.

264 *Vischer thought of* einfühlung: See S. Lanzoni (2018), *Empathy: A History* (New Haven: Yale University Press).

264 *"a pinecone falling on a garden bench":* S. J. Ebisch et al. (2008), "The sense of touch: Embodied simulation in a visuotactile mirroring mechanism for observed animate or inanimate touch," *Journal of Cognitive Neuroscience* 20(9): 1611–1623. doi:10.1162/jocn.2008.20111.

265 *"calming and organizing effects on our brains"... "even its structure":* O. Sacks (2019), "Why we need gardens," in *Everything in Its place: First Loves and Last Tales* (New York: Alfred A. Knopf), pp. 245–24.

265 *an effect of calming and focusing the mind is seen:* S. D'Andrea, M. Batavia, and N. Sasson (2007), "Effects of horticultural therapy on preventing the decline of mental abilities of patients with Alzheimer's type dementia," *Journal of Therapeutic Horticulture* 2007–2008 XVIII.

265 *attention deficit disorder:* F. E. Kuo and A. F. Taylor (2004), "A potential natural treatment for attention-deficit/hyperactivity disorder: Evidence from a national study," *American Journal of Public Health* 94(9): 1580–1586 (doi:10.2105/ajph.94.9.1580). See also: A. F. Taylor and F. Kuo F (2009), "Children with attention deficits concentrate better after walk in the park," *Journal of Attention Disorders* 12(5), 402–409 (doi:10.1177/1087054708323000).

265 *increasing levels of alpha waves:* R. Nakamura and E. Fujii (1990), "Studies of the characteristics of the electroencephalogram when observing potted plants: *Pelargonium hortorum* 'Sprinter Red' and *Begonia evansiana*," technical bulletin of the Faculty of Horticulture of Chiba University 43(1): 177–183. See also: R. Nakamura and E. Fujii (1992), "A comparative study on the characteristics of electroencephalogram inspecting a hedge and a concrete block fence," *Journal of the Japanese Institute of Landscape Architecture* 55(5): 139–144.

266 *Fractal patterning makes the brain's task easier:* C. M. Hägerhäll, T. Purcell, and R. Taylor (2004), "Fractal dimension of landscape silhouette outlines as a predictor of landscape preference," *Journal of Environmental Psychology* 24(2): 247–255. doi:10.1016/j.jenvp.2003.12.004.

266 *"fluent visual processing":* Y. Joye and A. van den Berg, *Nature Is Easy on the Mind: An Integrative Model for Restoration Based on Perceptual Fluency*, at 8th Biennial Conference on Environmental Psychology, Zürich, Switzerland, 2010.

267 *"the tree which moves some to tears of joy":* From a letter Blake wrote to Reverend John Trusler in 1799, in A. Kazin (ed.) (1979), *The Portable Blake* (New York: Penguin Classics).

267 *extraordinary encounter she had with a tree:* E. Ensler (2014), *In the Body of the World* (New York: Picador).

271 *"A pure and intense joy":* O. Sacks (1991), *A Leg to Stand On* (New York: Picador), pp. 133–135.

273 *designed the garden for maximum variation:* G. Souter-Brown (2015), *Landscape and Urban Design for Health and Well-Being* (Abingdon, UK: Routledge).

274 *ratio of green to hard surface:* C. Cooper Marcus, and N. A. Sachs (2013), *Therapeutic Landscapes* (New York: John Wiley & Sons).

Chapter 13: Green Fuse

277 Dylan Thomas quotation is from "The force that through the green fuse drives the flower," published in 1934 in a collection entitled *18 Poems.*

281 *97 percent of which have disappeared:* https://www.plantlife.org.uk/uk/about-us/news/real-action-needed-to-save-our-vanishing-meadows.

282 *plants warn other plants to defend themselves:* For example: D. Spencer et al. (2018), "Glutamate triggers long-distance, calcium-based plant defense signaling," *Science* 361: 1112–1115. 10.1126/science.aat7744.

282 *Trees . . . form communities:* P. Wohlleben (2016), *The Hidden Life of Trees: What They Feel, How They Communicate—Discoveries from a Secret World,* J. Billinghurst, trans. (Vancouver, Canada: Greystone Books).

282 *sunflowers go out of their way to accommodate their root systems:* M. López Pereira et al. (2017), "Light-mediated self-organization of sunflower stands increases oil yield in the field," *Proceedings of the National Academy of Sciences* 114(30): 7975–7980. doi:10.1073/pnas.1618990114.

282 *crisis of biodiversity:* Climate change and agricultural management are the two biggest causes. https://nbn.org.uk/wp-content/uploads/2019/09/State-of-Nature-2019-UK-full-report.pdf.

282 *monitoring the life of domestic gardens:* R. W. Cameron et al. (2012), "The domestic garden: Its contribution to urban green infrastructure," *Urban Forestry & Urban Greening* 11(2): 129–137. doi:10.1016/j.ufug.2012.01.002.

283 *front garden is disappearing:* Royal Horticultural Society, *Greening Grey Britain,* www.rhs.org.uk/science/gardening-in-a-changing-world/greening-grey-britain.

283 *The density of birds in city gardens:* K. Thompson and S. Head, *Gardens as a Resource for Wildlife,* available at: www.wlgf.org/linked/the_garden_resource.pdf.

283 *supports a healthy diversity:* J. L. Edmondson et al. (2014), "Urban cultivation in allotments maintains soil qualities adversely affected by conventional agriculture," *Journal of Applied Ecology* 51(4): 880–889. ISSN 0021-8901

283 *Topsoil is a precious resource:* https://ec.europa.eu/jrc/en/publication/soil-erosion-europe-current-status-challenges-and-future-developments.

283 *degradation of soil through a failure of care:* D. R. Montgomery (2008), *Dirt: The Erosion of Civilizations* (Berkeley: University of California Press).

284 *"The more beautiful and striking the experience":* N. Klein (2015), *This Changes Everything: Capitalism vs. the Climate* (New York: Penguin Books), pp. 419–420.

284 *Depression has recently overtaken respiratory illnesses: Depression and Other Common Mental Health Disorders: Global Health Estimates* (Geneva: WHO, 2017).

284 *"Il faut cultiver notre jardin":* Voltaire, *Candide, or Optimism,* T. Cuffe, trans. (2006) (New York: Penguin Classics).

287 *took on a neglected estate at Ferney:* I. Davidson (2004), *Voltaire in Exile* (New York: Atlantic Books).

287 *"I have only done one sensible thing in my life":* Quoted in Clarence S. Darrow, Voltaire, lecture given in the Court Theater on February 3, 1918, p. 17, University of Minnesota Darrow's Writings and Speeches, http://moses.law.umn.edu/darrow/documents/Voltaire_by_Clarence_Darrow.pdf.

Illustration Credits

Title page image: Tammy Marlar

Chapter 1: Author's collection

Chapter 2: Tammy Marlar

Chapter 3: Courtesy of California Department of Corrections and Rehabilitation

Chapter 4: Marianne Majerus

Chapter 5: Milstein Division, The New York Public Library

Chapter 6. Author's collection

Chapter 7: Tammy Marlar

Chapter 8: Courtesy of the New York Botanical Garden and Mitchell Harris-Dennis/Bronx Documentary Center

Chapter 9: Imperial War Museum, catalogue number Q 6131

Chapter 10: Author's collection

Chapter 11. Author's collection

Chapter 12: Marianne Majerus

Chapter 13: Andrew Lawson

Acknowledgments: Author's collection

Index

Page numbers of photographs appear in italics.

Achuar tribe, Upper Amazon, 121–22
addiction, 151–55, 175, 176
adrenaline, 72, 142, 241
aging
    Athill in old age, gardening and, 218–19
    Edinburgh Garden Partners program, 222
    Erikson's generativity concept, 219
    Freud and his gardens, 225–31
    gardening and, 217–22
    Harvard Grant Study, 219–20
    Kunitz and gardening, 216–17, 219
    loneliness and, 220, 222–24
    Montaigne's strategy, 228
    plants and emotional health, 219, 222–23
    residential care, pets, plants and, 223
    threshold spaces in gardens and, 232
    Vaillant on relationships and, 220
    Winnicott's "growing down," 221
Aging Well (Vaillant), 220
Alnarp Rehabilitation Garden, Sweden, *237*, 244
Alzheimer's disease, 265
Anderson, Edgar, 117
Andreas-Salomé, Lou, 147

Antaeus myth, 195–96, 197
Appleton, Jay, 70, 77
Athill, Diana, 218–19, 222–23
attachment, 18–19, 81, 148, 154, 203
attachment theory, 18–20
attention, 25, 75–76, 98–99
    attention fatigue, 98
    Attention Restoration theory, 98
    "tuning in" to a garden's needs, 31
attention deficit disorder (ADD), 265
auriculas, 45–46, 157–59, 160, 188
autism, therapeutic garden for, 274

Babylon, hanging gardens of, 89
Baker Cresswell, Anna, 73
Bar Ilan University, Israel, 213
Barn, the, Hertfordshire, England, *1*, 6–7
    Athill visits, 218
    garden at, 6–11, 23–24, *23*, 45–46, 66, 109–10, 135–36, 157–59, 183–84, 238–39, 257–58, 275–76, 280–81
    hammocks in garden, 67–68, *67*
    lupines at, 87–88
    meadow at, *277*, 281
    rose garden, 11
    tulips at, 257–58, *257*
    winter at, *209*
Beard, George Miller, 92–93, 192
beauty, 136
    as both calming and revitalizing, 138
    brain activity and, 137

beauty (*cont.*)
  as consolation, 269
  as ephemeral, 147–48, 149
  flowers and human need for,
    143–44
  Freud and, 137, 225, 228, 231, 234
  Kant's concept of "free" beauty, 136
  Klein on, 284
  as nourishment for the psyche, 161–62
  Scruton on the pleasure of, 224
  as therapeutic, 155
  urban green spaces and, 89
  in wartime, 184, 186–91
  Zeki's experiments, 137–38
bees, 3, 10, 85, 139–41, 143, 164, 202, 287
  euglossine bee, 140–41
Being Mortal (Gawande), 223
Benedict, St., and order of, 27–28, 41
Berman, Marc, 96
Bible, 26, 213, 214
biodiversity, 94, 133, 282–83
biophilia concept, 100, 106, 150–51
  "urgent biophilia," 191–92
Bird, William, 39
birds, 18, 58, 60, 136, 207, 264, 275
  in city gardens, density of, 283
  meadows as habitat, 281
Birkenhead Park, Liverpool, England,
  91–92
Blake, William, 267
Body of the World, The (Ensler), 267
Bonaparte, Princess Marie, 229
Boscawen, Sir Arthur Griffith, 204
botany, 161, 178, 193, 282
Bott, Katy, 273–74
Bowlby, John, 18–19
Bowlby, Sir Anthony, 187
brain
  amygdala, 71, 76, 78, 85, 247
  beauty's effect on, 137, 138
  beta-endorphins, 37
  brain-as-computer metaphor, 32–33,
    285
  childhood development of, 33–34
  cortisol and, 75
  dopamine system, 78, 101–2, 138,
    140, 142, 151, 247
  effect of flowers, gardens on, 265
  effort-driven rewards circuit,
    254–55
  endogenous opioid systems, 138, 142

  evolution and, 71, 77, 78, 97–100, 177
  filtering out plants by, 179
  garden metaphors and, 33–35
  hemispheric specialization, 99
  hippocampus, 104
  McGilchrist's study of, 98–99
  memory, and place, 242
  microglial cells, 34–35, 80, 242
  mirror neurons in, 264
  nature changing physiology of, 265
  need to manipulate environment,
    254
  nested hierarchy, 71
  neural networks, 32–35, 71, 104–6
  neurogenesis process, 34–35, 104
  neurotransmitters, 34, 102, 247
  nonacceptance of death and, 213
  nurturing of, 33
  olfactory center, 79, 85, 141–42
  perception of time and, 240
  physical exercise and, 35, 39, 78–79
  physical surroundings and, 104–5,
    264
  physiology of, 71, 97, 102, 104
  placebo effect in, 262
  plasticity concept, 34
  as a predictive organ, 240–41
  pruning in, 34
  as "relational organ," 151
  resemblance to plants, 33
  serotonin and, 78–79, 80, 138, 142,
    247
  states of mindful awareness and, 76
  stimulation from nature's patterns,
    266
  synapses, 33–34
  working with one's hands and, 255
brain-derived neurotrophic factor
  (BDNF), 34–35, 75, 78, 104, 247
Branas, Charles, 173
Bratman, Gregory, 97
Bridewell Gardens, Oxfordshire, 41–42
Britain's National Health Service,
  39–40, 210–11, 237–38
British County Homestead Association,
  203
British Medical Association, 261
Brock, Arthur, 193–95, 197, 203, 206
Brodie, Charles, 198–99
Brodie, Theodore, 198
Brown, Estelle, 165

Buchan, William, 160–61
Buried Soul, The (Taylor), 213–14

camas, death camas, 124–25, 126
Candide (Voltaire), 284–87
caring activities, 31–32, 76, 123, 132–33
  gardening and, 62, 177, 248
  in hospitals, 262–63
  for the land, rooting ourselves and,
    131
  neurochemistry of, 37–38
Central Park, New York City, *87*, 91
Centre for Research on Environment,
  Society and Health (CRESH), 95–96
Chapple, David, 270
Chapple, Horatio, 270
Chapple, Olivia, 269, 270, 271
Chase Memorial Nursing Home, N.Y.,
  223
Chicago, Ill., 176–77
  "Large Lots" program, 173
  urban farm youth projects, 175–76
  Windy City Harvest Youth Farm
    Program, 175–77, 178, 180
Chicago Botanic Garden, 175–77
Childe, V. Gordon, 111–12
childhood
  at-risk for criminal behavior, 62–63
  attachment theory and, 18–19
  author's memories of, 5
  babies and moving objects, 264–65
  being held and, 68–69, 234
  brain development in, 33–34
  experience during, as formative, 12–13
  experiential learning, 64–65
  "facilitating" process and, 50
  gardening in schools, 51–52, 55,
    164–65
  garden's significance during, 6, 12, 19
  Growing Options project, 63–64
  mother-child relationship, 16–17,
    48–49, 234, 264
  parental illness and, 12–13
  play and, 16, 17, 19
  Pollan's memory of, 47–48
  reparative activities in, 30–31
  seeds recommended for children, 51
  self-belief and, 48–50
  social learning and, 177–78
  technology and dependence, 65
Churchill, Winston, 185, 197

Civilization and Its Discontents (Freud),
  150
Clairvaux Abbey, France, 28
Clear, Mary, 163–66
climate crisis, 279, 283–84
cognitive science, 177
colors, 74, 136
  human response to green, 74, 90
  recovery from illness and, 259, 260
community gardening, 162–72, 179–80,
  250
  allotments, England, 160–61, 162,
    251–54
  in France, *Incroyables Comestibles*,
    166
  Geddes's gardens in Edinburgh, 193
  See also urban gardening movement
contemporary life
  consumerism, 20, 32, 288
  disconnection and, 131–32, 150,
    245, 166
  erosion of food sharing, 177
  fragmented social networks, 32
  indoor environment as predomi-
    nant, 106
  internet as a retreat from the world,
    77
  lack of attachment to place in, 18
  lack of caring stance, 32
  loneliness and, 166
  loss of rituals and rites of passage, 20
  malaise of "uprootedness" and, 131
  mood disorders, mental disorders
    and, 14
  pace of, effects of, 32, 241–43,
    250–51
  playing outdoors as rarity, 19,
    62–63, 65
  technology and, 14, 32, 65, 99, 106,
    288
Coral Gardens and Their Magic (Malinowski), 119
Cowper, William, 237
Craiglockhart Hospital, Edinburgh,
  192–96
creativity, 21, 150, 217–22
  death, existence, and, 217
  empowering illusion, 48–51, 65
  gardening as, 20, 26, 46, 160
  self-belief, small children, and, 48–49
Crete, 87–88

crime and criminology, 61, 93, 96, 169,
173
children at risk, 62–63
"condemnation" script and, 61
"generative narrative," 61
urban farms and, 175, 176
urban green spaces and, 96, 174,
175, 180
Csibra, Gergely, 177
Csikszentmihalyi, Mihaly, 247

Darwin, Charles, 139
Dash, Robert, 133
death (last season of life), 209–35
afterlife beliefs, 214
consciousness and awareness of, 144
consolation of nature and, 231
Dunmore's poem on, 234–35
fear of, 210, 213, 215, 216
Freud and, 212–13, 231, 233
gardening in old age and, 217–22
hunter-gatherer societies and, 212
Kunitz's view of, 216
Lifton's work on psychology of
dying, 231
as loss, 210, 215–16
Montaigne's view of, 210, 216
naturalness of, 211–12, 215–16, 233
as a return to the earth, 211–12,
234–35
seed germination and rebirth,
213–14
"symbolic survival," 231
Winnicott on, 220–21
Defence Medical Rehabilitation
Centre (DMRC), Nottinghamshire,
England, 73
Defiant Gardens (Helphand), 191
delphinium, 135–36
depression and anxiety, 14, 24–25, 93,
250
BDNF and, 34–35
gardening as therapeutic, 24–26, 31,
35–40
loss of connection to nature and, 150
newly greened spaces and, 174–75
pessimism of, 286
rising levels of, 39, 284
slow time and recovery, 250
workplace-based stress and, 243
Descola, Philippe, 121, 122

Dessert, The (painting, Matisse), 259
Dickens, Charles, 42–43
dopamine, 78, 101–2, 138, 140, 142,
151, 247
Douglas, James, 124–25, 126
Duke of Cornwall Spinal Treatment
Centre, Salisbury Hospital, England,
269–70
Dunmore, Helen, 234–35

Eagleman, David, 240
Edinburgh, Scotland, community gardens by reformer Geddes, 193–94
Edinburgh Garden Partners, 222
education
experiential learning, 64–65
gardening programs, 51–53, 55,
164–65
life skill activities, 178
in prisons, 54, 61, 62
social bonds as facilitating learning,
178
social learning, 178–79
special needs children, 51–52
theory of "natural pedagogy," 177
urban farms and, 175, 177
Egypt, ancient
Gardener's Tomb, 214
flowers and, 144
Osiris beds, 214–15
tomb inscription, 209
seed germination and rebirth,
214–15
Eliot, T. S., 5
emotions
babies being held and, 69–70
"benign" or virtuous circle and, 31
capacity to love, 30–31
Erikson's generativity concept, 219
flowers, gardens and, 143–44, 146,
265
lifetime restoration and repair of, 30
nature's awakening of, 267
needs of spinal injury patients, 269
plants and emotional health, 222–23
recovery from illness and, 262
reparation and, 29–30
tending like a garden, 35
therapeutic horticulture and, 247–48
empathy, 78, 99–100, 107, 264
endorphins, 37, 78, 247, 262

Ensler, Eve, 267–68
environmental issues, 13, 29, 283, 284
    nature as a living system and, 285
    politics of food, 167–72
    See also climate crisis
environmental melancholia, 283–84
environmental psychology, 150–51
Erikson, Erik, 67, 219
eucalyptus tree, 83
Evelyn, John, 89–90
evolution
    brain and, 71, 77, 78, 97–100, 177
    care's neurochemical rewards and, 37
    co-evolution, 80, 115–16, 139–40
    color, responses to, and, 74
    desire to see without being seen, 77
    human consciousness and, 122–23
    human environmental preferences,
        70, 75
    humans as grassland species and, 35
    role of pleasure and, 143
    sharing of food and, 177
exercise, 35, 39, 78, 79
    gardening as, 79, 81, 86, 160–61
    green exercise, 79
    urban green spaces and, 94

farming
    Borneo jungle, burned ground and,
        114
    destruction of prairies and, 283
    industrial, topsoil loss and, 283
    origins of, 111–12
    Romans and, 283
    Sumerians and, 128–31, 283
    U.S. history and, 170
    See also urban farms
Faust (Goethe), 150
Fenton, Norman, 206–7
Ferney, France, 287
Fiacre, Saint, 27
fig tree, 113, 214, 225
Finley, Ron, 169–70
Flannery, Kent, 116
flower pots, 158–59
flowers, 135–55, 258
    as agents of continuity, 144
    brain's electrical activity and, 265
    bulb planting, 184
    co-evolution with insects, 139–40
    cultivation of, 143

earliest grave with, 143
early choice for seeds, 143
florist societies, 160
Freud and, 141–42, 145–46, 149–50,
    224–25, 227, 228, 231–32, 233
in hospitals, 258–61
human need for beauty and, 143–44
human unconscious and, 141–42
hunter-gatherers and, 142–43
Industrial Revolution and, 159–61
Kant on, 136
loss of English wildflower meadows,
    281
mathematical beauty and, 138
Monet on, 135, 136–37
moods influenced by, 146
nectar, 140
nineteenth-century flower shows, 161
oldest in hunter-gather settlement,
    143
pollination, 29, 85, *135*, 139–41, 283
recovery from illness and, 260,
    261–62
scent of, 74, 75, 89, 140–41, 142
self-sowers, 110, 143
stress reduction and, 261–62
supernormal stimulus and, 140
symbolism and, 144, 145, 217
as therapeutic, 155
of Vancouver Island, 124–25
on World War I, Western front,
    186–91
    See also orchids; *specific types*
flow states, 246–47
foraging, 110, 114, 164
Fournier, Eliza, 175–76, 177, 178–79
Frazer, James, 82
Freud, Alexander, 224
Freud, Anna, 149, 230, 231, 233
Freud, Ernst, 149, 230, 232
Freud, Lucian, 229
Freud, Lucie, 233
Freud, Martha Bernays, 141, 142, 145, 146
Freud, Martin, 141, 149
Freud, Sigmund, 6, 144–49, 233
    antiquity collection, 228–31
    beauty and, 137
    Craiglockhart Hospital and, 192–96
    death, dying, and, 212–13, 233
    flowers and, 137, 141–42, 224–29,
        231–33

Freud, Sigmund (*cont.*)
  gardens and, in old age, 225–31
  at Grinzing, 225–26, 234
  in London, 228–30
  on mourning, 148
  nature's restorative powers and,
    147, 149
  orchids and, 141, 147, 149
  Paradise Garden, Torre del Gallo,
    224, 234
  plant life in dream interpretation,
    145–46
  sublimation and, 41
  theory of Eros and Thanatos,
    149–50, 192
  unconscious mind's denial of death,
    231
  World War I and, 149–50
Freud, Sophie, 149
Freud, Stephen, 229
Freudenberger, Herbert, 243
Freud Museum, London, 230
Fromm, Erich, 150
Fuller, Dorian, 112
Fuller, Richard, 94–95
Furrows in the Desert initiative, 277–29
future orientation, 66, 76, 239, 255, 288

Gallese, Vittorio, 264
Gandhi, Mahatma, 157
Garden, The (Sackville-West), 191
"Gardener's Mortal Sin, The" (trans.
  Kramer), 129, 130
gardening
  aggression during, 9
  as ancient and modern, 287–88
  attitude of care and, 31–32, 37–38,
    76, 155, 248
  balance between doing and being,
    280–82
  Benedictines and, 27–28
  benefits, 36, 38–42, 77–78, 79, 80
  bulb planting, 184
  calming effects, 7, 13, 14, 15, 35–38,
    56–58, 62, 73–86, 103, 274
  catharsis and, 9, 248
  Churchill and, 185
  coping with death and, 216–17
  as counterbalance to warfare,
    183–92
  as counterculture, 61

  as creative act, 20, 26, 46, 160
  cultivating the soul or self and, 33
  cycle of life and, 19, 21, 24, 148,
    216, 217, 234–35, 241
  destructiveness during, 8–9, 11,
    41–42
  digging and smell of wet earth
    (*geosmin*), 79
  eating produce in situ, 109–10, *109*
  emotions and, 35, 247–48
  as empowering, 181, 195, 254–55
  as exercise, 78–79, 81, 86, 160–61
  existential processes of, 13–14, 215
  future orientation of, 66, 76, 239,
    255, 288
  garden time, 237–56
  "getting to know" and, 11
  as global social movement, 167
  "green thumb," 49
  grief, loss, and, 4, 13, 14, 19–20, 21,
    81, 88–89
  growing from seed, 8, 45–48, 51,
    57, 239
  hope and, 10, 61, 66
  introspection, insight and, 13
  jobs of, attitude toward, 7–8
  Jung as advocate of, 161–62
  Maurilius and, 26–27
  May, Ted, and, 3, 4, 204–6, *289*
  Mother Earth, symbolism and, 213
  as nurturing activity, 14, 21–22, 31,
    37–38, 132, 180–81
  in old age, 217–22
  opinions of, as polarized, 26
  origins of culture and, 115, 118–23
  overlap of "me" and "not me" and, 20
  patron saints of, 27
  as play, 252–53
  pleasures of, 7, 8, 79
  as political resistance, 167–72
  as popular hobby, 14
  as reclamation, 217
  rehabilitation through, 14, 195, 204–6
  as a reiteration, 10
  relationship with plants, the earth,
    and, 14, 17, 86, 132–33
  as reparative activity, 26–27, 28, 29,
    31, 36–38, 61, 253, 282
  restorative effects of, 4, 23, 27
  rhythm of, 239–40, 241, 249, 253
  as ritual, 20, 125–27, 128, 130, 132

St. Hildegard of Bingen's *viriditas*, 29, 35, 279
sanctity of manual labor and, 27–28
self-worth and, 25–27, 31, 40, 51–52, 62–64, 86
social prescribing schemes, 39
as space-time medicine, 249–50
subconscious effects of, 14
symbolism of, 20, 215, 216, 217
therapeutic effects, 24–27 (*see also* therapeutic horticulture)
as transformative, 9, 42, 51, 52, 65
Wordsworth and, 15–16
gardening history, 109–34
"agricultural mindset," 127
burning and, 114, 125, 126
as domination of nature, 124–25
European settlers in America and, 124–27
Fertile Crescent and, 111, 114, 129
"high-value foods" and, 112–13
hunter-gatherers, 97, 102, 111–23, 142–44
hybridization and plant-breeding, 117
Maori gardens, 127–28
in Mesopotamia, 185
in Mexico, 113
Neolithic Revolution, 111–12
Ohalo II camp, 113–14, 143
origins of culture and, 115, 118–23
origins of gardening, 110–23, 280
Paleolithic era, 110, 112
ritual and, 117–19
understanding of death and, 213
on Vancouver Island, 125–27
garden magic, 65, 119–22
gardens
in antiquity, 112
apothecary, 163
the Barn Garden (*see* Barn, the)
Benedictine monastery gardens, 28, 41
bostan, of Turkey, 286
brain's electrical activity and, 265
Bridewell Gardens, Oxfordshire, 41–42
calming effects of, 15, 38, 51, 57, 58, 69, 71, 73–86, 142, 205, 234, 265, 274, 279
in children's lives, 7, 12, 19

Churchill's, Hoe Farm, Surrey, 185
Clairvaux Abbey hospice gardens, 28
combining enclosure and openness, 15, 70–71, 279
community plots, 162–72, 179–80
as connection to life, 16
cyclical narrative of, 241
designers, 91–92, 185, 243, 245, 262, 269–70, 273–74
enclosed, 54, 70–71, 73, 75, 244
as expression of the gardener, 16–17
Freud's, in London, 229–30
front gardens lost to parking places, 283
Garden of Eden, 26
Headley Court, Surrey, England, 73–76
herb garden, 7, 15, 28, 163–64, 244
in hospitals, 269–75
imagined or remembered, 68, 218
Insight Garden, San Quentin, *45*, 61–62
Jung's, Bollingen, 250
Kunitz's, Provincetown, Mass., 216–17
Lady Beaumont's winter garden, 15–16
as living poem, 217
meditation and, 28
memories evoked by, 87–89
as non-pharmaceutical therapy, 265
Paradise Garden, Torre del Gallo, 224–25, 234
pre-agricultural, in China, 112
as re-creation, renewal of life, 208
as refuge, 16, 77–78, 254
as restorative, 14, 16, 28, 74, 271–72
as safe or protected space, 9, 13, 16–17, 28, 67–87, 234, 239, 241, 244, 279
shamba gardens, 278
social leveling effect of, 55
in spinal injury centers, 269
sublimation and, 41–42
symbolism of, 81, 121, 122, 234–35
Syrian refugee camps, 143–44
Tager Centre, for autism, 274
therapeutic gardens, 28, 41–42, 60–61, 73–76, 81–82, *237*, 273–74
threshold spaces in, 232
as transformative and transcendent, 62

gardens (*cont.*)
    as in-between or transitional spaces, 16, 17, 232–33, 272
    of the Trobriand islanders, 119–20
    Voltaire's, at Ferney, 287
    Wordsworth's, at Dove Cottage, 15
    of World War I, *183*, 186–91
Gaskell, Elizabeth, 161
Gawande, Atul, 223
Geddes, Patrick, 193–94
    "Place-Work-Folk" concept, 194
Gell, Alfred, 120
Gergely, György, 177
Gillespie, Alexander Douglas, 188–90
Goethe, Johann Wolfgang, vi, 150
Golden Bough, The (Frazer), 82
gooseberry, gooseberry clubs, 160
Grahn, Patrik, 243, 245
Great Expectations (Dickens), 42–43
Greek mythology, 129, 180, 213
green fuse, greening power, 277–88
    climate change and, 279, 282–84
    Furrows in the Desert initiative, 277–79
    gardens as wildlife habitats, 283
    St. Hildegard of Bingen's *viriditas*, 29, 279
    human nature, green nature and, 280
    sustainable lifestyles and, 284–88
    union doing with being, 280–82
GreenHouse project, Rikers Island, N.Y., 52–60, 61
greenhouses, 8, 9–10, 133, 159
    at Alnarp therapy garden, 244
    in asylums, 38–39
    author and healing, 238–39, 275–76
    author's grandfather and, 3, *289*
    at the Barn, 275–76
    in Headley Court garden, 75–76, 77
    in Hørsholm Arboretum, Copenhagen, 81
    prison projects and, 52–60
    at Salisbury Hospital, 269
    at Sarisbury Court, 205–6, 208
Greening the Red Zone (Tidball), 191
green rebels, 167–72
    Diggers, 170
    Green Guerrillas, 170, 171
Greenstone Design UK, 273
grief and loss
    attachment and pain of, 19

automatic responses to loss/trauma, 24
    consolation of nature, 5–6, 19–20, 231
    as creative motivation, 21
    environmental melancholia, 283–84
    Freud on, 147–48
    gardening and, 4, 13, 14, 19–20
    hidden feelings and, 13
    isolation and, 5, 24
    Klein, Melanie, on nature and, 19
    Klein, Naomi, on inevitable loss, 284
    loss and restoration cycles, 148, 149
    love and vulnerability, 148
    motivation to create and, 21–22
    mourning and the cycle of life, 19
    mourning as hardest emotional work, 148
    re-finding a safe haven and, 19
    rituals, rites and, 19–20
    traumatic wrench of loss, 215–16
Growing Options project, 63–64

Harding, Mark, 167–69
Harvard Grant Study, 219–20
Haviland-Jones, Jeannette, 143, 258
H.D. (poet), 224
Headley Court, Surrey, England, 73–76, 81
Heiser, Charles, 117–18, 128
Helphand, Kenneth, 191
Herbert, George, 23
herbs, herb gardens, 7, 15, 28, 113, 136, 161, 163–64, 165, 244
Herman, Judith, 72
Hibberd, Dominic, 195
HighGround gardening program, 73–76, 81
Hildegard of Bingen, St., 29, 35, 279
"Hold Out Your Arms" (Dunmore), 234–35
hope, 50
    gardening as hopeful act, 61
    nature's restorative powers and, 149
    for personal change, 61–62
    prisoner gardening projects and, 52
    recovery from illness and, 262
    urban green spaces and, 96
Horatio's Garden (UK charity), 269–71
Hørsholm Arboretum, Denmark, 81–82
Horticultural Society of New York, 52–60, 62

hospitals, 257–76
  design of, 259–60, 262
  design placebo effect and, 262
  effects of art in, 259, 263
  flowers and recovery, 258–61, 262
  fresh air, daylight as antibiotics,
    259–60
  patients' contact with nature as
    therapeutic, 262, 264–65
  psychological awareness in design,
    261–62, 269–70
  window views, 258–59, 261, 267–68
How the Mind Works (Pinker), 142
human nature
  as connection-seeking, 35
  dual aspects of, gardening as uniting,
    181
  green nature and, 23–43, 280
  twin poles: warrior and cultivator,
    185
Humphrey, Nicholas, 122–23
hunter-gatherer societies, 98, 102, 111–23
  awareness of surroundings, 97, 263
  dump heap theory and gardens,
    116–17
  flowers and, 142–43
  Lekwungen tribe, 125–27
  Ohalo II camp, 113–14
  proactive or "managed foraging," 114
  storytelling and, 240

identity, sense of, 86, 169
  gardening programs for schools
    and, 52
  memory, and place, 242
  recovering, through nature, 271–72
  rooted relationship to place and,
    17–18
  sense of place and, 85–86
  St. Maurilius's story, 26–27
immune system, 34, 35, 75, 79–80
*Importance of Nature in Coping with a
  Crisis, The* (Ottosson), 245–46
Incredible Edible movement, 163–67
Industrial Revolution, 159–62, 167
Ingold, Tim, 123
insects, 85, 116, *135*, 139–40, 281, 283
Inside the Wave (Dunmore), 234
Insight Garden Program, San Quentin
  State Prison, *45*, 61–62
International Rescue Committee, *157*, 171

Interpretation of Dreams (Freud), 145
Isabella Plantation, Richmond Park,
  Kingston upon Thames, England, 12

"Jack and the Beanstalk," 180–81
Jencks, Charles, 262
Jiler, James, 54, 60
Johns Hopkins Center for a Livable
  Future, Baltimore, Md., 172
Jones, Ernest, 137, 229–30
Jones, Glynis, 127–28
Journey of Recovery, The (Pálsdóttir), 248
Jung, Carl, 131–32, 161–62, 178, 250, 256

Kant, Immanuel, 136
Kaplan, Rachel and Stephen, 98
Keller, Terry, 171
Kipling, Rudyard, 197
Klein, Melanie, 19, 30, 223–24
Klein, Naomi, 32, 284
Kolk, Bessel van der, 195
Kramer, Samuel Noah, 129, 130
Krus, Hilda, 54, 58, 59
Kunitz, Stanley, 216, 219
Kuo, Frances, 96–97, 107

Lambert, Kelly, 105–7, 254–55
Lampl-de Groot, Jeanne, 230
lavender, 89, 142, 163
learning disabilities, adults with, 273–74
Leg to Stand On, A (Sacks), 271
Leibniz, Gottfried, 285
Lekwungen people, 125–27
Lemon Tree Trust, 143
L'Enfant et les Sortilèges (Ravel), 30
Lifton, Robert, 231
limpets, long-spined, 115–16
Lisbon earthquake (1755), 284–85
loneliness, 166, 220, 222–24
love
  beauty and, 137
  brain development and, 33
  brain regions and, 138
  children and, 30, 31
  fear of, 284
  of flowers, 136, 137, 142–43
  of gardening, 4, 8, 15, 58, 289
  of nature, 85
  overprotectiveness and, 58
  scent of roses and, 142
  vulnerability to loss and, 148

Lowry, Christopher, 79–80
lupines (*Lupinus perennis*), 87–88
Luton, England, gardening project,
   52–53

Maggie's Cancer Care Centres, UK, 262
Malinowski, Bronislaw, 119–20
Manchester, England, 161
Man Makes Himself (Childe), 112
Maori people, 127–28
Maruna, Shadd, 61
Matisse, Henri, 259
Maurilius, Saint, 26–27
May, Alfred Edward "Ted," 1–4, 204–7
   horticulture training, 204–6, 207
   orchid growing by, 208, *289*
   recovery of, 3–4, 206
   World War I and POW experience,
     2–3, 4, 184, 196–202, 286
May, Fanny, 2, 3, 202, 207
McGilchrist, Iain, 98–99
McGuire, Terry, 143
meadows, 281–82
   biodiversity of, 281
   loss of wildflower meadows, 281
   as wildlife habitat, 281
memory, 11, 71, 72, 75, 80, 85, 88, 104,
   203, 234, 275, 276
   collective, 112
   passage of time and, 240, 242
   place and, 242
   Pollan's, 47–48
   scents and, 142
Menninger, Karl, 86
"Mental Cases" (Owen), 192
mental health
   aging and, 222–24
   asylums in parkland settings, 38–39
   burnout, 242
   community gardening benefits, 250
   contemporary life and, 14
   contraction of time, focus and, 250
   daydreaming, play, and, 17
   dissociation, 195
   gardening for, 14, 15, 38–42, 180–81
   loneliness and, 166
   modern "quick fix" mentality, 32
   nature and, 14–16, 38, 191
   pharmaceutical approach, 39
   physical exercise and, 86
   POWs and, 203

relationship with income level,
   95–96
Rush's manual for treatment, 38
"social prescribing" schemes, 39
soil bacteria and, 80
therapy at Bridewell Gardens,
   40–42
trauma and, 207
Tuke's approach, 38
urban green spaces and, 90–91,
   174–76
urban life and, 92–97, 100–102
Milner, Marion, 48, 49, 64, 65
mind (consciousness)
   attention fatigue, 98
   awareness of mortality and, 144
   calm state, processing emotion and,
     15
   evolution of, 122–23
   gardening and, 13, 14, 35
   Jung on, 161–62, 178
   nature and animation of, 14–15
   social intelligence and, 123
Mind (UK charity), 39
Mitchell, Richard, 95–96
Monet, Claude, 135, 136–37
Montaigne, Michel de, 210, 216, 228
music, as non-pharmaceutical therapy,
   265
Mycobacterium vaccae (*M. vaccae*), 80
myths, legends, and folk tales, 82, 119,
   122, 128–31, 180–81, 195, 213, 240

nature
   asylums in parkland settings, 38–39
   attachment and, 18
   behavior changed by, 107
   biophilia concept, 99–100, 106,
     150–51
   brain's physiology or structure
     changed by, 265
   classic fairy tale of, 21–22
   clockwork universe and, 285
   collective survival and, 282
   communion with, 85
   consolation of, 5–6, 19–20, 231
   contact with, effects, 14, 29
   domination of, 124, 128, 131–32,
     281–82
   ecological niches, 115–16, 117
   emotional impact of, 16, 37, 267

experimental neuroscience and, 105–6
as free and universal, 60
garden as union of wild and cultivated, 17
gardening and connecting to, 216
geometries, patterns in, 138, 266
growth force of, as divine, 29
as healing or restorative, 15–16, 43,
 74, 147, 191, 193, 248, 262, 266
health benefits of, 94
hospital window views and, 258–59,
 261, 267–68
human empowerment and, 21, 50
human interconnection with, 17,
 28–29, 91
human limitations and, 50
human response to green, 74, 90
hunter-gatherers and, 97, 102,
 111–23
illness and, 39–40, 258–76
interconnection of life and, 29, 31, 35
Jung on, 131–32, 161–62, 256
link with human thriving, 35–36
as living continuum, 211–12
as living system, 285
loss and restoration cycles, 148, 149
loss of connection to, effect of,
 131–32, 150, 162, 211–12, 245
memory and, 85–86
mental health and, 14–16, 38–42, 265
paradigm shift in understanding, 282
partnerships/symbiosis in, 115–16
rebirth, renewal, and, 43
St. Hildegard of Bingen's *viriditas*,
 29, 35, 279
slower rhythms of, 32
social prescribing schemes, 39–40
spiritual connection with, 255–56
stress reduction and, 38, 39, 73–75,
 94, 104, 106, 176, 251
subconscious effects of, 14
urbanization and, 56, 62–63, 106
"urgent biophilia" and, 191–92
Wordsworth and, 5, 14–15
nervous system, 32–35, 71, 75
 green environments and, 105–8
 music and gardens as non-
  pharmaceutical therapy for, 265
 neurological disorders, 265
 perception and, 14–15

sensory stimulation as necessary,
 265–66
sympathetic and parasympathetic,
 75, 80, 241, 246–47
neurasthenia, 92, 93, 106, 192–93, 194,
 202, 203, 207
neurobiology, 132
neuroscience, 96, 104–6
 Lambert's experiments, 254–55
 Wordsworth's intuitions confirmed
  by, 14
New York Botanical Garden, New Roots
 Community Farm and, *157*, 171
Nightingale, Florence, 260–61
Norfolk, England, 6
Notes on Nursing (Nightingale), 260
Nutt, David, 78

Obama, Michelle, 169
Ohalo II, 113–14, 143
O'Keeffe, Georgia, 144
Olmsted, Frederick Law, 87, 91–92, 96, 98
On Not Being Able to Paint (Milner), 48,
 64, 65
"On Transience" (Freud), 147, 149
optimism, 65, 151, 255, 286
Oranjezicht urban farm, Cape Town,
 South Africa, 167–69
orchids, 139, 141, 149–50
 Freud and, 141
 May, Ted, and, 208, *289*
organic gardening, 39, 168
Ottosson, Johan, 245–46
Owen, Wilfred, 192–93, 195–96
*Oxford Textbook of Nature and Public
 Health* (Bird), 39
Ozinsky, Sheryl, 168

Pálsdóttir, Anna María, 248–49
Pamela Barnett Centre, Ravenswood
 Village, Berkshire, England, 273
Pankejeff, Sergei (Wolf Man), 146
Panksepp, Jaak, 71
Parkinson's disease, 265
Paxton, Joseph, 205
Pennsylvania Horticultural Society,
 173–74
Persian empire, 280
Pfister, Oskar, 146–47
Philadelphia, LandCare Program, 173–75
Phocas, Saint, 27

Piaget, Jean, 64–65
Pinker, Steven, 142
Planting for Justice, 62
plants
    caring for, 31–32, 76, 103, 155, 177
    communication by, 282
    cultural information about, 178
    dump heap theory, 117
    earliest domesticated, 113, 117
    growing from seed, 239
    highly scented, for urban parks, 89
    human affinity with, 123
    human reproduction and plant
      regeneration, 121–22
    inward quality of, 58
    life force of, 31
    mutating and hybridizing, 117
    non-food, cultivation of, 113
    prisoners' sympathy with, 58
    with psychoactive properties, 117
    relationships with, 31, 103, 112,
      116, 132–33, 218, 245, 248,
      267–68
    seed germination, 209–10, 213–14
    self-seeding, 110, 117, 143
    speaking to, 57
poetry, 5, 15
    garden as a "living poem," 217
    Wordsworth's essence of, 15
    See also specific poets
Pollan, Michael, 47–48, 50–51, 65
post-traumatic stress disorder (PTSD),
    72
    Antaeus myth and, 195–96
    "barbed-wire syndrome," 203
    calming scents, 74, 75, 142
    colors and, 74
    dissociation and, 195
    exercise for, 79
    Fenton on therapeutic horticulture,
      206–7
    gardens and, 71, 73, 74, 75, 77, 85
    HighGround program, 73–76, 81
    Hørsholm Arboretum project, 81–82
    hypervigilance and, 72
    mindfulness practice for, 76
    mind's processing of time, 76, 194
    need to reground, 195, 203–4, 207
    olfactory triggers, 74
    patient, Eddie, 83–86
    recovery as slow, 83–84, 85, 202–3

    regaining a sense of safety, 72
    as serotonin system dysfunction, 78
    shell shock, 70, 192–93
    "therapy by stealth," 76
    Thrive gardening project, 83–86
    trauma, effects of, 83–86, 194
    treatment at Craiglockhart, 192–96
    trees and healing, 81–84
    violent crime levels and, 93
potatoes, 21, 124, 132, 250
Poulsen, Dorthe, 81–82
Pretty, Jules, 98, 250–51
Priapus, 180
prison gardening projects, 46–47, 52–62
Rikers Island, New York City, 52–56, 60
psychology and psychotherapy
    aging, emotional well-being, and,
      219–20
    Appleton's "habitat theory," 70
    art, effects on the psyche, 262–63
    attachment theory, 18–20
    attention restoration, 98–99
    automatic responses to loss/trauma,
      24
    cognitive behavior therapy (CBT),
      40, 101
    cognitive development, 64–65
    control and, 50–51
    daydreaming and playing, 17
    desire to see without being seen, 68,
      70, 77
    dissociation and, 246
    environmental issues and, 284,
      285–86
    feeling of being unheld, 70
    flow state or the zone, 246–47
    Freud's Eros and Thanatos, 149–50,
      192
    imaginative projection, 263
    infantile omnipotence, 48–49
    learned helplessness, 254–55
    Lifton's work on psychology of
      dying, 231
    mourning and, 19, 148
    negative thoughts and, 24
    psychoanalytic psychotherapy, 12,
      194
    refuge vs. retreat and, 77
    reparation, 29–31
    ruminating on negative thoughts, 97
    sublimation, 41–42

transitional processes, 16
trees, psychological effects of, 68–69, 96
Wordsworth and, 14–15
See also specific psychologists
pumpkins, 46, 52, 169

Ralfsia verrucosa algae, 115–16
Ravel, Maurice, 30
Rees, Goronwy, 69
religion, 118–19, 128
afterlife beliefs, 214
ancient Egyptian, 144, 214
Christian attitudes to gardening, 26–29
spirituality of gardens, 85
spiritual connection with nature, 255–56
tree worship, 82
Retreat asylum, York, England, 38
Reynolds, Richard, 170–71
Rikers Island, New York City, 52–56, 60
Rilke, Rainer Maria, 147
Rivers, William, 194
Roman Empire, 28, 283
Roosevelt, Theodore, 92
rosemary, 89, 142, 163
roses, 11, 142
Royal Horticultural Society (RHS), 51
gardening in schools programs, 51–52
Rule (Benedict), 27
Rush, Benjamin, 38

Sachs, Hanns, 141, 227–28, 230, 232
Sacks, Oliver, 257, 265, 271
Sackville-West, Vita, 183, 191
Sales, Carol, 73–74, 75–76, 81
Salvation Army, 204
San Patrignano, Italy, drug rehabilitation program, 151–55
Sapolsky, Robert, 79
Sarisbury Court, Southampton, veteran horticulture training at, 204–6, 208
Sassoon, Siegfried, 185, 196
Schussler, Elisabeth, 179
schizophrenia, 100–104
Scruton, Roger, 224
Searles, Harold, 69, 245
seasons of the year, 8, 9, 10, 149, 239
consolation of, 241

cycle of life and, 19, 148, 216, 241
Second Nature (Pollan), 47–48, 51, 65
seeds
author growing plants from, 45–46
future orientation, 239, 255
dormant life and growth force of, 8
recommended for children to grow, 51
self-belief and, 45–66
setting life in motion and, 10
transformation and, 58
Segal, Hanna, 21
self-belief
in children, 48–49
gardening for self-worth, 62–63
Pollan and, 47–48
prisoner, Samuel, and, 46–47, 52
school gardening projects and, 52
seeds and, 45–66
Sempik, Joe, 256
Serge Hill, Hertfordshire, England, 6
serotonin, 78–80, 138, 142, 247
flowers, gardens and, 79, 265
raphe (in brainstem), 78
scents and, 142
soil bacteria and boosting, 79–80
Seveso, Italy, chemical leak, 13
sex, sexuality
flowers and, 144–46
Freud and, 145–46, 150
gardening and, 129–30, 132, 180–81, 217
Sumerian myth and, 129–30
Sheffield, England, 159–61
Sherratt, Andrew, 113
Smith, Bruce D., 114–15
snowdrops, 23–24, *23*
social deprivation
gardening in schools and, 51–52, 55, 57
health and income levels, 95–96
intergenerational cycles, 60
newly greened spaces and, 173–75
psychotic illnesses and, 93
unhealthy lifestyles and, 168, 169
urban environments and, 168, 172–73
urban farm projects for, 167–72, 175–80
urban housing, green spaces and, 96
soil bacteria, 79–80

Solent, The (strait), 6
Sontag, Susan, 249
Souter-Brown, Gayle, 273
Spencer, Carita, 188
spinal injuries, 269–71, 272–73
Sternberg, Esther, 74
Stiggsdotter, Ulrika, 81–82
stress
    abstract art promoting, 263
    city living and, 93, 96, 100
    cortisol and, 74–75
    damaging effects of, 79
    positive anticipation vs., 255
    reducing, beauty and, 138
    reducing, exercise and, 79
    reducing, flowers and, 261–62
    reducing, flower scent and, 142
    reducing, gardens and, 57, 75,
        180–81
    reducing, greenhouses and, 57
    reducing, nature and, 38, 39, 73–75,
        94, 104, 106, 176, 251
    workplace-based, 237–38, 242
Stuart-Smith, Ben, 6
Stuart-Smith, Harry, 6, 7
Stuart-Smith, Rose, 1, 6, 7
Stuart-Smith, Sue, 1, 4–6, 7
    environmental awakening, 13
    father of and his death, 4–5, 6,
        11–12, 13
    gardening and rooting herself, 7, 15
    gardening and unity with nature, 17
    grandfather of (see May, Alfred
        Edward "Ted")
    growing plants from seed, 45–46
    hammocks in the garden and, 67–68
    herb garden of, 7
    Isabella Plantation and, 12
    as psychiatrist in NHS, 7, 60,
        237–38
    psychoanalytic psychotherapy and,
        12–13
    rose garden of, 11
    suffers fractured hip, 258–59,
        275–76
    work in cardiology unit, 210–11
    workings of the unconscious and,
        12–13
    work related illness, 237–38
Stuart-Smith, Tom, 1, 6, 7, 47, 68, 88,
    183–84, 238, 277

Sullivan, William, 96–97, 107
Sumerians, 89, 128–31, 132, 283
sunflowers, 10, 46, 51, 282
sunlight, 35, 65, 74, 78, 81, 91, 196
supernormal stimulus, 140, 151
sustainability, environmental, 39, 60–61
    Furrows in the Desert initiative,
        277–79

Tager Centre, Ravenswood Village, 274
Taylor, Anne-Christine, 121
Taylor, Timothy, 213–14
technology, 32, 288
    brain-as-computer metaphor, 32–33
    dependence on, 14, 65
    internet as retreat from world, 77
    and modes of attention, 99
    as supplanting industry, 167
    ubiquitous screen culture, 99, 106
therapeutic gardens
    Alnarp Rehabilitation Garden, 237
    garden design and, 245, 269,
        273–74
    gardens as health intervention,
        273–74
    gardens for autistic adults, 274
    gardens for the learning disabled,
        273–74
    gardens for spinal injury patients,
        269–73
    Hørsholm Arboretum, 81–82
    natural complexity for, 275
    ratio of green to hard surface and,
        274
    as safe enclosure, 15, 59, 67–86,
        244, 245
therapeutic horticulture, 28
    addiction and, 151–55
    Alnarp model for, 243–49
    Bridewell Gardens project, 40–42
    burnout and, 242–47
    clinical trials, 40–41
    in conflict zones, after disasters, 191
    at Craiglockhart Hospital, 193
    depression and, 24–26
    expression of emotions and, 247–48
    Fenton on, 206–7
    HighGround program, 73–76, 81
    intensive interaction therapy and,
        274
    Menninger and, 86